Personalisation and Learning Disabilities

A handbook

Edited by
Andrew Tyson

in ☼ Control®

Pavilion

Personalisation and Learning Disabilities

A handbook

Edited by
Andrew Tyson

Personalisation and Learning Disabilities: A handbook

Published by:
Pavilion Publishing Ltd.
Richmond House
Richmond Road
Brighton, BN2 3RL
Tel: 01273 623222
Fax: 01273 625526
Email: info@pavpub.com
Web: www.pavpub.com

Part of OLM Group

First published 2011

A Catalogue record for this book is available from the British Library.

ISBN: 978-1-908066-13-8

Editor: Sanaz Nazemi
Cover design: Emma Garbutt
Cover photo: Caroline Tomlinson
Page layout: Emma Garbutt
Printed on paper from a sustainable resource by Charlesworth Press

Contents

Foreword

My name is Nicola Smith and I live in West Sussex, and I have been
involved in the self-advocacy movement for many years now. I was chair
of Bognor and Chichester Voice and then I became the first co-chair of the
West Sussex Partnership Board. In 2006, I got the job of co-director of the
Valuing People Support Team with Rob Greig. I worked in that role for two
years before I moved back to work in my home town of Chichester where
I am now working on equal access to transport and health. In this role I
conduct some training for professionals and help with interviewing as well
as doing other things.

West Sussex was one of the first areas in the country to start self-directed
support back in 2006. I don't have a personal budget myself but I know lots of
people who do and I've talked to them about what is good about it and what
the problems are. I think that one of the best things about personal budgets
is that they enable people with learning disabilities to employ their own staff
to support them if that is what they want. This means they are in charge.
One person I know who does this is Alan. He is a shy person who lives with
his sister. He now employs personal assistants who support him to go out to
work, something he couldn't do before. Sometimes his personal assistants go
with him to work and talk to his manager about how he is getting on there
and what help he needs. Another friend of mine, Sally, works as a community
service volunteer at the hospital. She wouldn't be able to do this without the
staff she employs to help her and boost her confidence. So I think one of the
best things about personal budgets is that they allow people with learning
disabilities to contribute to society.

Other people I know have used their personal budget to have support to
live in their own home instead of a hostel or a group home. This is very
important: I have my own flat and it is very important that we all have a
place we can make our own and where we feel safe and happy.

One thing I often say is *'don't label us, we're not jam jars'*. Everyone is an
individual and has different things they need and different things they can
offer to others. Personal budgets and self-directed support mean lots more
people can plan what they want and then get it because they are in charge of
their own budget and not someone from social services or a family member.

I know there are some problems with personal budgets as they are still quite new. One person I know had a personal budget to help him do certain things and then he broke his leg and couldn't do those things, and the social worker said he had to give some of the money back. He thought this was very unfair because there were lots of other things he could use his budget for – his parents didn't have a lot of money and he was at home with a broken leg and less money. He could have used the money to save up for a holiday or to buy a bit more support or even give his parents a break when he was better. If a person is given a personal budget it should be their money to do what they choose with it.

I know things are difficult with the credit crunch, but give people a personal budget and this will make them healthier and happier and then they will stay out of hospital, and that will save the government money.

I hope that this book helps everyone to learn more and also make a success of personal budgets and self-directed support right across the country. People with learning disabilities need them!

Nicola Smith
Former co-director of the Valuing People Support Team

Introduction

Key points:

▶ Personalisation is about people, not as passive recipients of services, but as active citizens with preferences and with a contribution to make. An example is people with complex needs: their 'contribution' is unlikely to be 'productive' in the usual sense, but many people with complex needs are loved hugely and love back. They can give back emotionally, give great joy, especially as they become happier with support that really meets their needs and wishes. This is the greatest change resulting from personalisation and many families are seeing this.

▶ To move from the old system to a new personalised system, we need leadership. This book is about leadership.

▶ It is also about personal budgets, but it is important to remember that personalisation is about much more than personal budgets.

▶ Personalisation is about more than individuals with money to spend on the support they need. It's about people as members of communities and about how those communities can change to make life better for people.

▶ Not all views of personalisation are the same. Some are overly simplistic, being little more than accounts of disabled people with more purchasing power. In Control focuses on the concepts of *citizenship* and *real wealth*, both of which are described in this book.

▶ If we follow this approach to personalisation, we save money because we are bringing into play new 'social capital' from a variety of sources.

▶ Personalisation drew its inspiration from the *independent living movement* (direct payments for people with physical and sensory impairments) and was taken up by people with learning disabilities and their families, who quickly came up with evidence that personal budgets can work well if properly implemented. This led in due course to policy change in *Putting People First* (Department of Health, 2007).

▶ There is an important relationship of personalisation to *Valuing People Now* (Department of Health, 2009) and other government policy, but just because something is policy doesn't mean it will happen.

▶ Personalisation is about people and their lives, more than it is about systems and processes. Systems and processes do have to change (and have changed to some extent) but that is relatively easy – what is more difficult is to shift the power and the ideas people have that underpin power. The main shift required is to the view that people with learning disabilities are citizens with real rights.

Jessica is a young woman with very complex needs. Her brain was damaged at birth and as a result she has multiple impairments, which means she doesn't use speech, she can't walk and she has difficulties eating and drinking and using the toilet. She lives at home with her mum, dad and younger brother and sister, who all love her very much and worry about her future. Until recently, she went to a council day centre in a minibus five days a week where she was a member of what was the 'special care unit' renamed as the 'special people club'. A year ago, after a lot of pressure, the council agreed that she was entitled to a personal budget. Jessica's mum manages the budget for her with some help from the local Centre for Independent Living and the family now employs a small team of personal assistants to support Jessica with her personal care at home. They take her out to a hydrotherapy pool and to a local riding school where Jessica sits in on grooming sessions and spends time in the yard around the horses. She has now begun spending time in the office with the administrator who has befriended her. The administrator has just joined Jessica's circle of support along with her mum, dad and brother, two family friends, one of the personal assistants and the person from the Centre for Independent Living. The circle is now planning a trip to the races and a summer holiday in Ireland and is discussing different options for long-term support when they hope Jessica will be able to live in her own home, away from mum and dad. Because of this Jessica is 'giving back', she smiles more, she has stopped biting the back of her hands and 'wailing' and she clearly loves contact with the horses. She is engaging and making a contribution and her dad recently described her as 'our number one daughter ... special but not different'.

This book is written with people like Jessica in mind, some who have needs that are less 'complex' but all who have been 'labelled' and – in the past – confined to institutions and to living situations that are (at best) 'safe', safe but often also dull, boring and uniform. 'Personalisation' is a horrible word but what it tries to convey is that everyone is different, everyone has different needs and wishes, and indeed everyone has something unique to offer, whether it is a smile, a shoulder to cry on, or in some cases an extra contribution in the form of voluntary or paid work, doing something they care about.

This book is the third in a short series on personalisation from Pavilion Publishing. The first one, *Personalisation: Practical thoughts and ideas from people making it happen* edited by Sam Newman (2009) was aimed at staff working with people across the whole spectrum of 'social care needs'. This handbook is specifically for those working for people with learning disabilities (the term learning disability will be used rather than the alternative 'people with learning difficulties' because the latter sometimes causes confusion and can be interpreted as excluding those with multiple or more complex needs). It will be helpful for support staff and their managers, but also for the families and friends of people with learning disabilities and perhaps for training and development of staff and for anyone who wants to know what personalisation means in practice or who wants to play a part in it. This is a book about 'leadership'; leadership by all of the people in this list and many others to get from the old system of health and social care for people with learning disabilities where they were excluded and marginalised to the new one where they are in control. We need strong, committed, well-informed leaders.

The book isn't written in 'easy read' format, but it does use straightforward, everyday words and gives lots of examples, illustrations and case studies where appropriate, rather than try and be an academic text. It is a book with multiple authors, and that means multiple voices: 'personalisation' is about individuality and we have not tried to make everyone sound the same or write in the same way. We have encouraged people to write from their own experiences, sometimes very personal experiences, but also to reflect on what others have found, and to draw general conclusions.

This is not to say that the book doesn't have a point to make. There are many different approaches to 'personalisation', some more or less radical, some more or less rooted in evidence from practice.

Personalisation and Learning Disabilities unashamedly adopts the values and thinking of the organisation In Control, which pioneered the development of self-directed support and personal budgets, initially in Scotland, and from 2003 onwards in England. This organisation was the result of a group of people, family members and professionals coming together in the town of Wigan in Lancashire and taking up the challenge of making choice and control real, first for disabled people they knew and cared about, then as they saw it working for others too. The organisation was led first by Simon Duffy and now by Julie Stansfied: both Simon and Julie say clearly that the real leaders are the disabled people and families who remain so determined to change things. There is more about how these ideas developed throughout the book, especially in Chapters 2 and 16.

This approach – self-directed support – has in some respects become 'mainstream' in that it was adopted as policy in England through the *Putting People First* cross-government concordat in December 2007, and made real for many people with the help of the social care transformation grant and the local authority circulars that followed. But this is very far from saying that what we now see across the land is In Control's approach in practice. In fact, In Control remains very concerned that in many local authorities we see 'transformation' in name only and that the key message about the absolute necessity of shifting power from paid staff, managers and professionals to ordinary people is being quietly forgotten or undermined.

Many aspects of In Control's approach are reflected in the different contributions that follow. We can introduce what is distinctive about that approach in five points, as follows.

▶ Personalisation always puts the individual (the person at the centre) first. So to the greatest extent possible, the individual needs to define what is important to them, the support they need to get this and how they should organise and manage that support.

▶ The individual needs assistance to do this, sometimes they need help to think through what they want, almost always they need help to plan and manage. The best people to help are very often those who know and care about the person, probably family members. This fact is to be welcomed and not treated with suspicion.

▶ To achieve success, we need to be clear that the person at the centre is a citizen, with all the rights and responsibilities that go with this. Simon Duffy wrote about what citizenship means in his book *Keys to Citizenship* (2006) where he talks about self-determination, direction, money, home, good support and community life. These ideas recur in what follows.

▶ We also need to be clear that to work, personalisation must be seen as being about much more than a money-based 'personal budget'. In fact, we have now learnt that it is the individual's 'real wealth' that makes the real difference. This important concept focuses on the individual's resilience, their capacity to deal with the problems of everyday life using the strength they have, their health, character, and how they feel and think; together with all the things that support this resilience: skills, connections, information and so on as well as income or other financial resources. Personalisation will only work if we see the 'whole person' in this way. It is also only if we see the person in this way that it will be affordable. Chapter 14 talks much more about 'real wealth'.

▶ It follows that personalisation necessitates a profound change in the hearts, minds and power relationships of those who work with and for local authorities. 'Systems change' is important, which is why In Control developed and tested the Seven Step Model of self-directed support, which was then adopted in most localities in the country. But systems change has to be underpinned by a shift in mindset away from the view that managers and professionals know best and towards a realisation that ordinary people – citizens – can and must be trusted to look after their own best interests.

To sum up, In Control's approach has three distinct aspects:

1. It is an *ethical* approach to personalisation in that it does what it does because it is the right thing to do. It is rooted explicitly in a series of value statements, and these remain the touchstone of success.

2. It is an *affordable* approach: in the late 1990s it became apparent that the old system of social care was broken, it was not working for many people who continued to live impoverished, segregated lives in residential care homes or day centres, and it was increasingly unaffordable as improvements to medical technology meant more disabled people survived longer into adulthood as the expectation of a good life for all grew. We tried 'block-commissioning' of large services and a variety of other forms of contracting, but whilst some of these brought slightly lower unit costs for a while they did not change anyone's life for the better – and these approaches were only ever a finger in the financial dyke. As we hit the credit crunch of 2009 and public spending cuts of 2010 this becomes even more important.

3. It is an approach that builds upon the *connectedness* of individuals. This is important to note because some people have criticised personalisation on the basis that they believe that it treats people as isolated consumers,

with purchasing power to buy support, but little more. In reality, In Control's approach does the opposite; it builds from the person as the member of a family, a friendship group and a community. The approach requires that we overturn the trade off we have had with certain 'special people' in our society, a deal which has gifted them 'care' so long as they show that they can behave well and replace it with a contract that should in fact apply to everyone in society. This new contract is about the fact that we are all 'members of each other' (as Julie Stansfield puts it in Chapter 16, quoting from Wendell Berry (1986)), and that we respond when people expect things of us and when people appreciate us or give us 'strokes' (to use a term from transactional analysis), and we shrivel and die when we are ignored or are told that we have nothing to offer.

Not everyone agrees with this approach, which has its roots in the *independent living movement* of people with physical disabilities and sensory impairments who fought for direct payments; and in the 'inclusion movement' of people with learning disabilities – and which took its operational principles from the person-centred planning techniques which grew from this. Some people believe that real inclusion is a pipedream or that it is too costly, or they continue to assert that the answer lies in better commissioning, and that personal budgets are for those few people who want day-to-day control of their support services, but that for most they are too much trouble or impossibly complicated. Some people also believe that an important part of the answer needs to be a new type of professional – usually known as a 'broker' – whose job is to guide people through an increasingly complex maze of services. Why this is not the perspective taken in this book will emerge in the chapters to come. The point for now is that 'personalisation' encompasses many perspectives and approaches, and that this book favours In Control's approach which makes bold claims to be radical, open and inclusive but by no means 'finished'.

A book about personalisation must of necessity centre on personal stories of change. A part of my personal story was as a commissioner of services for adults with learning disabilities in West Sussex in the 1990s and early 2000s. West Sussex was a good, well-led authority with strong partnerships between health and social care and a highly professional ethos amongst its staff. We went out of our way to talk with and involve people who used services and their families. We developed a strong, inclusive partnership board and tried hard to deliver the high aspirations for rights, independence, choice and inclusion of the government's *Valuing People* strategy in 2001. Some people got better lives as a result, but it became increasingly clear that there was insufficient money to provide this for the whole population of people with learning disabilities, relying on the old models of commissioning. It is true that quality services cost money (particularly if you pay support staff decent wages), but it is when you have no expectations of people on the receiving end, when you ignore their contribution and those of their families, friends and communities that costs really start to become astronomical and politically untenable.

When self-directed support came along in 2005, we began in West Sussex by focusing on a group of 12 young people with complex support needs who were of an age to move from children's services to adult services. Over a period of time, with help from Carl Poll of In Control, we assisted the young people and their families to develop support plans; we allocated them personal budgets based on a fair, open and clear set of rules; and we helped them find ways to use those budgets to get what the plans said. Instead of the pathways into long-term care, sometimes in 'specialist placements' away from friends and family that faced this group at the outset, they developed their own, local solutions based on their own individual needs and preferences.

This was the right thing to do for this group of people. It was also the cost-effective thing to do; at a conservative estimate the support for the 12 young people cost the authority between £200 000 and £250 000 a year less than it would have done had we commissioned residential care for them. And it was an approach that made the most of the connection, of the contribution of family, friends and community – building on these foundations rather than ignoring and discounting them and uprooting the young people.

The chapters that follow bring this story up to date and show how thinking and practice have flourished in the five years that have followed. This is a handbook, that is to say it is designed to help the readers not only to think about and make sense of 'personalisation' but also to change their behaviour and practice so that it is 'more personal'. This is demanding of the practitioner because it asks more of them in terms of 'personal authenticity' and engagement with the people they are employed to support. As Bronwen Williams and I discovered in our conversations with social workers in the London Borough of Newham, it involves a rediscovery of the 'emotional depths' (Williams & Tyson, 2010). As Pippa Murray puts it in Chapter 4 on working with the families of disabled children, we need an approach that is 'relational', and that makes it clear that we are all of equal value, irrespective of gender, impairment, ethnicity or age.

The book tries to do this by covering the key areas and topics that we need to think about when we are introducing personalisation or self-directed support to a locality, and by showing how leaders can be inspired and how they can then go on to inspire others.

In the first part of the book, we give a voice to some of the *leaders by experience* whose energy continues to drive self-directed support. These include people leading through experience as 'self-advocates' or 'service users', and as families all striving to change health and social care systems so that they get a decent life. The important message here is that ultimately self-directed support will be created by people themselves, this is the beginning and end of the matter, and in one sense the rest of the book is a footnote to this.

This is not to say that others do not have a critical part to play. The second part of the book focuses on some of the ways these others can help to create the conditions that make self-directed support possible. It focuses on the roles played by support planners, 'brokers', commissioners and providers, social workers and local and central government. These people have 'managed' the old social and health care systems, systems which have now had their day; many now accept this and are clear that they have a part to play in what comes next. Some prefer to see the flaws and continue to resist, but we remain hopeful that we can still win them over by the force of argument and evidence.

We have no doubt that existing 'policy', *Putting People First* and *Valuing People Now* is (mostly) quite positive and helpful for personalisation, but the law which governs adult social care is less so. This was made clear in many of the points made in conversations with the law commission in the course of their recent review of adult social care law. It is also the case, as it always has been, that what 'policy' says should happen and reality on the ground are two very different things – the road from number 10 'any street' to number 10 Downing Street and back is a long one, and things tend to get lost or changed along the way.

These chapters spell out how each group of staff and stakeholder are beginning now to think about these issues and to define or redefine their role.

The final part of the book takes a step back and examines some of the broader issues about personalisation. One of the difficulties in thinking and writing about this topic is that we very readily 'lose the plot' as we get sucked into technical detail about how to: how to design the *resource allocation system*; how to provide information that is easy to use; how to make sure that people get the support they need to employ personal assistants and so on. As we have seen, personalisation is about much more than a technical change from one way of spending money to another. It is about some big ideas that are changing society, changing the relationship of individual citizens to the state. The third part of the book looks at some of these ideas: 'whole life' approaches; what is happening in our communities; and what we really mean and intend when we talk about 'outcomes'. The book finishes with an important chapter by Julie Stansfield, the Chief Executive of In Control, which argues that what we are seeing is in fact very much more than an adjustment in the way people experience health and social care services in this country; it is a new 'social movement', a movement for radical change in the way we all think, feel and relate to one another, which will take us beyond the ideas and the systems of the old post-war welfare state.

We have tried to include stories about real people and their lives and how they have changed as a result of self-directed support throughout the book. Many of these 'stories' come directly from the lives of our contributors, others are about people they know or have worked with. We have tried hard to include examples that *make a point* or add to the narrative. We have also included a couple of extended case studies, one about home by Sam Sly and one about paid work by Graeme Ellis because these are such critical issues for us all, and because we cannot really write about personalisation for people with learning disabilities without referring to them.

Finally, a few words about terminology: the title of this book includes the word '*personalisation*' and we have used the word liberally in this introduction. 'Personalisation' is a useful but not a particularly friendly word: it is useful because it describes a necessary change – things most certainly do need to become 'more personal' if we are to create helpful conditions to assist people to get better lives. But the word itself is a 'system word', it seems to suggest that if only we could change the way certain processes work – perhaps if we instructed the staff on our front desk to be a little more 'customer friendly', or tried a bit harder to get hold of someone's mum on the phone when it is time for their review then things will be all right. As the readers of this book no doubt will have realised by now, this is not what we mean here when we use the term 'personalisation'.

Some time ago In Control suggested that we use the terms 'self-direction' and 'self-directed support', which are also perhaps not perfect terms, but at least make it clear that it is the 'self', the 'person' who is running the show. Generally, when we use these different terms now, we use the word *personalisation* when we are talking about the whole system, and 'self-direction' or 'self-directed support' when we are talking about health and social care.

There are similar issues with other terminology used in this book. In Control has used its website and other publications to try and explain and iron out some of these difficulties. For the most part, we have not insisted that the contributors to this book use words in exactly the same way, and we have asked them to explain any technical terms they do use. We hope this works.

I would like to thank everyone who helped with the production of this book: Jan Alcoe and Sanaz Nazemi, editors at Pavilion Publishing; all my colleagues at In Control, particularly Julie Stansfield; Ali Gardner of Manchester Metropolitan University, who shared ideas about social work and writing; Nicola Smith who generously wrote the foreword; and most of all the contributors to this book who gave their time and experience to help with this small step on our journey together to a better world for Jessica and those many people in similar circumstances who rely on our systems of health and social care and who are now demanding a better, fairer life for all.

References

Berry W (1986) *The Wild Birds: Six stories of the Port William Membership.* San Francisco: North Point.

Department of Health (2007) *Putting People First: A shared vision and commitment to the transformation of adult social care.* London: Department of Health.

Department of Health (2001) *Valuing People.* London: HMSO.

Department of Health (2009) *Valuing People Now.* London: HMSO.

Duffy S (2006) *Keys to Citizenship: A guide to getting good support services with people with learning disabilities.* Birkenhead: Paradigm.

Newman S (2000) *Personalisation: Practical thoughts and ideas from people making it happen.* Brighton: Pavilion Publishing.

Williams B & Tyson A (2010) Self-direction, place and community, re-discovering the emotional depths: A conversation with social workers in a London borough. *Journal of Social Work Practice* **20** (3).

Extended case study 1: Home

Hands Off, It's My Home – A path to citizenship

Sam Sly

Sam Sly works as a consultant in health and social care and in 2007
she was seconded to the change team in Cornwall, which supported
the health and social communities in the county to put into action the
recommendations made following the investigation into the care provided
for people with learning disabilities by Cornwall Partnership NHS
Trust. This contribution is based on 23 years of experience, working with
people with learning disabilities and their families, and in particular,
on her experience in developing and using the *Hands Off, It's My Home*
(2008) training pack. This is the first of two extended examples, this one
demonstrating the importance of a home.

Introduction

'Home' is really important for all of us. It's our base, a place of security and
somewhere we can relax, unwind and express our personality and what
is important to us. Recent history for people with learning disabilities is
characterised by life in institutions of one sort or another. People haven't
had proper homes in the sense that we describe them here. Institutional
life began with the large long stay hospitals of the 19th and 20th centuries,
many of which were then broken up to form the smaller campuses and
hostels of recent decades. Then many people were moved to residential care
homes and most recently on to 'supported living' in all its forms.

When given information and the support to make real choices, most people
with learning disabilities now say that they just want to live in their own
homes, in their own communities, with the people they choose and if needed

get some support to do what they want to do. It's what the *Valuing People Now* policy refers to as 'getting a life' (Department of Health, 2009). People will only get a life in this way if we:

▶ give people the information and tools needed to make informed choices about their lives

▶ take those groups important to a person (often families and support workers) on the journey. To do this we need to understand and address their anxieties and fears and build on their hopes

▶ have a framework with which to continually check and improve how we support people so that an institutional culture does not continue to permeate future support.

This chapter discusses the development and learning from implementing *Hands Off, It's My Home! – A path to citizenship*, which is helping change culture and shape practice around the country. It includes feedback from staff who have made the move from more institutional care practices to supporting people in personalised ways, and the aim is to encourage others to make those first steps. This is a critical element in the 'personalisation' of support.

Key points

▶ 'Home' is really important in meeting our emotional needs and allowing us to express ourselves.

▶ Cultural change requires a framework from which to think, check and improve current practice.

▶ Getting support wrong for people with learning disabilities can put their homes at risk, with rights and choices being significantly curtailed.

▶ We need to reflect on poor practice to ensure 'support' does not slip back to become institutionalised care.

▶ When given informed choice most people with learning disabilities choose their own homes with support over residential care.

▶ If the cultural shift is to be effective, those people working with a person who is moving into their own home need their own guidance and support.

▶ The fact that people have lived in institutions for years before moving into their own homes in the community does not mean things are bound to fail.

▶ Workers' fears can stop them embracing change.

▶ The 'supporting' role we now expect of workers is vastly different from the 'caring' role of the past.

▶ Workers who have been empowered to change see the benefits that come from their new roles and enjoy their work more.

Hands Off, It's My Home – a framework for change

Hands Off, It's My Home! is a training pack based on Simon Duffy's *Keys to Citizenship* (2006) and on some of In Control's work since that date (see Chapters 14 and 16). Our expectations of support are now much changed. We expect people to be supported to achieve the following.

1. **Self-determination** – to be treated as a person who can speak up for themselves.

2. **Direction** – to have a purpose or plan for their life. To have a lifestyle that offers satisfaction and personal fulfillment.

3. **Money** – to have money to buy what they need, and have control over how they live and how others treat them.

4. **Home** – to have a place that belongs to them and where they have control over every aspect.

5. **Good support** – that the support received contributes to the person being seen as a fellow citizen by others. That the person has the support they need provided by those they choose. That the support enables them to do what they want, and does not control what they do.

6. **Community life** – that the person plays a part in the community. This means working, learning and enjoying leisure pursuits with other fellow citizens whilst making friends along the way.

We expect workers to support people to get a good life through building on the person's strengths, skills and gifts, to make and sustain those connections that are important in anchoring them into their communities and developing their citizenship. We expect workers to support and facilitate access to communities and finally we expect workers to maximise the person's income whether through state benefits or better still through employment so that the best opportunities are available to them.

These changes need to be made by workers who have supported people previously in a number of institutional settings; hospitals, campuses and residential care homes and though most are willing to change, the ability to shift deep-seated cultural views requires a long, slow process. This process requires patience, careful management and understanding.

The pack provides a framework to enable workers to support people with learning disabilities to get the homes and the lives they desire. It includes a toolkit, guidance and a self-monitoring checklist. The checklist enables organisations to develop an action plan to improve the support they deliver and it addresses common themes that recur in 'institutional' settings. It provides the means to achieve a culture shift in a support service.

Workers, who have been given information on the future, kept informed, had some training before and after moving, and have been supported by their employers find it easier to make such a shift in culture. Amanda Wenden a support co-ordinator for the Brandon Trust said, *'Hands Off, It's My Home! had a major impact on how people saw the homes and tenancy rights of the people they supported, until these changed, houses were run as mini care homes, places of work primarily, rather than people's own homes. On transfer it was not easy to unpick this. The staff were in some ways as institutional as the people we supported. We are continuing to evolve'*.

The themes which the toolkit *Hands Off, It's My Home!* covers are:

Tenure of accommodation: checking that people have the best possible housing and tenure options and understand their rights and responsibilities as home owners or tenants.

The way support is provided: ensuring that people have choice about how and by whom support is provided, and checking that people are being 'supported' as individuals and not 'cared for' as a group. Also looking to make sure workers do not have restrictive practices and mindsets. Making sure support options are not just restricted to paid support.

Support planning and records: checking that planning and recording is person-centred and that plans give the level of detail to enable workers to practice consistently and empower people to do as much for themselves as possible. This should include setting and achieving goals and understanding that risk is a positive part of having a full life. Ensuring that people have individual budgets where possible and always know what support costs, what support they are paying for, and being able to complain if they are not getting it.

Support with financial management: checking that the right people are involved in managing a person's finances, especially when they lack the capacity to manage money themselves, and ensuring that the people who are involved in their money management are up to the job.

The environment: making sure that every aspect of a person's home reflects that it is their home and not a place of work for workers (especially where 24-hour support is provided). Checking that the person makes all the decisions and takes charge of what goes on in their home, and this includes holding the key to their own front door.

Communication: ensuring that workers understand how someone communicates and that this is reflected in how information and decision-making are presented to the person; checking that people know how to complain.

Decision-making with regard to people who lack capacity: checking that workers understand and practise within the framework of the Mental Capacity Act; and that they ensure that people are as involved as possible in decision-making about their lives. Adrian Kennedy, a manager from Lifeways, attended a *'Hands Off, It's My Home!* training workshop and summarised the changes within someone's home and life that should take place in the move from institutional living: *'If we keep thinking, checking and improving we can achieve our goal and people can "get a life"'.*

The history of *Hands Off, It's My Home*

Government policy makes it clear that people with learning disabilities should no longer have to live in institutional settings. The *Hands Off, It's My Home!* toolkit helps people to achieve this. It is also an attempt at implementing the aims of 'Enough is Enough, Time 4 Change!' as a result of the formation of a leadership group which Geoff Baines the former director of the change team started in August 2008. The group consisted of individual champions and leaders (people receiving services, family members, individuals from the independent, health and social care sectors) who came together following the Health Care Commission/Commission for Social Care Inspection (HCC/CSCI) investigation into Cornwall

Partnership Trust in 2006. The phrase 'enough is enough' was used to model appropriate challenge and to provide skills to support people faced with resistance and denial of others around them. In addition, the 'time for change' phrase signaled the intention of positive action.

In 2006, Cornwall Partnership Trust supported over 200 people with learning disabilities of which 166 people lived in 45 houses, which together was called a 'supported living service'. This may well have been an accurate term at the time it was developed. A substantial amount of supporting people funding (money for housing-related support) was invested in the scheme. The term 'supported living' is now widely used and abused to describe a range of support services, many of which have come to constitute little more than small institutions, and this is certainly what had happened in Cornwall by the middle of the decade.

The investigation concluded that 44 of the 45 houses were *'unregistered care homes because accommodation was being provided together with personal care'* and that *'the services must be redesigned, based on the assessed needs of people who use them – or registered as care homes'*.

Some of the key areas of concern for CSCI and the HCC were:

▶ staff had little expectations that people would develop and move on

▶ there were no tenancy agreements

▶ areas of the houses were used to store records and medication

▶ people were not routinely involved in the selection and recruitment of staff

▶ people lacked choice and control over their care, where they lived and who they lived with

▶ people could not refuse entry to their homes

▶ there were restrictive and institutional practices

▶ staff, and not tenants held keys to their homes

▶ staff 'cared for' rather than enabled and empowered people to be as independent as possible

▶ there was a risk averse culture

▶ staff had difficulty accessing training and supervision

▶ there was a lack of monitoring and review by management

▶ there was little evidence of person-centred planning and poor records

▶ staff had considerable control over people's finances

▶ there was evidence of pooling of people's money for household expenditure, and paying for staff expenses and home improvements.

A 'change team' began work in Cornwall in early 2006 following the investigation and report. The team aimed to provide leadership for whole-systems change in the way people with learning disabilities received support in the county. The team was made up of people from outside the county with up-to-date experiences, expertise and most importantly values, principles and ideals. The team worked alongside the existing health and social care agencies, self-advocates and carers to make improvements to the lives of people with learning disabilities.

Sam Sly was part of the team and her role included:

▶ enabling people and their circles of support to make informed choices about whether they wanted to live in residential care or to continue to live in their own homes with support

▶ registering and running a part of Cornwall Partnership Trust as a domiciliary care agency and thereby enabling the staff to continue to support people in their own homes

▶ developing a process so that people and their circles of support could choose new domiciliary care agencies

▶ working with the new domiciliary care agencies and housing providers to improve the quality of support and the home environments for people so that they moved from 'quasi-living' to real living.

Making choices

The first step in the process agreed with the registration authority was to give people living in the homes some choices, these were to either register each house as a care home or to substantially improve on what was being delivered, and ensuring people had a tenancy and appropriate support.

Of all the 166 people given this choice, every one of them categorically said they wanted their own home with support and not to have their home registered as a care home.

As people had been living with the old 'institutionalised' culture for so long, many of them – workers, families and the tenants themselves – all found it really difficult to define exactly what features defined their 'own home with support'. Tenants knew broadly what they wanted, and what it would feel like, but not in any depth or detail. This lack of understanding meant that staff found it hard to pinpoint when things were going wrong, when abusive practices were occurring and when they needed help from the outside to heal or improve things.

Many of the people being supported did not have the capacity to make choices about these things unaided, so advocates and circles of support were created and involved in making decisions. To assist the process a number of easy-read documents were developed to describe the differences and to help people make informed choices (see **Table 1** below).

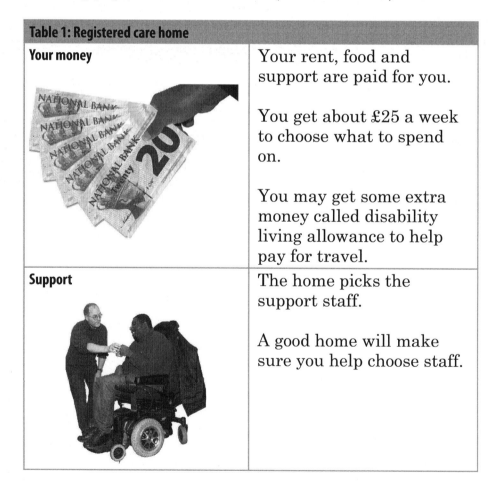

Table 1: Registered care home	
Your money	Your rent, food and support are paid for you. You get about £25 a week to choose what to spend on. You may get some extra money called disability living allowance to help pay for travel.
Support	The home picks the support staff. A good home will make sure you help choose staff.

Management	Your support staff will have a manager who will have an office at the home.
	A support plan and other records about you will be kept at your home.
Records	You will be told about what is written. You can see them if you like.
	The manager will decide what meetings are held at the home.
Paying for your support	Social services will pay for your support.
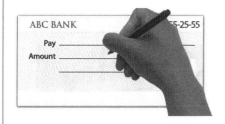	You may pay towards the support.

People you live with 	The home will decide who lives there. You will have your own bedroom. A good home will ask if you are happy with a new person moving in.
Checking the support is good 	The manager of the home will ask you if you are happy with the support you get. The care quality commission (CQC) will check the home regularly. CQC might ask you if you are happy with the home. Social services will check you are happy with the home.
Activities  	The home will arrange and pay for your activities. A good home will involve you in deciding what to do. You may pay towards activities or social services may pay.

Who comes in to the home	It is up to the home who comes in.
	A good home will give you a key to the front door and your bedroom.
Your rights	You will have a contract with the home.
	The home can give you four weeks notice if they want you to leave.

Living in your own home with support

Your money 	You get money to pay for rent, food and bills. You (or your family or support circle) must make sure bills are paid. A support worker can help you. You choose what to spend left over money on.
Support 	You are involved in choosing who supports you.
Management 	Your support staff will have a manager who will visit your home. A support plan and other records about you will be kept at your home. You will be told about what is written. You can see them if you like.

Records	Meetings are only held at your home if you agree.

Paying for your support	You will have to pay for support.
	You can choose how to pay.

Social services can help. Or you can have a direct payment/individual budget. Or you can mix both.

You may get extra money to help pay from the independent living fund. |
| **People you live with** | You are involved in choosing who you live with. |
|  | |

Checking the support is good 	The manager of your support staff will ask you if you are happy with your support. The manager and staff will be checked by the care quality commission (CQC) at least every three years. CQC might ask you if you are happy with your support. Social services will check you are happy with your support.
Activities 	You will choose what to do every day.
Who comes into your home 	You and the other people you live with will choose who comes into your home. You will have the key to the front door and your bedroom if it is a shared house.

Your rights	You have a tenancy agreement with your landlord.
	Your landlord must give one to six months notice if they want you to leave.

(Images courtesy of Pete le Grys. Available at: www. Photosymbols.com)

Once choices were made we needed a framework for the changes in people's homes and lives. It was at this point that the toolkit, *Hands Off, It's My Home!* was developed and in order to make the changes work, it was critically important that those fundamentally involved in people's lives, families and support workers needed to make the journey too. People with learning disabilities and their families needed to be encouraged and supported through the changes or they tended to revert back to their pre-existing ways of thinking and acting. During training on *Hands Off, It's My Home!* a fear regularly expressed by workers is that particular groups of people have been institutionalised for so long that they cannot change and that we are setting them up to fail if we try. This is not borne out of experience: but it is true that things can go wrong if the right measures aren't taken. To protect against this, people need information about what they should expect to empower them; to know what they need to do to reject poor support and to have a clear understanding of their rights. *The Hands Off, It's My Home!* toolkit includes easy-read information about these issues, both for people with learning disabilities and their families.

Often families become disempowered whilst their relative is in an institutional setting: they are often marginalised and excluded from contributing to important decisions about their loved one. Sandy Collington, who is the mother of a woman with learning disabilities remembers, '*We were told that from now on the NHS Trust would manage my daughter's finances, her medical problems and that they would be her guardians and at that time we were afraid to rock the boat and challenge*'.

After her daughter moved from institutional care to support in her own home she said, '*My hopes and dreams for the future are that all people have the opportunity to take control over their lives, choose where they live and do what they want to do like my daughter*'.

Support workers: a changing role

Nick Brown and Sue Weldon are team managers for United Response. Amanda Wenden is a support co-ordinator and David Collier a senior support worker for Brandon Trust. These four people were all formally employed by Cornwall Partnership NHS Trust, and like approximately 600 others, over the past three years in the south west, have transferred or are transferring by Transfer or Undertakings Protection of Employees (TUPE) regulations to domiciliary care agencies. They share some of their experiences below. (These regulations are designed to protect people whose job stays largely the same but whose employer changes.)

The role of the support worker has changed beyond all recognition over the past two or three decades. Training programmes based around the *Hands Off, It's My Home!* model over the last few years have often been attended by workers who have not received the support, training and guidance to understand and keep up with these changes. This means that if quality monitoring and improvement is not on the agenda, then staff tend to revert back to older styles of 'caring for' people because it is easier and it is what they were trained for and understand. Amanda reflects, '*I guess it is all about confidence. Staff were given the confidence to try new things. In the past we were definitely risk averse*'.

Sue said the journey is a '*work in progress – the changes are immense from the perspective of both the staff and individuals we support. Where once it was four people sharing a house and being seen as a group it is now four individuals who chose to live together but are unique and it's their home now – no longer a workplace for us*'.

In the 1980s the support worker role was very much about making sure people got the personal care required to be physically well and safe, to get to their day placements, to have suitable meals on time (usually cooked by workers), to get their medication, to keep the house clean and tidy (usually done by workers) and to get out in the community too if there was time. However, excursions out were usually all together in the minibus and timed to fit in with meals and the shifts of workers. For example, trips to the pub ended at 10pm in order to get back for the worker's sleeping-in shift. This was a very institutional way of working, very similar to the sort of routines from the old long-stay hospitals and it was an approach that was acceptable at that time.

Amanda said, *'We managed B's money, medication, shopping, diet, car, and contact with family, everything. Now we use the phrase "nothing about me without me" and she is involved in every decision that is made about her life'.*

Nowadays a support worker role has changed enormously. David said, *'The sad thing was that we had worked in the NHS for so long doing what we were doing that we were as institutionalised as the people we were supporting'.*

Nick says, *'At United Response we now have great training, regular 1:1 meetings, yearly appraisals, and staff have their own developing excellence folder enhancing skills, experience and performance – none of this was available in Cornwall Partnership Trust'.*

When given leadership, support and praise, teams come on in leaps and bounds and enjoy their new roles. David said, *'The facts are that myself as a team leader and my team have reached what we thought 12 months ago was absolutely unreachable; it has galvanised myself and my team to reach for the next "unreachable"'.*

And most importantly, people being supported flourish. Nick said *'K came with a reputation of being physically aggressive and challenging. K now attends college, accesses and uses the community, engages with family again, has her own small car whereas before she had to be driven around in a large transit van. Her self-esteem on a scale of 1–10 must now be 10!'* This is only achievable if managers actively support and encourage their staff to change.

Helping workers change: using the toolkit

Workers have many fears around supporting people with learning disabilities to live more independently and move on from institutional care. Some of these fears are echoed by concerns about changes in their own roles, which make it hard sometimes to distinguish who they are most concerned for. There is also often a fear of the unknown. David remembers thinking that, '*It was the unthinkable; we were being sold off to the private sector. The worries and concerns for ourselves, our jobs, our pay, mortgages, pension, redundancies and the anger and frustration that the NHS could make these radical changes was beyond belief*'.

The fear of change is real for everyone involved; people with learning disabilities, their families and support workers – and this has to be acknowledged as a real concern if we are to move forward. Workers who experienced the training said they benefited from hearing real stories from people in the same positions who have moved on already. In the words of Martin Luther King, this has enabled people to move from being part of the problem to being part of the solution.

In training sessions based on the toolkit, workers transferring from institutional care settings have expressed their hopes and fears about the move.

Hopes

▶ People will get the **right staff** to support them

▶ People will **get more out of life**

▶ Excitement about the **opportunities** for people and workers

▶ People will show **fewer behaviours** that will challenge

▶ Peope will have more **independence and choice**

▶ People will be **accepted** in society

▶ People will make **new friends**

▶ People will have more **choice and control**

Fears

▶ Isolation of both workers and the people being supported, as most work would be on a 1:1 basis. Some workers felt that working with one person after working in a unit or a large home would be boring for them and for the person they are supporting who would be used to having lots of company. (The trainer explains to workers that the job may isolate the worker more, so and this needs to be considered if they want to continue with their employment, but the person being supported will only be isolated if the worker does not help them access things to do and places to go.)

▶ Loneliness and lack of stimulation for workers and people with learning disabilities. (The trainer points out that if the person is not supported to find things to do, people to meet and places to go they may well get lonely but this is the support worker's job to facilitate.)

▶ The public will not accept people, and they will not be safe in the community. (The trainer explains that people are more likely to be accepted and less likely to be at risk from the public if they have firm connections and are visible in the community and this is a major part of the support worker's role.)

▶ What happens if it fails – where will people go? (The trainer makes clear that there must be good community back up from teams of professionals, but this does not mean building more hospitals and assessment units or we are back to square one again.)

▶ There will be a lack of monitoring, and abuse may occur with staff being open to accusation when working alone and people open to abuse by staff. (Many workers are unaware they will be working for a domiciliary care agency monitored by the Care Quality Commission, and that there will be safeguarding strategies in place in each agency.)

▶ People have been institutionalised for so long now that they cannot change. The move is setting people up to fail. (This is a sad reflection on the sometimes low expectations workers have about people. David sums this up: *'the changes were not difficult for the tenants to deal with, but we ourselves had difficulty in thinking positively and implementing that change'*.)

Training that allows workers to voice their concerns and work through them helps them on their journey. Following *Hands Off, It's My Home!* training, workers provided comments about the changes they plan to make to their practice. These comments included the following.

▶ It will encourage staff to promote positivity and empowerment of individuals.

▶ I will concentrate on the positives and look forward to the future.

▶ I will be aware of giving more choice to people.

▶ I will begin to change my attitude and working practices.

▶ I will try to facilitate more rather than doing things for people.

▶ I will change my attitude for a better future.

▶ I will try to involve clients in everyday activities ie. laundry.

▶ I have a better understanding of the importance of offering as much choice as possible and treating individuals' homes with respect.

▶ I will consider tasks in smaller chunks and not take on the entire task myself.

▶ I will try to be more positive.

▶ I will be more aware and think more deeply about the residents' needs/choices – it's their life.

▶ I will stand back a bit more and make the service user more independent.

Also, moving to employers who embrace individualisation and person-centred support, and value innovation and the skills and knowledge workers bring, has enabled many staff to support people with learning disabilities to gain more out of life. The bonus is that workers tend to enjoy their own jobs more too. Amanda says, *'We used to lock B's clothes away. In fact we locked everything! Gradually all the locks were removed – the last one being the kitchen cupboard last year. B and a worker filled the lock in together with Polyfilla! It was a wonderful moment and we all felt a real sense of achievement'.*

HANDS OFF – IT'S MY HOME

I don't have a rota blu-tacked to my wall
I don't expect to find one anywhere at all
If the telephone is ringing, I pick up to see who calls
I don't have great big posters about slips and trips and falls

I decide what happens, when I go to bed, or eat
I decide who enters in, which people I will greet
I decide on furniture, which bed, which bath, which seat
I decide the temperature and when to turn up heat

All the things around my house, they all belong to me
I don't have strangers coming in changing channels on TV
All the post I get is opened by the addressee
I have dominion in my castle, I have my privacy

I don't use my home for meetings, training or interviews
The colours in my carpet are my favourite chosen hues
All records kept about me are accurate and true
And, if I really want to, I will own 100 shoes

I will make my choices; I will make my own decisions
And any plan I make contains my own wishes and visions
Any person in my home is only here from my permission
No office do I have here, no rules and no restrictions

I decide who to employ to a vacant situation
I decide on where I want to store my medication
I have the right to keep my mother out of my accommodation
And I don't need to have a weekly fire evacuation

No risk assessments stop me from trying something new
I make my own mind up about everything I do
When I need support I will let you know if it is you
Hands off, it's my home – or Sam Sly and I will sue!

Adrian Kennedy, Lifeways
(January 2009)

(Taken from In Control www.in-control.org.uk (accessed November 2010))

References

Department of Health (2009) *Valuing People Now* [online]. Available at: www.dh.gov.uk (accessed November 2010).

Duffy S (2006) *Keys to Citizenship* [online]. Available at: www.paradigm-uk. org (accessed November 2010).

Enough is Enough, Time 4 Change (2010) [online]. Available at: www. enoughisenough.org.uk (accessed November 2010).

Hands Off, It's My Home! – A path to citizenship! (2008) toolkit [online]. Available at: www.in-control.org.uk/HandsOffItsMyHome (accessed November 2010).

In Control (2010) [online]. Available at: www.in-control.org.uk (accessed November 2010).

Further resources

Brandon Trust is a progressive charity that exists to improve lifestyles and deliver greater independence for people with learning disabilities. Available at: www.brandontrust.org (accessed November 2010).

Cornwall Partnership NHS Trust (CQC) provides joint investigation into the provision of services for people with learning disabilities. Available at: www.cqc.org.uk/_db/_documents/cornwall_investigation_report.pdf (accessed November 2010).

United Response is a charity that supports people with learning disabilities, mental health needs and physical disabilities to live in the community, across England and in Wales. Available at: www.unitedresponse.org.uk (accessed November 2010).

Section one:
Leaders by experience

The handbook starts with experiences and reflections from different individuals and groups of people who are directing their own support. In Control has long argued that self-directed support is the most effective and efficient approach in providing people with what is currently referred to as 'social care' support, and to many aspects of 'health care' too. In fact, the majority of people do not make the distinction between social care and health care – most just want a decent life. They want to have a reasonable standard of living, to have friends and sometimes a paid job. They want to be accepted as valued members of their community, and they want to stay healthy. We have gathered evidence from many people in different parts of the country and in very different circumstances which shows that this really is possible and achievable. The chapters in this section explore some of the challenges and dilemmas people have come up against in their lives, and set out things they have found to help as self-directed support has been introduced.

In Control has argued that 'getting a personal budget' is not in itself enough. There is a danger that a local authority introducing a system for personal budgets changes nothing, except the label: it's still the same old product, with a different name. Managers still go on deciding how much money someone is entitled to (often the person who shouts loudest or longest gets most) and what they can spend it on. Ordinary people continue to feel excluded from the important decisions about their own lives; family members are still expected to provide 24 hour 'care', or at the other extreme are shut out of the picture when they have had too much to cope with, and their loved one then has to leave and go into a home.

A personal budget is not enough if it is not understood as a means to an end. That end is citizenship for the person at the centre. Simon Duffy has written about what he calls the 'keys to citizenship' and the first key is 'self-determination'. In this title, *Keys to Citizenship* (2006) Simon says, '*The first thing you need to do if you want to be treated as a citizen is to be recognised by those around you as someone who can be treated as a fellow citizen. This means being someone who counts, someone who has their own voice, their own interests and a life that is genuinely their own. We all want people to treat us as an individual, as a person in our own right.'*

The chapters in this part of the handbook are about people struggling to achieve citizenship. Part of that struggle is the struggle of individuals themselves – what I need in my situation to get a decent life; and part of it is collective – what people with learning disabilities (or other people, in other situations) need to do *together*.

The chapters in this part of the handbook are also about *leadership*. This is important because we are still at an early stage in the process of introducing self-directed support, and the people writing here are the pioneers, pushing the boundaries, trying things out, taking risks. Leadership is especially critical at this stage because many people using health and social care services have been ground down by life and by 'the system', and they need inspiration. In Control and its friends have sometimes been accused of being too upbeat about self-directed support and personal budgets, and of not seeing the very real problems the new approach brings. In fact, the evidence from the chapters here and from elsewhere is that – in common with great leaders in other fields – families and citizens leading this change process are extraordinarily creative problem busters. What they bring is a set of positive attitudes and a shared belief in the values of rights and responsibilities, family, community and inclusion that together provide an incredibly powerful medicine for the health and social care systems – and bit by bit they are beginning to change the world.

Chapter 1

Leading through experience: remembering who personalisation belongs to

Tricia Nicoll

Tricia Nicoll has a history of work in the advocacy movement. She is a long-term user of mental health services and is foster carer for two young disabled people. She worked for the Department of Health's Valuing People Support Team and then the national Having a Voice programme. She now runs her own consultancy and works part time for In Control.

Introduction

This chapter reminds us who the real leaders of personalisation are and where the drive for change and many of the most important ideas came from – disabled people themselves. It traces some of the early history of the disabled people's movement and it focuses on the need to see disabled people as more than just *people with certain labels* or with certain *needs*. In doing this it sets out some of the roots of personalisation and introduces many of the themes that recur in later chapters. It makes the case that if self-directed support is to succeed, then professionals need to really believe and act from the belief that disabled people are best placed to make the key decisions about their lives.

Key points

▶ The fundamental ideas and philosophy behind personalisation and self-directed support come from disabled people themselves. These ideas are not something that central government dreamed up; they are not a passing fad or a simple change in bureaucratic processes and procedures. They are the product of an historic process of change, led by disabled people and their families with the aim of them 'claiming back their lives'.

▶ To make the radical changes that self-directed support demands, services need to work in partnership with disabled people and their families. Working in real partnership means seeing people with learning disabilities (and other disabled people) as more than just 'labels' or 'people in need of help and support', but as people with a concrete contribution to make to society – skills and gifts that they can use and share.

▶ If the system is to benefit from real partnerships with disabled people then those people need the opportunity to understand the system they are joining in order to make effective contributions.

Remembering the history

Through history disabled people have been treated as objects of pity, of fear, of fun or as deserving of contempt. They have been ridiculed and have experienced segregation, oppression and discrimination.

▶ In Greek and Roman times, with their culture of the 'body beautiful', it was common practice to kill disabled babies.

▶ The Middle Ages saw institutions quarantine people with leprosy and the killing of women who were accused of being witches – many of these women were disabled and their impairment was seen as proof that they are evil.

▶ The Priory of St Mary of Bethlehem had been operating as a hospice and hospital from 1329. From 1377 it began to take people who were 'mentally ill'. Records show that by 1450, it was being called by the name that we are more familiar with: 'Bedlam'. By 1700, people were being charged a penny for the privilege of coming to watch the patients.

▶ The Industrial Revolution in the18th and 19th centuries saw social changes away from a situation where most people worked on the land to one where most worked in factories, with no role for disabled people. Institutions and asylums grew in number and size and began to have a 'profcooional' otaff.

▶ By the early 1900s the eugenics movement took hold and '*mental defectives*' were seen as a '*terrible threat to the race*' (Churchill, 1910).

▶ During the Second World War, around 140,000 disabled people were murdered as part of Hitler's plan to create a perfect master race.

It is easy to think of this as awful, but also as 'just history' and something that happened in the past. History, however, continues to shape the present: think of the images our children see in Disney movies where 'evil' witches and other villains are characterised by physical imperfections.

The large number of soldiers coming home disabled by injuries from the two World Wars led to the Disabled Person's (Employment) Act (1944) and a raised awareness and focus on support for disabled people. In 1948, with the National Health Service Act and National Assistance Act, the 'welfare state' was born.

All this meant a range of services that whilst not so overtly barbaric as those in the centuries before, still kept disabled people segregated from the rest of society, and were still clearly controlled by managers and professionals.

In the 1950s, parents and families of disabled people began to find a voice to express their unhappiness with the way their loved ones were required to live their lives, and we saw parent-led charities setting up (Mencap and Mind in 1946 and the Spastics Society in 1954). The 1960s saw the beginnings of demands for deeper change from disabled people, and in 1972 this took the form of a letter written to the *Guardian* newspaper by a disabled man called Paul Hunt.

THE GUARDIAN

London **Wednesday September 20 1972** **5p**

Sir, – Ann Shearer's account of the CMH conference *of* and not *on* the so-called mentally handicapped, challenges our patronising assumptions about such people. It also has important implications for anyone who genuinely wants to help other disadvantaged groups. For instance, practically every sentence in her article could apply with equal force to the severely physically handicapped, many of whom also find themselves in isolated and unsuitable institutions, where their views are ignored and they are subject to authoritarian and often cruel regimes.

I am proposing the formation of a consumer group to put forward nationally the views of actual and potential residents of these successors to the workhouse. We hope in particular to formulate and publicise plans for alternative kinds of care. I should be glad to hear from anyone who is interested to join or support this project. – Yours faithfully,

61 Chettle Court,   **Paul Hunt.**
Ridge Road,
London N8.

(*Taken from www.disability_archive.leeds.ac.uk*)

Paul Hunt developed his ideas while he was living in an institution. He and some other residents had been involved in a long struggle with the local authorities that paid for their care over their rights to have control over their lives. His letter was a call for disabled people to come together and form a collective voice. Several disabled people responded to it, going on to set up the Union of the Physically Impaired Against Segregation (UPIAS).

In the years that followed, disabled people living in specialist homes began to demand the right to live independently by taking control of the money used to fund their care.

'The pioneers of "Project 81" were Philip Mason, John Evans, Philip Scott, Tad Polkowski and Liz Briggs, based in the Cheshire home in Hampshire. They then went about applying the principles of independent living, ie. asserting control about the decisions of their lives, empowering themselves, taking more responsibility about what was happening to them and developing their choices. They were then able to successfully negotiate a financial package which enabled them to move out of the institutions and into the community. They struck a deal for their freedom! This was achieved by coming to a social and financial agreement with their appropriate authorities who were sponsoring them to live in the institutions. In other words, their authority provided them with the amount of money agreed through an assessment, which they could then use to pay for the support they needed through employing their own personal assistants. This enabled this group of people to move out into the community in the early 1980s. This was the start of independent living in the UK. It would change the lives of generations of disabled people to come.' (Evans, 2003)

So, the first direct payment in England was actually made long before the 1996 Direct Payments Act was finally implemented in April 1997.

A partnership of equals ... or everyone is equal, but some are more equal than others?

When you live with a label, it is easy for that label to become who you are. For example, 'John's got Down's syndrome'; 'Cathy's got challenging behaviour' etc. It's like a slightly warped version of the dinner party introduction, 'I'd like you to meet John and Jane – John's a Solicitor and Jane's a GP'. While the dinner party introduction might get you some slightly irritating questions about someone's dispute with their neighbour or their dodgy back, it is unlikely to have people telling you what they think is best for your life – something disabled people get all the time.

Labels make it really easy to start making assumptions. If you asked a sample of a hundred 'ordinary people' to say something about people with Down's syndrome or people with autism, it wouldn't be surprising if they came up with the myths or stereotypes they have grown up with. 'People with Down's syndrome love music and are always happy'; 'People with autism have challenging behaviour'. Labels like these don't help us know *who* a person is: 'John is a really good painter and loves dogs', 'Cathy loves travelling by train and has an amazing capacity to make people laugh'. Think about how you would want to be introduced; by the fact that you have diabetes (and have people watching what you eat!) or by the fact that you're working on your family history?

The media doesn't help as we still hear people described by their 'mental age', perpetuating the notion that people with learning disabilities are eternal children. We also have a media that loves stories where 'vulnerable people' have come to harm because 'the authorities' (whoever they are) didn't do their job and make sure they were safe from harm and protected.

It is important to be clear about this point: self-directed support doesn't ignore or down-play risk, the evidence is quite the opposite in fact, people who control their own support with help are generally much safer than others. Self-directed support in fact comes from a very clear starting point that *people know best what they need* and that everyday life for all of us involves making decisions about risk taking and how best to stay safe.

> When Jake moved with his mum and dad from the city to live in a village in the countryside they wanted to help Jake become part of his community and have people see him as more than the 'odd kid'. Jake is 14 years old and has the label of complex autism. He is very tall for his age and does a few unusual things like flap his arms when he is excited or quote lines from Disney movies. Jake loves being outside and going for walks and this was the main reason for the move to the country. In their early days in their new home, as they were busy unpacking and sorting the new house out Jake and his family would often go to the local pub for dinner. There they got talking to the landlord, Jeff, and found that he had two large dogs. In fact you could often hear the dogs

barking upstairs, and Jeff admitted that finding time to give them the long walks they needed was difficult, as running a village pub is a full-time job. Jake's dad offered to take the dogs three times a week for a long walk with Jake after school, and once with the whole family over the weekend. Getting out and about with the dogs was a great way for the family to get to meet people and soon lots of people knew Jake's name and would say hello. Tom, one of the boys from Jake's school also walked his family dog and they often used to see him to say hello too. After a few weeks, Jake got an invitation to go swimming with Tom and some of his friends after school and soon he had other invitations too.

A few months after they had moved to the village, Jake's mum had a phone call from his school to say that there had been an incident on the school bus and Jake had been bullied. It turned out that one of the kids from another village had been making Jake do silly things and filming it on his mobile phone. As soon as Tom had realised what was happening, he had stood up to the bullies and taken the phone from them. When they arrived at school he had gone with other kids from the village to the head of year and reported the bullies. That evening, Jake's mum went round to say thank you to Tom and he told her, *'It was nothing. Jake is my friend and I won't stand for anyone being mean to my friends!'*

Jeff said that Jake walking the dogs had made a huge difference to their lives. It certainly got Jake the friends he needed and a really great reputation in the village. Jake's mum and dad really liked the arrangement as they often got a free pint when they went for dinner in the pub!

Even when professionals accept that they need to work in partnership with people who are using services, they often invite people because of their label, not because of particular skills or strengths those people might bring. I wonder how many of us when drawing up a list of people we need to invite to a meeting have said (or thought) 'we better ask two users and two carers'. I call this the Noah's Ark principle where we bring people in two by two to represent others 'like them.' At its worst this is no more than ticking boxes; and even at best it is no more than the feeling that 'morally' we perhaps should have 'end users' present. What it is *not* is an approach to get the right people in the room in order to get things done.

Personalisation and Learning Disabilities: A handbook © Pavilion Publishing (Brighton) Ltd 2011

One personalisation project board decided to do some basic 'asset mapping' of the people who were members. They asked everyone to share:

▶ things they could do

▶ things they know about

▶ people and connections they have

▶ things that they would really rather people never asked them to do.

They found that members of the board had worked as accountants and computer programmers, but who were actually there because of their labels of 'mental health service user' or 'family carer'. They also found that people who were there as part of their paid role also had skills that no one knew about – one person had a passion for graphic design and another for photography. In this way they found that they had people with the skills they needed to make many of the huge changes that personalisation demands. To give one example, the family carer who was an accountant was quickly recruited to the group working on the resource allocation system (RAS).

Getting the right people to do the job is sometimes about recognising that as 'professionals' we need to stop, reflect and ultimately sometimes hand a piece of work over to the real experts – people with direct experience.

Quality Checkers are part of the It's My Life Project at Skills for People in Newcastle upon Tyne. Quality Checkers is a social business, which works to:

▶ make sure that people with learning disabilities all over the country get the support and housing they need to live happy and full lives

▶ ensure that people with learning disabilities have more control in saying if their support is good enough

▶ help service providers find out what the people who use their services think of them

▶ provide training and work opportunities for people with learning disabilities.

Quality Checkers monitors services using the Reach Standards in Supported Living – a set of quality standards for supported housing co-designed by people with learning disabilities. They use questionnaires, home visits, telephone conversations, meetings, and talks with close friends and relatives to find out if services are doing a good job. Then they write reports about what action should be taken, and check to make sure the changes that are needed are happening.

The special thing about Quality Checkers is that at least half of each team are people with learning disabilities themselves who know what it is like to receive a service in their home, and *'This means we know what to look for, and people often find it easier to talk to us about their lives and their support.'* (Suzie Fothergill, a member of the Quality Checker group).

The Tickers Award is a partnership between Skills for People and North Tyneside Council. The Tickers Award is an award that is given to services and organisations (doctors, youth clubs, leisure services, short break services etc) that meet a set of standards known as the Tickers Standards. The standards were designed by disabled young people to make sure that services:

▶ include disabled young people in all the activities

▶ are welcoming to disabled young people

▶ listen to the ideas of disabled young people and plan their developments based on the young people's needs and wants.

The standards take into consideration the building, the information available about the service, the staff and the inclusion of disabled young people in the planning and shaping of the organisation. Services are checked by a team of young disabled people using a structured format that includes a self-assessment by the organisation itself as well as interviews and observations. The Tickers team will then decide whether the organisation should receive the Tickers Award. The aim is that information about local services will be held on a website that young people and their families can access to help them select services to buy with parts of their personal budget.

Knowing the job

Have you ever been asked to go to a meeting or event on behalf of someone else and realised really quickly that you're not quite sure what's going on? Have people started using abbreviations or jargon words that you didn't understand? For example, *'We've talked to the JIP and they're going to work with the SMT to agree the RAS....'* Often, when we invite people who use services to get involved in strategic planning processes or service evaluation, we do so without making sure that they have all the knowledge and information they need to have their say. Most of us have built our knowledge of how the system works over several years and it is of course totally unrealistic to expect people outside that system to just step in and get on with it. We also sometimes forget to tell people what they are signing up for; an invitation to 'join the programme board for personalisation' is great but what does that mean I have to do, and for how long?

One of the messages of this book is that what we call 'personalisation' is much more a movement of ordinary people demanding change than it is a series of technical changes in the way local authorities organise services and allocate resources. This movement is powered by programmes like Partners in Policymaking, of which there is much more in the chapters to come. This sort of programme is so important because it addresses the issue referred to here – how ordinary disabled people and their families can get 'up to speed' with information about how the system works so they can make the most of what they have to offer and make a real difference.

Tomorrow's Leaders is part of the family of courses that come under the umbrella of Partners in Policymaking. It was first developed in partnership with the National Forum of People with Learning Difficulties in 2005 because they wanted to understand more about the job they had all signed up for.

The course includes the following.

▶ The history: how disabled people have been treated throughout history and how people came together to fight for change.

▶ Understanding oppression and discrimination and how disabled people are stereotyped.

▶ How policy is made and how government works.

▶ How to be the strongest leader you can.

Some of the important things about the course are as follows.

▶ It is always run by people with learning disabilities in partnership with non-disabled people.

▶ Tomorrow's Leaders' graduates always speak and share their experiences.

▶ People come to the course with a learning partner to offer support during and between sessions.

▶ All sessions run over two days and include an overnight stay (for some people this has been their first night away from home or a service) and there is lots of time for sharing stories about how life can change.

'Tomorrow's Leaders changed my life – it's as simple as that! I didn't know about any of the history stuff, like the awful things that Hitler did to disabled people. I didn't understand how services are planned and how social services have to make decisions about what to spend the money on. I didn't really even think of things like the day centre or the short breaks place costing money – once you know that it costs about £50 a day to go to a day centre you can easily think about better ways to spend that £50! Most of all, Tomorrow's Leaders has given me confidence as a leader because I know how things work and I know the best ways to make change happen.'
(Tomorrow's Leaders graduate, 2010)

Tomorrow's Leaders is now supported by Inclusion North and courses have now run all over the country.

Conclusion

In this chapter, we have traced some of the important history – how disabled people have been seen over the centuries, what this has meant for their lives, and how services developed. We have also seen how disabled people themselves fought for things to be different and won the right to direct payments. In the last chapter of this handbook, Julie Stansfield picks up this story and shows how the independent living movement and the inclusion movement became the drivers behind self-directed support and personalisation.

The key things to take from this chapter are:

▶ remember the importance and power of history

▶ we all need to challenge assumptions (including our own) and see behind the label to find the person and *who they really are*

▶ we need to invite people to the table to help us figure out how to make these huge changes happen in ways that are right for people, but we must invite them for the skills and knowledge they bring, not to tick a box; and we need to make sure they have had the opportunity to learn about and understand the job they have signed up for

▶ we need to recognise when a job would be better done by someone else, someone with direct experience, then we need to hand it over to them.

Reference

Churchill W (1910) [online]. Available at: www.winstonchurchill.org (accessed November 2010).

Disability Archive [online]. Available at: www.disability_archive.leeds.ac.uk (accessed November 2010).

Evans J (2003) *Independent Living Movement in the UK* [online]. Available at: www.independentliving.org/docs6/evans2003.html (accessed November 2010).

Further resources

The Council of Disabled people, Coventry and Warwickshire has a detailed historical timeline of the disabled people's movement compiled by Peter Millington [online]. Available at: www.cdp.org.uk (accessed November 2010).

Leeds University, the disability studies page hosts a large archive of information and articles on the history of the disabled people's movement [online]. Available at: www.leeds.ac.uk/disability-studies (accessed November 2010).

Tickers Award. [online]. Available at: www.northtyneside.gov.uk/browse-display.shtml?p_ID=508817&p_subjectCategory=1022 (accessed November 2010).

Tomorrow's Leaders, for more information contact: info@inclusionnorth.org

Quality Checkers, for information on contact: info@skillsforpeople.org.uk

Chapter 2

Leading as a family

Caroline Tomlinson

Caroline Tomlinson lives in Lancashire with her husband Robert and three children Joe, Rosie and Jacob. Caroline became involved in the world of services as her eldest son Joe contracted meningitis and was left with a huge range of complex disabilities. In her attempt to get a good life for her son, Caroline home educated Joe, she also developed a wide range of inclusive play opportunities, accessed a wide range of learning opportunities including Partners in Policymaking, got several user-led organisations off the ground and was one of the co-founders of In Control. This chapter describes what family leadership means and offers some ideas to make it happen in your own backyard.

Introduction

When disability happens in your family it is like you wake up in a place you never knew existed, a place that many families refer to as 'service land', where things are often done to you rather than with you. The search for an accurate diagnosis takes over your life, believing that if you have a name for what is wrong this will give you the passport to the support and services that you need. We have created a system which has put people in competition with each other, because our social care system is neither equitable nor transparent, we have made people dependent on the system by reinforcing that 'the state knows best', yet we have a population of people with learning disabilities many of who will outlive their families; this has never happened on such a huge scale before (Walker & Walker, 1998). Our systems and services have over complicated the lives of people with learning disabilities and their families, and we now need to return to the important task of helping people to get the ordinary things in life – and for this to apply to everyone, not just the fortunate few. The time has come for a very different conversation by having policy which really does make a difference in people's front rooms.

Key points

▶ Why families are like they are – our pain, our guilt, our love and most of all why facing our mortality is such a scary thought.

▶ How to encourage people to believe in possibility – why self-determination is essential to making this happen.

▶ What the key components are to making change happen – ideas to stimulate people's thinking.

▶ Believing the resource already exists in every community and identifying ways to find it.

▶ Using information technology to make our resources much more efficient and in line within the modern world.

▶ Plan or be planned for – creating a sustainable future for the people we love and care about.

Getting to grips

This was the challenge we had in 2003, two years after the launch of *Valuing People* (Department of Health, 2001). As a family we had to think really hard about do we sit and wait for things to change or do we bring the solution for our son Joe to the table. After all, who was really interested in creating a good sustainable life for our son?

Joe had contracted meningitis at six months old which had left him with complex learning disabilities. Our path was very different to the one we had planned, we had one of two choices – do we sit and wallow in self-pity or do we take control? We chose the latter. The early years were tough but heading towards the dreaded 'transition' phase (from children's services to adult services) was going to be the biggest challenge yet. It felt like heading towards the edge of a cliff, but we didn't know if we would fall into a big black hole or if we would be given a parachute and fly off into the adult social care world and everything would be fine (Heslop *et al*, 2002). Our biggest concern was how do we truly create a life for Joe that is worth living and a life that would continue if we were no longer here. Of course we had two other children, but haven't they a right to live a good life too without having to take practical responsibility for their brother? Peace of mind was all that we wanted.

The main issue for us was not coming up with a person-centred whole life plan, but actually making the plan happen. We had been planning with Joe for years, but we had the impression that the plan had to fit into the service system, a service system that didn't work well for people like Joe who expressed many challenges. Joe was in a minority within a minority, he was one of those people the system has struggled with for years.

If we accepted what had always been done we would get what we have always got – a society that still can't welcome or celebrate difference. On a personal level we also knew that Joe would become increasingly anxious, with his challenges becoming significantly worse and potentially spiralling out of control.

We were willing to play our part – we had no expectation that others would do it for us but we needed some real help to make fundamental changes happen. What we saw was needed was a new way of working with us as a family, a way that was much more equal, a way that encouraged people to take more responsibility and that helped those who were willing to help themselves.

Leading the way

Changing a system shouldn't be done on the back of one person's opinion. What we had by the early 2000s was a consensus of families from across the country, from many different networks, who all thought that the system didn't really work in a way which gained the best outcomes for the people they loved and cared about. These networks included traditional support groups from organisations like Mencap, Scope, Carers UK etc who had all found that when past changes had been made they didn't provide the families with confidence for the future. They also included networks around people with specific needs such as autism and those who relied on technology to keep them alive, who felt that the system had let them down and often failed to provide good local support. There was also a very new and perhaps different network of individuals and families emerging, the people who had experienced a family leadership course such as Partners in Policymaking, who were less focused on the problems and more on designing the solutions.

The system we had didn't make sense for people – you got the prescribed services, either as pre-bought or as provided by the council.

From the late 90s, direct payments became available for people with learning disabilities and this was the first time ever you could get cash in lieu of services. The implementation of this was very different across the country, but for many people once they found out about it they soon discovered their local direct payments scheme was so restricted, it didn't work at all for many people with learning disabilities. This was because of limits on how much you got per hour and because of restrictions on how you could spend it, plus the fact that you were scrutinised to the hilt. Or for people considered very 'complex' you were sent out of the borough to an extra special type of placement, soon discovering that the only thing that was really special was the astronomical cost.

There had to be another way, a different approach to using the same amount of money, but spending it in a way that brought good outcomes for people. Self-directed support was the obvious way to make this work. This had been described by Simon Duffy in his book *Keys to Citizenship* (2006) and had been tried and tested albeit in a small way in Scotland.

Seven steps to change

We managed to persuade a small group of people, including the CEO of our local council to test out the ideas in Simon's book: to question whether they did indeed make for a way to provide support for people to achieve better outcomes, whilst spending no more money. We had a legal framework that we could work with and we had a small group of 15 families who were ready for the change. We brought together some of the best people in the country to work out how to do this and so the early concept was born.

The seven steps of self-directed support were created and they were simple.

1. Find out how much money you can have.
2. Develop your support plan that describes how you will spend your money, keeping your loved one healthy, safe and well and using it in a way which brings about good outcomes.
3. Get the council to agree to your support plan.
4. Organise your money.
5. Organise your support.
6. Live your life.
7. Review and learn.

The money

In the early days a crude resource allocation system (RAS) was developed, enabling people to know how much their estimated amount of money was. The RAS was designed to allocate people with a fair and equitable resource.

When we first looked at how local authorities actually allocated money out to people in the traditional way, we expected people to get an amount of money or service according to their needs: a high level of need would mean more money spent on you, a low level would mean less. What we very quickly established was this wasn't so, in many cases local authorities couldn't actually even tell us how much they spent on individuals, and when they did there was no correlation to need. In fact the only conclusion you could come to was, 'those that shout the loudest get the most'. Surely, this wasn't a fair system for people? The RAS was therefore developed to provide a fairer and more equitable way of allocating the resources and over time it has become much more sophisticated as it has been tried, tested and refined. To date there is still a debate as to whether a national RAS is appropriate and as yet no final decision has been made.

Plan or be planned for

One of the real challenges in this approach is how we stimulate people's thinking about what is possible; for how on earth can someone choose from a rainbow of colours if all they have ever known is red? Getting people to think beyond 'service solutions' is a big challenge and we began by reflecting on how we make choices in other aspects of our lives, how we make choices when shopping online in particular. Wouldn't it be great to have not only the Amazon or eBay of social care, but the Trip Advisor rating system all built into one?

This idea led us to approach Valueworks, an expert IT company, and to work with them to set up a social enterprise, which we called Shop4Support. What we wanted to design was a sophisticated e-market place where you can buy services and other products and find out what is going on in your local community. The website: www.shop4support.com is now live and is slowly building council by council to give people real choice and control over their lives.

The support plan needs to explain how the person can keep healthy, safe and well, who the appropriate decision maker is and how the money would be spent to enable the person to achieve the outcomes they required. For some people control of all their support money was simply too much, and they needed to try and 'dip their toe in the water' first to have a go in a small way. One family came to the conclusion that there simply wasn't enough money available and they would have to negotiate a larger amount. This was, however, different to the old style conversations: it wasn't a question of fighting about 'my disability being worse than yours', it was more a question of demonstrating very clearly through a support plan why this individual would not be kept healthy, safe and well with the money allocated and how just putting in that little bit more could help him to achieve significant outcomes. As self-directed support has developed since those early years it has become clear that individuals and families want what is needed for a decent life, but no more than necessary.

The support plans are all agreed by the local authority, and this process needs to be communicated well with people. People need a clear timeframe to understand what will be done and by when. We also need to ensure we keep things simple – the more complex we make the planning process the less likely people are to help themselves. Equally, people need to be clear about what they need to tell the local authority – so councils need to communicate what they need to know in order to make a judgement and agree support plans.

When the plans are completed people then start to live life. How people manage their money and what support they choose varies enormously. Some people choose to take full control and employ their own staff, some choose to have a provider and some take the care management route but with more choice. The evidence showed that when good plans were made, great outcomes were achieved. The question then arose how do we scale this up when frontline staff are struggling with care plans, day-to-day enquiries and doing reviews?

Keeping people at the heart of what we do

The answer to this question lies in getting families to work with other families to work out what a good life would look like. I visited a group of families in Worcestershire who were really cross at the implementation of self-directed support locally. They were bewildered and very confused by the idea of having a personal budget. I couldn't understand why the families were being so negative initially, but then realised they couldn't see possibilities as they had been given no real help to step back and plan. I offered to spend two days, one month apart so I could see if actions were starting to happen with the families to get them to see possibilities and to make positive change happen on one condition, that if it worked they would help another family in a similar situation. They willingly agreed and so 'Pass It on Support Planning' was born.

Pass It on Support Planning has been modelled on Jamie Oliver's Ministry of Food where recipes were passed on from person to person across a community. The concept of good planning is certainly much more difficult than simply passing on a recipe and we had to understand why Jamie found some of this so difficult. We discovered that the recipes failed to be passed on if people were unenthusiastic about food, had no interest in cooking and no determination to make it succeed.

After working this out and sitting down with the group, things started to change for the families very quickly – it was like I had given permission for them to start to seek opportunities for their sons and daughters. Once a family had a taste of the good life they were more than willing to help others.

Interestingly, this strength still remains several years on and what amazes me is the positive change, not only for the people with learning disabilities, but for their families too. One couple hardly spoke through the training, although I could see they were interested and engaged throughout. They were farmers and practical, salt of the earth type of folk. They were given some simple tools and some real belief over those two days which encouraged them to build an amazing future with their son. He now has his own business making and selling pet bedding and the family is happy as they see a positive future. Mum has grown in confidence and she simply looks much happier and has described how the many years of depression has now been lifted.

Another group of families in the southwest of England had been promised a personal budget from their local authority as part of a pilot but were still waiting. I had been asked by the college they were at to do some support planning with them. We spent two days together and we quickly started to talk about what the young people were going to do all day when they left college. I suggested ways of contributing to their communities and very quickly we were on a roll. The group of young men had a great bond and were interested in doing something productive together. It was soon very evident that they needed ideas about planning and setting up a business, not a personal budget and so that is what they are in the process of doing.

Of course they will all need elements of support, but for now the plan is that they set up their own social enterprise with the help from a supportive employment organisation. Self-directed support is much more than having a personal budget, it is about self-directing your life. We now ask, what has happened to some of the young people on the original pilot, seven years on?

Craig's story – control to the end

Craig had been known to the service system for many years, he was 17 years old when he embarked on self-directed support and his 'transition' into adult services was imminent. By this point Craig has already lived much longer than had been expected when he was an infant. He lived his life in and out of hospital and used the local children's hospice for respite. He had attended special school since the age of two and was in the further education division of the school. His mum, Lynne, was known for asking for more and more respite.

Craig was offered a personal budget based on the very crude resource allocation system. We started to develop a support plan with Craig and his family, and Lynne felt it would be too difficult to be the employer and take all the responsibility on as a family, and so decided that a service provider was needed. However, it soon became clear that the cost would be above the indicative amount. Using the support plan we were very able to clearly demonstrate why Craig needed a higher allocation. This enabled a very clear conversation to take place with the council and the revised amount of money was offered.

The family chose a provider which worked very well, but over a period of time the family gained confidence in managing the support themselves. After less than a year they decided to cut out the 'middle man' and become the employers. Craig's life was transformed overnight – he had his own team to enable him to do all the things that his peers take for granted. He went swimming, abseiling, canoeing, did voluntary work, went to college and line dancing to name a few things. He no longer went 'to respite' but had a break from his family, or his family had a break from him by using their caravan near Blackpool. His health improved significantly and his constant seizures almost disappeared and he put on weight. It was evident that his team of personal assistants were providing continuity of care and support that Craig had never experienced before and this was the vital ingredient that significantly improved his quality of life.

His family could live their life, but be together whenever they chose. Mum went back to work, she hadn't worked since Craig was born and chose to use her skills to help other families. Dad could retain his job and developed a much more intimate bond with Craig.

Craig maintained his health, well-being and a good life for six years and the family very clearly said that these were the best years of his life. Sadly, Craig died aged 23 years old on 13 July 2009 from pneumonia. However, his team were at his side constantly, they provided a personalised service until the very end of his life.

Katie's story – control – gaining it, losing it and getting it back

Katie was one of the early adopters of self-directed support and her family was hugely supportive of the idea. She was the second eldest of four children and had significant challenges with her behaviour, in particular at home with her younger siblings. Having their own personal budget meant the family could employ their own staff and Katie's life changed dramatically, in particular during the school holidays when she could do her own thing and her siblings (who were much younger) could do the things they enjoyed, and everyone was happy.

As time went on Katie left school and the family chose a mix of support from both the council and her own directly employed staff which seemed to work well. The next obvious step was for the family to plan for Katie to leave home. With support from a variety of people and a few struggles with the council about Katie living on her own, the family finally agreed on Katie living in a shared tenancy. They agreed to Katie sharing with two other people as long as Katie and her family had a choice of who she lived with and who supported her. As Katie was the first person to move into the tenancy, the family got involved in the recruitment of a provider organisation. In hindsight, the family says that this was the point when they started to lose control. The providers were chosen from three organisations who applied from the council's preferred provider list. The family was clear that none were very good, but felt stuck between a rock and a hard place so they went ahead with one of the providers. They believed that it was more about the people who supported Katie rather than the organisation which employed them, and as they had some say in the recruitment of staff they felt it right to go ahead.

At first Katie moved into the property on her own and the support worked well – it was very person-centred and of course revolved around Katie. A friend of Katie's was planning to move in with her over the coming months and so things were looking positive. Then almost out of the blue the social work team had an emergency placement to make, before anyone could catch their breath a young man had moved in. Initially Katie and her family were OK – after all who wants to see anyone struggling? But it wasn't appropriately planned and no real matching had occurred to see if Katie and this young man were compatible, it was simply another case of 'here is a vacancy'.

Very soon the situation deteriorated with the young man proving very demanding. He constantly made derogatory remarks about Katie and her anxiety levels increased; her challenging and self-harming behaviours got worse. The family tried to negotiate with the local authority but they were insistent it could work, suggesting that Katie may like to spend more time in her bedroom. The staff were struggling too but the provider organisation had a contract to deliver. The situation finally broke down completely and the family had no choice but to remove Katie from the property. The family felt so very low, they had taken their foot off the accelerator and had lost control.

Eventually a new personal budget was offered and a new support plan developed. This new plan was acted on very quickly. Katie got the keys to her new apartment at the end of July 2010 and in the words of her mum, '*So we can now get on with it, Katie is happy, we are back to using staff she loves, yes Katie really now is in control'*.

The question posed by Katie's story is why do we set people up to fail? As parents of our non disabled youngsters we wouldn't let our sons and daughters move in with someone they have met twice at McDonalds for tea so why on earth do we think this is ok for people with learning disabilities?

But it's all right for you

As people hear the stories of how the new system is working for so many people there is a comment that keeps recurring time and time again, '*but it is alright for you*', the feeling that personal budgets will only work for those articulate, well educated, middle class people.

The fact is, personal budgets will work for those people who want them to work. The very concept means that it should work for everyone if the arrangements are truly personalised, and if they aren't, then we are not doing things right. Personalisation is about developing a new relationship between the citizen and the state. For many years we have had a system where people have become more and more dependent and have contributed less and less. The state system has become the answer to everything as it has attempted to be all things to all people. The system cannot continue in this way, it needs to encourage, nurture and grow a new culture of help for those who are willing and able to help themselves.

When my son was very young a senior health visitor gave me some very good advice: she told me that no one was really interested in my son but me. At the time the words seemed harsh and extremely hurtful but as time moved on I started to discover she was right. If we think about who are the consistent people in the lives of people with learning disabilities, for most it is their family. What we also know is that as a person gets older, the facts of old age and death mean that family networks start to diminish, and for many people they end up totally reliant on paid staff.

How are we investing in real families, in family leadership, in creating a sustainable life for people when their families are no longer around? We have for years fudged the issue with the 'carer's agenda' patting families on the head in a patronising, non-meaningful way that has offered no real resource apart from the odd head massage or pedicure. The real fact is that we need practical help and information to ensure the lives of our grown up children are as good as they can be.

Families making change happen

Partners in Policymaking and associated courses have offered individuals and families an excellent lesson in helping themselves. The course takes people on a journey of discovery which gets them to look at why things are the way they are. It gives people the tools to make change happen in their own lives, builds up their confidence and self-esteem to influence and help others in their community. The course brings the best speakers from across the world and gives a real flavour of what is possible. There is no doubt that it inspires, motivates and can visibly change the attitudes of the participants to their own families, to each other and most importantly to themselves.

The course is based on a US model and I was privileged to be on this first course and it gave me the practical tools that I needed to do what felt right in my own heart. The course has now helped over 1500 people in England, as it has been delivered in various formats across the country (Chapter 16 expands on this further).

Self-efficacy is the academic term for believing in your own capabilities to achieve your goals and being able to succeed regardless, whatever barriers or challenges are put in your way.

'*If people experience only easy successes they come to expect quick results and are easily discouraged by failure. A resilient sense of efficacy requires experience in overcoming obstacles through perseverant effort. Some setbacks and difficulties in human pursuits serve a useful purpose in teaching that success usually requires sustained effort. After people become convinced they have what it takes to succeed, they persevere in the face of adversity and quickly rebound from setbacks. By sticking it out through tough times, they emerge stronger from adversity.*' (Bandura, 1994)

I'm absolutely convinced that had I not had a child with a disability, my sense of strength and self-efficacy would have never evolved and I certainly know that I never really appreciated the saying 'try and try again'. I also firmly believe that talent is often overrated, it is how much you want something, how determined you are and when you can't possibly lose that will make you succeed.

My personal example of this was when I had experienced Partners in Policymaking, it started me on a journey, and eventually we were fortunate to be the first people in the country to experience how personal budgets worked and then things just started to take off. The early visioning we had done with person-centred planning on the course was that Joe would have his own house, his own car and would be doing something like a job – yet in my heart as much as it was a goal or dream I didn't believe it would actually come true.

How wrong I was – having the taste of something good but when we got the control we started to explore things for ourselves. Joe could have his own micro business and start doing something productive all day by contributing to his community. We set up The Odd Socks Enterprise which quickly evolved into a successful social enterprise providing a useful service to the community. We understood that for him to have a real quality of life transport was essential and so we got an open insurance policy on his mobility vehicle so his team could go with him anywhere. The real icing on the cake though came with his ability to own his own home. We got a mortgage for Joe and he lives in the house next door to us, meaning he can choose who moves in with him and who moves out, but more importantly no one can ever kick him out of the property.

Looking ahead

So what about the future? This is the scariest, most difficult issue for many families. Many older family members were told that it is likely their child will die before them – and we know many hoped they would because the thought of dying with your adult child being supported by the state is a fear that many people simply do not want to face. The fact is that we are now being out lived by our disabled sons and daughters in significant numbers, and so this is a fear we need to face.

We need to understand that the biggest disability most people will face in this country is isolation and loneliness and being disconnected has a huge negative impact on any individual's mental health and well-being. Yet what are we doing to prepare for the inevitable? This question bothered me significantly: what would happen to Joe in the future and who would know his real story?

When I say who will know his story it is that I'm convinced that the assessments gathered by the state over the years will not reflect the real story for Joe. If people don't really know him well what will happen when I am gone?

To illustrate this, about 18 months ago Joe visited London with a couple of friends and his PAs. He has an unexplainable obsession with carrier bag handles and he especially loves Sainsbury's carrier bag handles. They all decided to go to the South Bank on the tube and in the carriage there was a man taking a small party of school children on a trip. He was holding the rail above him and carrying a Sainsbury's carrier bag full of sandwiches.

As Joe stepped on the tube he launched at the man and grabbed his bag, ripping it from the terrified man's hand. Immediately his team stepped in, they caught the sandwiches, and offered the man a new carrier bag and explained the situation. Just imagine the scene if the people supporting Joe didn't really know him – my guess is that the situation would have escalated out of control and Joe could have been taken away never to be seen again. This isn't an extreme thought, we know it has happened to many people over many years but now we have a chance to get it right.

My experience of seeing what has happened to individuals without a plan scared me senseless. I knew a story of a father who supported his daughter with learning disabilities and he one day died in the supermarket, unexpectedly. The young woman was quickly taken off to the local respite centre where she could only stay for 10 days and then she was shipped into a hostel where the average age of the 25-plus residents was 64 years old, and this young woman was 24 years old. Eventually her brother who lived on the other side of the country tried to help her out but needed her to move close to him, but neither his local authority nor where the young woman lived would fund her if she moved. Eventually after several years she moved into a house with friends she went to school with and all was well, but perhaps if only her dad had planned for her future after his death could she have stayed in the family home.

It was this story that pushed me to ensure that this would not happen to my son and so I continued to search, until eventually I came across an organisation called PLAN based in Canada. They have developed sustainable circles of support for many families across Canada in a way that I thought could be replicated in the UK. I then found out that in Scotland they had set up an organisation which did something similar called Equal Futures. After some research we started to develop something similar in England and Our Futures was born. We set up the co-ordination with a strong, family-led organisation, Embrace Wigan and Leigh, which was supported by In Control. We now have six groups working in various places across the country and these are small groups of families with one core common aim: to secure a good life for their son and daughter when they are no longer here. Circles are evolving and are getting stronger by the day; the small groups are becoming self-reliant and offer mutual support to each other. Families are learning the importance of developing wills and trusts, looking into the Mental Capacity Act, handing over their stories to others and preparing for the inevitable, but most importantly a sense of peace of mind has started to evolve. Interest in the model is growing and a progress report will be written in late 2010.

What next

The problem with personalisation and the transformation of social care is that it is a bit like a Rolf Harris painting in that no one knows what it looks like until you stand back and look at it once it is finished. Not one local authority has totally transformed their social care system, some are getting near and some are light years away. However, the one thing we know is that you simply can't just change the process or fiddle around at the edges, it has to be driven from the heart and led from the top as a clear values-led agenda. We know it can bring efficiencies, it can make us work much smarter but ultimately it has to change lives. Remember the only way the people think a policy or government directive is any good is *if it makes a difference in your front room.*

As a final note from me: personalisation is the only thing that has made a difference in our front room and not only for Joe and our family but the biggest difference can be seen in the community. Joe has friends and I don't even know who they are, but then what's so extraordinary about that – it is how it is with my other children!

References

Bandura A (1994) Self-efficacy. In: VS Ramachaudran (Ed) *Encyclopedia of Human Behaviour* Volume 4. New York: Academic Press.

Department of Health (2001) *Valuing People: A new strategy for the 21st Century*. London: Department of Health.

Duffy S (2006) *Keys to Citizenship*. Birkenhead: Paradigm.

Heslop P, Mallett R, Simons K & Ward L (2002) *Bridging the Divide at Transition: What happens for young people with learning disabilities and their families?* Kidderminster: British Institute of Learning Disabilities.

Walker C & Walker A (1998) *Uncertain Futures: People with learning difficulties and their ageing family carers*. Brighton: Pavilion/Joseph Rowntree Foundation.

Further reading

Equal Futures (Scotland) [online]. Available at: www.equalfutures.org.uk (accessed November 2010).

Pass it on Support Planning, for more help and ideas see the publication list and fact sheets [online]. Available at: www.in-control.org.uk (accessed November 2010).

PLAN [online]. Available at: www.plan.ca (accessed November 2010).

Shop4Support the My Life section [online]. Available at: www.shop4support.com (accessed November 2010).

Chapter 3

Leading in health: personal health budgets

Jo Fitzgerald

Jo Fitzgerald lives in the north west of England with her husband, Stan, and two sons, Mitchell and Daniel. Jo's life was profoundly transformed when Mitchell was born 18 years ago with a severe learning disability and complex health needs. The experience of being Mitchell's mum has largely influenced the direction of her life; it has shaped her beliefs, values and life choices.

Introduction

When my son was born 18 years ago, I joined a 'community' of parents whose lives have been profoundly transformed by the birth of a child with a learning disability and complex health needs. Like most women, I'd imagined giving birth to a lively, bouncing baby. Instead, my son cried day and night, had difficulty feeding, and never made eye contact. At one year old, an MRI scan showed there had been no trauma, no accident, no one to blame; his brain had simply grown in a unique and disorganised way that would shape and define both his life and mine. This chapter discusses some of the issues we faced as a family and sets out how the advent of self-directed support and personal health budgets are now helping. I also describe the challenges these new ways of working bring and suggest how we can address these.

Key points

▶ It is of absolute importance that professionals listen to individuals and families. People with complex health needs require expert clinical support, but they and their families are the 'experts' in their own life.

▶ People and families need access to the same information as commissioners and health care professionals.

▶ The transfer of power to people must be real – it is too easy at present to create a sham. A person is only empowered when they truly feel it.

▶ Timing is crucial. People need to be offered a personal health budget at the right time for them.

▶ We need to believe and trust in people; people are innately resourceful. It is the job of professionals to create the right conditions to utilise this resourcefulness.

Why we need self-direction in health

Giving birth to a child with complex needs is a stark reminder that we have limited control over our children's birth. Try as we might to mitigate the chances, every year families are confronted by the uncertainties and vagaries of life with a disabled child. Some children will be born with a learning disability and very complex health needs and throughout their lives will rely heavily on input from health care professionals. Whilst more children and young people are surviving into adulthood, the majority has a tenuous hold on life and families are faced with the previously unthinkable. They have little or no control over what will happen; lives can be limited and there may be many peaks and troughs. This shakes families to the core, lifting them out of their 'taken for granted' worlds and challenging them to live with feelings of uncertainty and powerlessness.

One way in which people manage this is by increased vigilance. They become attuned to the subtle nuances of a particular condition and become skilled at anticipating illness long before there are clear symptoms. They become expert at managing health needs and their expertise becomes integral to the good health and well-being of the child or adult they are caring for. When things are working well, it is usually because there is a good working relationship between the people who support someone on a daily basis and the professionals who provide ongoing health care. Everyone's knowledge and skill is valued and contributes to a clear picture of the whole person in their whole life context.

When things are not working well, it is often because the service they are receiving is not a good 'fit' or even 'one-size-fits-all'. We know that good services depend on listening to the person who needs support (or their representative) and understanding what is important to them and what is important for them, not only in relation to their health, but how they want to live their life and what a good life would mean to them. To do this, people need the freedom to make decisions and to have direct input into how support is delivered.

When people have large packages of health care support at home, the loss of privacy and control can be very problematic. As one mum said, '*It is a double-edged sword. As much as I have lost due to the nurses, I also need them greatly*'. Likewise, '*There are times when your home isn't your home. It's not really; it's so invasive isn't it? …. You pretend to be somebody who you're not…*'

What complicates the picture for people with a learning disability and complex health needs is the *degree* of support that is needed, the *type* of support required (which often includes clinical tasks), the necessary level of training, the perceived level of risk in providing the support and the need to ensure that the support the person needs does not obscure their hopes and aspirations.

These are the challenges we faced when my son was struggling to breathe and needed a tracheotomy to survive. The losses and gains were complex. A care package would support him to live safely with his tracheotomy but that support would mean a loss of privacy, freedom and control in our lives. The service he received for the first few years was hospital-based and did not meet his needs so we looked for an alternative. People were already directing their own social care support; we wanted to do the same for his health care.

There is strong evidence that self-direction in social care has brought consistently positive outcomes for people. Individual budgets and direct payments have made a great difference for people who need support to live a good life and to meet their aspirations. The In Control Third Phase report includes evidence from around 400 people who say life has got better for them (In Control, 2010). What is especially interesting is the fact that a significant number of people say their health has improved as a direct result of having more choice and control in their lives. Indeed, '*Good health depends on much more than just access to even the very best health care. It depends on active citizenship – a home, a job or opportunity to contribute, an income and friendships.*' (Brewis & Fitzgerald, 2010)

The evidence gathered from people with direct experience is very persuasive. Knowing that individuals with disabilities led the call for change is also a powerful testament to the commitment and enterprise of active citizens.

While self-direction initially developed in social care, the potential benefit to people with a learning disability and complex health needs and who are therefore in a large part dependent upon health services is very evident. We know that the split between social care and health care is artificial; people's lives do not slot into one of two parts. If we focus instead on the concept of 'whole people in their whole life context', then self-direction is readily transferable from one field to the other (see Chapter 14 for a detailed discussion of this point). That's not to say that social care models can be transposed onto health care; it is the concept of improved decision-making and a changed relationship between individuals and the welfare state that are the same.

A growing appreciation of the potential for more individualised health care built on a new relationship between individuals, families and professionals resulted in the launch in 2009 of a national pilot of self-direction in health (Brewis & Fitzgerald, 2010). In Control launched their Staying in Control project in spring 2008.

The aim of In Control's work in health is to improve the quality of:

▶ the conversation between people and health professionals

▶ decision-making and support/treatment planning to enable people to organise their support in ways that make sense to them

▶ health outcomes, through shifting power and decision-making closer to the person directly affected.

As with self-directed support in social care, there is a strong emphasis on improved outcomes. In Control's working definition of a personal health budget makes this explicit.

'A personal health budget is an allocation of resources made to a person with an established health need (or their immediate representative).
The purpose of the personal budget is to ensure the person is able to call upon a predefined level of resources and use these flexibly to meet their identified health needs and outcomes.

The person must:

▶ know how much money they have in their personal budget at any given time

▶ be able to spend the money in ways and at times that make sense to them

▶ agree the outcomes that must be achieved with the money.

The budget must be:

▶ used in ways that help the person achieve predefined outcomes

▶ targeted towards individuals with specifically defined needs.'

(Brewis R & Fitzgerald, 2010)

The Department of Health (DH) also launched a pilot programme in spring 2009 and as part of this programme the Department of Health is piloting direct payments for health care. Under the authority of the Health Bill passed in 2009, the Department of Health has developed regulations that allow direct payments in authorised pilot sites. They have set out some basic rules governing what a direct payment can and cannot be used for but have deliberately left room for great flexibility to enable maximum creativity.

The differences between self-direction in social care and health care

Whilst developments in social care provide some useful referents, it is important to acknowledge that there are significant differences in legislation, history, culture, numbers and a range of professional expertise. For instance, the NHS has at its heart three core principles:

▶ that it meets the needs of everyone

▶ that it is free at the point of delivery

▶ that it is based on clinical need and not the ability to pay.

For this reason, the DH has stated that a personal health budget should meet a person's agreed needs in full, not in part. An individual is not expected to use his or her own resources to purchase additional care.

The different histories and the vast cultural differences between health and social care services represent the biggest single challenge to the development of personal health budgets. There are often multiple 'voices' in the care and support of a person with a learning disability and complex needs. Our son has several hospital consultants: he has a consultant in paediatrics, respiration and long-term ventilation, neurology, orthopaedics, ear nose and throat (ENT), as well as a GP, physiotherapist, occupational therapist, specialist tracheotomy nurse, learning disability nurse and dietician. There is a vast degree of professional expertise which makes it all the more important that our son's voice is heard clearly amongst all the clinical voices so that he is known as a whole person in his whole life context.

This issue in many ways encapsulates the shift in thinking and culture that is needed: clinical expertise is absolutely critical to the health, well-being and day-to-day quality of life of the people we are talking about here. But no one in the group of highly skilled professional people who work to support my son is an expert in *his life*: that is the prerogative of the person and of those who love and care for him.

Another challenge to the implementation of personal health budgets is the legislative context. Currently, direct payments are only available in a small number of pilot sites approved by the Department of Health. This leaves two other ways of holding a budget.

▶ **A notional budget.** This is where the person knows how much money is available to plan with but where no money changes hands.

▶ **A budget held by a third party**. This can be an independent user trust, a social enterprise, a user-led organisation, a voluntary organisation of a private company.

Finding a third party to hold our son's personal health budget proved to be a challenge. Many of the organisations geared up to supporting people with a social care budget did not feel confident or competent to hold our son's budget. They cited anxieties about financial and clinical risk associated with our son's package.

Lastly, self-direction is not always practical in health care situations. Take the concept of 'co-production' for example, which means 'producing together'. Whilst this is crucial when developing a support plan, it is not appropriate for agreeing life-saving treatment after a road-traffic accident. In this situation, people want a skilled health care professional to make the best clinical decisions and to act swiftly on their behalf. There will always be health situations in which we seek to leave power and decision-making with expert professionals. At critical moments, having trust in others and their expertise can be essential for our health and well-being.

However, if a person has a long-term condition that requires ongoing management, a learning disability and complex health needs for example, it matters what they think, how they live and what they do. It matters to their health and to their whole lives. It is important to understand each person's deeply personal and unique perspective on how they experience their condition. Certainly we have always wanted our son's consultants to share best practice with us and discuss the latest clinical evidence but when it comes to decision-making, we want to work in partnership with them. A consultant might be an expert on neurological conditions but we are the experts on how our son experiences his condition and how it impacts on his daily life. We know how a particular medication affects his levels of alertness and ability to engage with his friends. We are also best placed to decide who supports him. It is crucial to our family that we are able to decide who comes into our home, when they come and how they support our son.

Five key messages about personal health budgets

Our son has had a personal health budget since September 2007. It has given us the choice and control we need to organise his support in ways that make sense to us and has taught us a lot about how personal health budgets work in practice. We learnt the following.

1. The importance of listening to individuals and families
Being listened to and understood very early on in the process of developing our son's personal health plan was especially transformative for us as a family. It enhanced our self-belief, enabled us to clarify our thoughts and crystallised our vision. It is widely acknowledged that clinicians and services will experience and need to embrace a huge culture shift as personal health budgets are introduced; this is also true for people and families. After years of being 'done to' by services, having the opportunity to talk intimately about their experiences and articulate their ideas for a better life with improved health outcomes is extremely important. It will help people engage with the process and explore what a personal health budget might mean to them in order to unlock potential.

2. People and families need access to the same information as commissioners and health care professionals

Unless people and families have access to the same information about personal health budgets as commissioners and health care professionals, they will continue to be disempowered by the system. The NHS white paper (Department of Health, 2010) reiterates the phrase 'no decision about me, without me'. It says, '*We will put patients at the heart of the NHS, through an information revolution and greater choice and control…. Shared decision-making will become the norm*'.

People need accurate information that empowers them to challenge the artificial barriers they face when the information they receive is inaccurate or when an organisation is reluctant to change or surrender power. Certainly, the NHS white paper acknowledges that 'bottom up' approaches that encourage people to share responsibility for their health care produce better outcomes for people and the welfare state.

3. The transfer of power to people must be real

My family and I learnt that it is often difficult for health care professionals, commissioners and providers to surrender power. Involving people in planning their own support is not the same as sharing power. We learnt this lesson when we entered into a third party arrangement based on a false set of assumptions. We assumed that what we meant by being 'in control' was the same as the organisation we had appointed to hold our son's budget. Sadly, within two or three months, it became clear that we were talking a different language. From their point of view as the third party, they were responsible for the budget and all important decisions. So what we actually experienced was no shift in power; it felt like what we were getting was no different to the service we had left behind. We have since brokered an arrangement based on shared values and aspirations which is working as we had always imagined.

4. Timing is crucial

People with a learning disability and complex health needs can experience many peaks and troughs in their long-term condition. Secondary respiratory infections are a particular hazard along with dysphasia, body shape distortion and epilepsy. Our son's tracheotomy came out of the blue and was a shock to us all. That's why the timing is crucial when a person is offered a personal health budget. When our son was discharged from hospital, we would not have wanted nor been ready to manage a personal health budget. We were adjusting to a life with an increased level of risk, a substantial package of support and the loss of his beautiful voice. However, things felt very different two years down the line. It seems important, therefore, that when people are offered a personal health budget that we attend to where they are, not only in relation to their health, but also in the context of their whole life. Is it the right time for *them* or would they rather wait to take more control over their health and support.

The concept of timing is particularly pertinent for young people with a learning disability and complex health needs who are going through transition. Young people who have benefited from a social care individual budget can face an arbitrary crisis at age 18 if they become eligible for fully funded continuing health care. They describe 'falling into a black hole or 'hitting a brick wall' when told that a change in funding means their support package must end. Having a personal health budget can ensure that existing support plans and their concomitant arrangements are transferable to adult services. Chapter 4 says more about some of these issues.

5. We need to believe and trust in people

It's my own personal belief and my experience as a qualified counsellor that people are innately resourceful. The majority of people I meet who care for someone with a learning disability and complex health needs are wholly committed to ensuring that the person they support stays safe, well and has a good life. The success of personal health budgets will largely depend on the investment we make in people directly affected by health conditions and their family members. We need to support people, give them good information and, above all, trust them to manage the budget and provide good support. By creating the right conditions, we will empower people to take control, be creative and make the best use of public money. Although it may feel difficult, commissioners and health care professionals will need to surrender some of their power, let go of their traditional role in decision-making, trust in people and work in partnership with them. Likewise, people who are used to being passive patients will need to accept that more power brings greater responsibility. They will need to make an active contribution to their own health and well-being.

There is huge potential for a better future for people with a learning disability and complex health needs. This will necessitate a significant culture shift, a changed relationship between citizens and health care professionals and systems and processes that put decision-making as close to the individual as possible.

References

Brewis R & Fitzgerald J (2010) *Citizenship in Health*. London: In Control.

Department of Health (2010) *Equity and Excellence, Liberating the NHS*. London: Department of Health.

In Control (2010) *A Report of In Control's Third Phase, Evaluation and Learning, 2008–2009*. London: In Control.

Chapter 4

The families of disabled children and self-directed support

Pippa Murray

Introduction

Since the inception of the welfare state, efforts to support disabled children and their families have been rooted in a paternalistic culture encouraging dependency. Personalisation challenges everyone to think and act differently. Rather than accepting what current systems offer, families are asked to think about what would work for them and how to put that in place; and professionals are challenged to put their trust in the solutions families come up with. This is a big change to the way things have worked, and we all need to adapt to this new way of working. This chapter explores two key issues raised so far as families begin to take control over their support:

▶ the cultural change that self-directed support demands

▶ the practical steps needed to support families.

The material presented is based on extensive work with families, and professionals in the voluntary and statutory sector.

Key points

▶ Personalisation challenges the prevailing assumption that families with a disabled child are 'at risk of breakdown' and says instead that they may simply need more support.

▶ Support should be designed around the needs of the whole family, which often means finding ways to help the whole family spend time together.

▶ We need a *relational model* to underpin the shift to self-directed support. This means an approach that affords everyone equal value.

▶ There needs to be a range of types of support available for families. Some of this support will be different to the types available to adults with personal budgets.

▶ There are a number of important practical things that families need to make the most of self-directed support. These include: good information; help and encouragement with support planning; the opportunities to meet and learn from other families; and the opportunity to hear stories about what is possible and achievable.

Section one: cultural change

State assistance for families is presently rooted in legislation, in child protection and 'children in need' processes. As far as providing *support* to families goes, social care is expected to deliver this through an opaque, subjective assessment system and allocation process based on parents demonstrating that they are struggling and heading towards family breakdown. Pulling families who simply want to take the best possible care of their children into systems focused on managing the risk of abuse creates unnecessary, time consuming and expensive processes that often have little benefit for those seeking support.

Personalisation within children's services challenges the assumption that families are at the risk of breakdown and acknowledges that families with a disabled child simply need greater support to achieve the same quality of life as do those without disabled children. In giving choice and control to families, personalisation requires the family to get involved in designing and managing their own support. Moving from traditional services to self-directed support is a big leap for families and professionals. In this section we explore the following key aspects of that cultural change.

▶ A family affair

▶ A relational model

▶ Developing the provider market

A family affair

In the past, services have attempted to support families by concentrating on the disabled child and typically by removing that child from the family for periods of time. This has had a damaging effect on relationships within the family, and often does not give the family the support they really need. Parents directing their own support report how they have been able to use self-directed support to strengthen the whole family. Parents appreciate support that enables the whole family to spend time together, and tell us that self-directed support is giving them this, and more: '*Having an individual budget has affected the whole family. We have had a summer like no other – we are a lot less stressed out and we have a lot healthier relationship with each other. All our children are happy. They are allowed to be just kids who are having fun together.*' (Parent)

What this approach means is that professionals have to widen their focus to take account of the issues affecting all family members and to provide the opportunities to meet the needs of all children in the family.

A relational model

Disabled children and their families report that effective support depends not so much on the model being offered, but rather on the quality of the support relationship.

'*We are open and ready to give anything a go as long as our children are treated with respect.*' (Parent)

A relational model is characterised by the understanding that we are all of equal value. As soon as we recognise others as being of equal value to ourselves, we relate to them with respect and empathy that allows us to transcend differences of gender, impairment, ethnicity, background or age. The impact of difficult life experiences such as living with impairment in a disabling world can be very distressing. The diversity involved in terms of families' health and social care needs, their personal and social circumstances and their perceptions of what might feel helpful in response to their practical challenges and emotional distress is extremely varied. In addition, the cultural diversity of families, demands openness to working with issues of difference in people's lived experience, their systems of meaning, beliefs and values. For these reasons it is essential that we place the support offered – money, access to universal and specialist services, developing community networks etc. in the context of a relational model.

Building trust is a key feature of a relational model and helping families establish trust in the motivation lying behind the move to self-directed support is particularly important in the current economic climate. As local authorities strive to adjust to reduced budgets, parents worry that the move to self-direction is little more than a smokescreen for a cost-cutting exercise. Politicians, managers and professionals have to be honest about the motivation for the introduction of self-directed support and where the savings, if any, will be made. Creating a safe space to discuss such issues openly with families is a necessary step in this journey.

Developing the provider market

Self-directed support was developed initially largely as a response to the needs of disabled adults, some of who find that they can improve their lives through an individual budget with which they pay for personal assistants. Although this is sometimes an appropriate response for families of young children – as in the world of adult social care – we must not suggest that this is the only option. Self-directed support requires that the support systems on offer to children and families should be flexible enough to meet the diverse expectations, needs and lifestyles of families from different cultures and with different views of the world. The messages in Chapter 7 on support brokerage apply just as much to work with families with disabled children as they do to adults needing social care support. Work with families indicates there are four broad categories of support that offer significant improvements for family life and these are as follows.

1. An extra pair of hands to do things around the house, in the garden, with the children or with the whole family. This is particularly appropriate to and relevant for families with young children.

2. Someone to take the children out to clubs and other leisure activities so parents can go out, take other children to their activities of choice, or stay at home to get on with household chores. This option is particularly welcomed by families with pre-teens and young teenagers.

3. A personal assistant or team of personal assistants, to support an older teenager helps all the family explore the possibilities of some genuine independence.

4. Ease of access to universal services, that is to say services that are used by everyone in the community. Chapter 9 explores this in more depth.

The needs of all families change enormously as children grow up, so it is not surprising to find a natural flow, from one age group to the next, between these categories. They are not of course, mutually exclusive or set in stone. They simply give an indicator of the types of support that families need, and therefore of the areas that local authorities and their partners need to work on if self-directed support is to be successful.

An issue affecting all four categories is finding people to support children to take part in activities – something parents are particularly anxious about. These concerns can present a considerable barrier to families going down the route of self-directed support, particularly as children grow up and begin to seek independence from their family. *'The organisation behind all this recruitment and managing the PAs is huge. I need to keep on top of timesheets, invoices, receipts, the weekly rota, holidays etc, I feel like I am a human resources department with no resources. I do this because it is the only way for us, but I can understand why other families don't want to do this. It is too much!'* (Parent)

Addressing the issues of finding such people and of helping with the role of employer are therefore crucial matters for local authorities to address. Unless local authorities invest in the development of agencies to provide support with people to help at home, buddies and personal assistants, the necessary infrastructure to support families will not be in place. If this happens many families will feel reluctant to embrace self-directed support, as they will perceive it as giving them as many problems as it resolves. As professionals begin to understand that self-directed support involves this developmental work, we will be able to introduce families to a way of working that is rich, nuanced and responsive to individual need.

Section two: Practical steps to support families

Families need practical help as they embark on self-directed support. This section covers a range of issues identified by parents and sets out some helpful measures that local authorities, PCTs and service providers put in place as responses. These include:

▶ the provision of information

▶ creative support planning

▶ networking opportunities

▶ sharing stories of what is possible.

Information

In order to get involved and shape the support they require, families need clear information about key aspects of self-directed support, including:

▶ what self-directed support means

▶ what an individual budget is

▶ eligibility and entitlements

▶ different routes to individual budgets (including use of 'health' monies, see Chapter 3)

▶ the process – the Seven Step Model (as set out in Chapter 2 and referred to elsewhere in this book)

▶ roles and responsibilities for parents and professionals

▶ the benefits self-directed support brings to children and families

▶ support planning

▶ how an individual budget can be spent, examples of what they can do with the money

▶ how to find someone to give the support they need

▶ information about 'legal rewards' and paying relatives

▶ contact details for local service providers in the specialist and universal sector

▶ local payroll services

▶ what is needed in terms of a record as to how money has been spent

▶ how we can capture the perspective of children and young people.

In giving families information about the process, it is not enough to show them a diagram of the seven steps and expect them to make sense of this. Families need clear, accessible, written information with an explanation of what each step entails, who is available locally to help them with particular tasks, and how long each step is likely to take. Having such information on its own is not enough though. Families need someone to talk them through the process, and to be able to answer their questions as they go along. Parents tell us it is much easier when they have one point of contact rather than different people helping with different aspects.

Creative support planning

A support plan outlines the needs of children and their families; it provides a 'flavour' of the family and what they find helpful; and outlines how the money available to them will be spent. The support planning process is a means to an end: it encourages families to think about wider aspects of their family life, particularly about the quality of their daily lives, what they want from life and how they might practically go about getting it. Support planning should actively encourage families to think about positive solutions to making life easier and more satisfying for each family member and for the whole family. Support plans need to be written and owned by families. However, families appreciate help with support planning and can gain a lot of confidence quickly when they are encouraged to think creatively. Professionals report that taking the time to listen well enables families to begin to think of creative ways of shaping their support.

A support plan is developed according to the interests of the children and all children should be enabled to take an active part in developing their support plan. Although local authorities may require specific information about the way the money is going to be spent, children can put together their section of the support plan in any way they like. For example, one child or young person might like to produce and edit a DVD; another may enjoy making a photographic scrap book showing all the things she likes to do and how she would like to spend her money; and another might write a story about her life and the things that she particularly enjoys.

For those very young children or those with significant communication impairments and learning difficulties, their preferences as expressed through body language and behaviour, must be documented in the support plan and taken into account when deciding on how the money should be spent. This is an area that professionals need to address with great sensitivity depending on how parents understand and view impairment. Work needs to be adapted according to the needs and sensitivities of each family. For example, support planning with teenagers and parents gives a valuable opportunity to help shift the power in the relationship between young people and parents as teenagers express their interests and wishes for the future (Chapter 16 has more on the process of support planning).

Giving families opportunities to network

'*We need to meet other families to have other parents who have been down the same road as us.*' (Parent)

Many parents express anxiety about the idea of being given public money to spend on their family and feel unsure as to how they might spend it. The words 'individual budget' and 'self-directed support' become less frightening when families are given opportunities to get together with others going down the same route. Parents can support each other to think creatively about the things that would make a difference to their lives:

'We came together as a group at the very beginning and we thought about the things that would make each day a bit easier. This really helped me understand that we don't need to be thinking about services, but more about what would make a difference to my family. Then the other parents helped me think about how I could make those things happen. We came up with all kinds of ideas that I would never have thought about on my own'. (Parent)

Parents in this particular group initially brought together through the support planning process, are now in regular contact with each other. Professionals working with them bring them together formally from time to time to help keep the network going. In the early stages it is important that groups are facilitated by someone with an understanding of the ethos of self-directed support and confidence in the improvements it can bring to family life. As parents gain this experience and confidence, they can be the ones to facilitate new groups.

Sharing stories of what is possible

Sharing stories about the benefits of self-directed support helps families and professionals think about what might be possible, rather than what is ordinarily available through disabled children's services. Giving families examples of ways in which others have spent their budget helps them to come up with their own solutions and encourages them to think outside the box. Many examples of the outcomes afforded by self-directed support demonstrate that it is often the smallest things that make the biggest difference.

Sometimes it's the smallest things that make the biggest difference

Grace has six-year-old twins called Jackson and Kyle. Jackson has complex impairments and the family has been awarded a modest budget to support him. The money is being used to pay for:

▶ family members to look after the twins when Grace is at work

▶ family members to accompany Grace and the twins on holiday

▶ a support worker to stay with Jackson while Grace takes Kyle to cubs

▶ someone to do the ironing

▶ someone to cook Jackson's meals.

Grace explains that the money she spends on domestic tasks makes the biggest difference to their lives: '*I spend £25 a fortnight on the ironing, and I can't put into words how fantastic that is! It is making such a huge difference to the quality of our family life. Before we had the budget, I would spend half a day every weekend doing the ironing, but now we go out together on that day – we hire bikes and go off for the whole day. We laugh so much on that day. The boys get exercise, we all do something together, and it is not just while we are doing the activity that we benefit. Jackson always sleeps that night, so I am more rested.*

'*And the same is true for the cooking. Jackson is on an unusual diet. There are loads of things he can't have and certain things he has to have. It was really difficult for me cooking two different meals every day, but now we have the budget I pay Sandra to cook Jackson's meals. I decide what he is going to have, buy the ingredients and Sandra comes round every Wednesday to spend the day cooking and putting stuff in the freezer. It is fantastic. I used to spend every evening cooking and cleaning but now I get the boys to bed, clean up a bit, and have time to get ready for the next day. I definitely feel less stressed and feel like I am being a better mum.*'

Sharing examples helps parents and professionals gain confidence. The information gathered can be used to support the development of self-directed support for families thereby creating a momentum for improvement with the voice of children and families at the centre.

Section two: Creating the right conditions

The second section of the book focuses upon 'the system' which is in place to help people who 'need health and social care'. It discusses how this system is changing with personalisation.

To say that people have 'health and social care needs' is to some extent a self-fulfilling prophecy. We all do certainly need certain fundamentals in our lives; the lists of these fundamentals vary slightly, but most lists include warmth, shelter, enough to eat and drink, and a connection with others. It is also a good idea to stay healthy, but beyond these basics what we 'need' is subject to definition by society, and to what it is deemed society can afford. We have had in place a 'system' that has 'delivered social care' and that is to say we have had arrangements to address a person's social needs, or some of them through the familiar process of assessment, followed by a judgment about 'eligibility' for state funded services, then (if the person is lucky) provision of those services. After a while the person has a review to see if they still have a 'continuing need' – or if they require more, less or different services.

This is a 'modern' system in that it grew in response to a situation in the middle 20th century where changes in the pattern of work and social and geographic mobility meant that the extended family was unable to cope with the demands and expectations placed on it, and where legislation was beginning to set certain standards for the 'care' of its more vulnerable citizens. This second section of the book describes the end of this system and what is now coming to replace it. We focus in particular on some of the key roles involved in this process, and how they are changing.

One way to think of someone's life is to think of concentric circles around the person at the centre. In the first circle there are those people in most intimate contact with the person. Most often this will be his or her family and hence we call this the 'family circle' by way of shorthand. But of course not everyone has a close family and it is certainly the case that whilst many people with learning disabilities have very loving families, others have lost close contact over years of institutionalisation, or the family has simply found it too difficult to cope and keep in close contact. In the second 'community' circle we would hope to see a wider group of friends, neighbours, colleagues and so on. Many of these people will be living in the same geographic community, but increasingly they will be far away, and sometimes now the connection will be a remote one or through email or online social networks. Again, people with learning disabilities tend to have fewer people in this second circle than most others. The outer-most circle is the 'professional circle', the circle which comes into play when we need special advice, support or help – as we all do at times in our lives. This circle includes doctors, nurses and health professionals, but also advice workers, social workers and now personal assistants. Under the old system of social care, some people with learning disabilities had this 'professional circle' but no other. Is it surprising that so many are lonely, frustrated or 'exhibit challenging behaviour?'

This section of the book looks at how self-directed support changes the responsibilities, roles and relationships of those who inhabit the three concentric circles. In Control has taken the strong view that self-directed support works best when things happen as close to the centre person as possible, when the person or those closest to them (in the family circle or failing this, the community circle) take decisions and take control. The professional circle, which is what this section of the book is about is always part of the picture, but it comes to play a major decision-making role only if inner circles need extra help.

This model explains why self-directed support is both more *effective* and more efficient than the old system. It is more effective because it turns first and foremost to the person and to those who really care about them, then it turns to their community where they live and are known, and only then – if need be – it turns to paid helpers. It is more efficient for the same reason by bringing families, friends and communities to the heart of the matter. It practises 'prevention' and only brings into play public funding when it is really needed. There is an important caveat to all of this, which some cash-strapped local authorities sometimes seem to ignore: family 'carers' are citizens, with the right to a decent life too, and the model does not and must not *depend* on them and *require* their input – to do so is to create another set of problems, and to perpetuate many of the failings of the old system.

Professionals in the 'outer circle' have another important role, which is largely the subject matter for this section, that of creating the conditions for self-direction to flourish. As these chapters each make clear in their own way, this is a little more complicated than 'getting out of the way' for citizens to take control. People with learning disabilities and their families have been ill-served by the system to date, many are isolated, despondent and disempowered; and what people with disabilities need is sometimes a little complex. People usually need support to complete a good self-assessment, to make a plan and design their service; and they need help to get what is in their plan and to review whether things are working. Perhaps most importantly of all, people need information about what is possible and what is available in their locality. They need images of possibility, they need inspiration and examples.

To be clear: people in the two inner circles may often be the best people to fulfill the roles we describe here, and where such people are not around for someone we can sometimes find substitutes (advocates or brokers) and when this isn't possible or appropriate either, there remain occasions where local authority staff, perhaps social workers are best placed to help.

There is another important role professionals have to help create the conditions. Where public funds are involved there is a responsibility incumbent upon the local authority to sign off the personal budget to fund someone's support plan. This process of signing off support plans can, if done well be very helpful in and of itself in assisting the person to think through what it means for them to devise a realistic plan that enables them to get what they want and to stay safe.

And finally and of critical importance at this stage, the service system and its culture need to change and to be managed in ways that are new, challenging and different. Each of the chapters address this central issue in its own way, and together the described changes constitute the fundamental transformation that is needed; a transformation in the way in which we think, feel and behave – such that the citizen rather than the state is in control. This section of the book therefore takes and examines some of the important roles in the new personalised system of support and reflects on how these now need to be established or to change.

Extended case study 2: Work

Getting a paid job: a good life – but not yet for everyone

Graeme Ellis

Graeme Ellis is 52 years old and lives in Lancashire. He does not have a learning disability but is physically and visually impaired and is recovering from mental health issues. In the second of two case studies, he offers his experience of attempting to take up employment after a number of years of being considered as unemployable. He also shares his experience as a volunteer of supporting people with a learning disability into paid work.

Introduction

I have always been a workaholic and gone the extra mile. I was devastated when I lost my job in the NHS where I had worked in various roles since I was 19 years old. My own personal experience gives me some insight into the experience of people with learning disabilities who are trying to get a job.

Key points

▶ Having a paid job is really important to help people to stay healthy and happy and to have the life they want.

▶ You can receive support to get and keep a job in a number of ways. A personal budget from the local authority or the access to work scheme from the Department of Work and Pensions can sometimes help.

▶ The government says that it wants more disabled people to work, but the system doesn't in fact always help.

▶ Only 17% of people with learning disabilities of working age have a paid job.

My story

After I lost my job I became depressed and more and more withdrawn and I felt as though I was on the scrapheap. I applied for hundreds of jobs declaring my disabilities and got no interviews. For a handful of jobs I applied for I did not declare my disabilities and got interviews. The look on the faces in front of me as I rolled in my wheelchair is an image I will never forget. Needless to say, I always lost out at the selection stage and I keep telling myself that it was their loss.

Finances were not a problem as the benefit system supported me adequately as my disabilities qualify me for the higher rate of disability living allowance. I also receive a substantial support package in the form of a personal budget from social services. Money did not fill the gap of wanting to work and earn a living. I started voluntary work with a local Citizen's Advice Bureau, but after undertaking the training I discovered that the IT systems could not be adjusted to take account of my visual impairment. I then approached another charity in Preston, known as Preston DISC at the time, which was looking for voluntary advisers. This was a turning point for me as the volunteer co-ordinator was very supportive in allowing me to use the skills and knowledge I had to help others. I volunteered there for a couple of years and my self-esteem and feeling of self-worth pulled me up from the depths I had sunk to. Unfortunately, as the organisation evolved and they had funding for more paid workers I began to feel pushed more into the background as I was unable to apply for any of the jobs because they required working more hours than I could sustain. I was determined to find a path to paid employment for myself.

I enrolled on a scheme with the Job Centre to test trade for self-employment. I decided I could support people who wished to be recipients of personal budgets from social services based on the experience I had gained as a personal budget user myself. At the end of the test trading I realised I had the energy to do this work only for a limited time each week. There was no funding available for me to do the work directly, but I was fortunate to be offered some work through the organisation In Control to go to various places around the country and talk about my experiences of personal budgets and about how they had turned my life around. There was also the added bonus that I got paid for this, which meant I could cover my expenses and I therefore had the opportunity to provide some free support to others who were looking to use a personal budget for the first time.

I applied for help through the access to work scheme and got personal assistant support for 13 hours a week and IT equipment to help me with my visual impairment. I also received a new power wheelchair that enabled me to travel independently whilst working in my local area. I didn't earn much but decided to go ahead and do permitted work as a self-employed person. The problem I now face is that my access to work finishes in October 2010 and cannot be continued as the entitlement is for one year only when doing permitted work.

Permitted work is the government's name for limited work someone is allowed to do whilst claiming employment and support allowance (previously known as incapacity benefit). It allows the person to test their own capacity to do some work, and perhaps learn some new skills.

Access to work can help you if your health or disability affects the way you do your job. It gives you and your employer advice and support with extra costs which may arise because of your needs. Access to work might pay towards the equipment you need at work, adapting premises to meet your needs, or a support worker. It can also pay towards the cost of getting to work if you cannot use public transport.

This means I will not be able to carry on supporting others after this date. Fortunately, I have a new volunteering opportunity that will help me build up skills in financial management and managing in a charity. So it remains to be seen what the future holds for me in terms of my employment prospects.

The government wants disabled people to work, and the majority of us want to work, but many of us have health limitations and the benefits system does not allow us to get the support to do the hours we can manage so we end up being written off. This feels very disheartening.

Some experiences of people with learning disabilities

As a volunteer I support disabled people in benefit appeals and with employment problems; many of these people have a learning disability. Everyone in the examples that follow has a learning difficulty of some description. The names and personal details have been changed.

Paul is a 25-year-old man who has worked in a warehouse in the Midlands since leaving school. He was able to manage stock in his area by keeping paper records as he could not manage to learn how to use the computer system. A few months ago after the company was taken over he was told that as he could not use the system he would be dismissed on capability grounds. He contacted the charity I volunteer for and after talking to the employer and making them aware of what help was available from access to work, a meeting was arranged. At the meeting it was explained that it might be possible for a support worker to be engaged through access to work who could sit with Paul and do the inputting into the computer with him. So Paul made an application to access to work. He was assessed and a support worker was appointed for 15 hours a week. Paul is now able to carry on using his paper system to then sit down with his support worker to do the inputting onto the system. His employer has a new insight to what Paul can achieve with support and his job is no longer under threat.

Janet is a 19-year-old woman with Down's syndrome. She was receiving incapacity benefit and after she had her assessment it was agreed that she could do indefinite permitted work and keep her benefits. She was introduced to the mangers of several large stores in the area of Lancashire where she lives. One manager agreed to take her on for 14 hours filling shelves during the store's opening hours. She was given a small defined area to look after. She has been very successful in doing this and is always a smiling cheerful face around the store and is able to help customers if they ask where things are. She loves her work; one huge highlight for her was going to the staff Christmas party at a local hotel. She often goes out with work colleagues for an evening pub meal. Her work colleagues see Janet as a person, and not as 'someone with Down's syndrome'.

Jim is a 22-year-old man who was identified as having a learning disability early in life. After leaving school he went to college to learn catering but dropped out as he could not cope with the course. After four years of casual work assisting a painter and decorator he got a job as a kitchen porter in a pub/restaurant. Here he demonstrated a flair for preparing starters and the owners agreed to give him an opportunity for taking responsibility for this. Jim is now settled into this job and is happy and feels he now has a purpose in life.

Alan is a 40-year-old man and has never worked. His experience is typical of people with a learning difficulty who have never had the opportunity to work. He has volunteered with local charities and has developed skills such as inputting records into databases. Despite applying for paid jobs based on these skills he has not secured paid employment. It seems that prospective employers have problems getting to grips with the fact that someone with an obvious learning disability can have skills that will help their business. Following advice he started on permitted work to collect printer cartridges for recycling. This has brought in enough money for him to work 20 hours a week and with his tax credits he is better off than he ever was on benefits.

There may be more negative stories than positive but I do not want to fill this chapter with them. I will summarise the problems, however. It is extremely difficult for people with a learning difficulty to find a job. The Disability Discrimination Act (1995) is ineffective in securing the employment rights of disabled people. There is no indication that the Equality Act (2010) will be any better. Discrimination against disabled people should be a criminal offence, not as it currently exists now, where the law gives a tiny slap across the wrists, with nothing to stop an employer discriminating against other disabled people in the future. My personal experience and that of many of the people I write about in these examples is that a paid job can make all the difference between a good life and a miserable one. This is what 'personalisation' should be all about, and until we have health, social services and the benefits system all working together to achieve this for everyone the journey will not be complete.

Here are some statistics to conclude.

▶ About 2% of the population has a learning disability.

▶ 17% of people with learning disabilities of working age have a paid job which means 83% do not.

▶ Children and young people with learning disabilities are six times more likely to have mental health problems than other young people. This makes it more difficult for them to get work in later life.

Chapter 5

Ordinary people, the real leaders

Wendy Gross

Wendy is a disabled person and has been using services for nearly 30 years as an individual in her own right and also as a disabled parent. She has been involved in the disability and advocacy movements for the last 15 years believing in the right of equality for all and the fundamental right for each individual to have choice and control over their own lives. Wendy was instrumental in the development of a disabled people's organisation in Northamptonshire and she has a long-standing interest in advocacy.

Introduction

This chapter gives another perspective on how disabled people are taking control of their money, their support and of their lives. It focuses particularly on making choices, an active process in every aspect of life. People with learning disabilities (and other disabled people) have the most to gain from these changes and they are the real leaders of the process.

Key points

▶ *Choice* is important in every aspect of life. The way we make choices and the support we need to do so differs from person to person.

▶ Most disabled people want the same things as non-disabled people. The key to providing good support for people is to ask them what they want from life.

▶ Ensure that people have the time and the support they need as individuals to express themselves and be heard.

▶ Ensuring that the person is genuinely at the centre of all decision-making that is about them and that the outcomes they want and need are delivered.

▶ Disabled people must be seen as the leaders of the change process. They have the most to gain from its success.

▶ It is important to work alongside 'user-led organisations' who know from first-hand experience what it is that disabled people need and want.

The importance of choice and control

We all live our lives in different ways and the life choices we make, and the ways in which we make them, can be compared to the way we choose chocolates from a box. Some of us leave it up to others to choose for us, while some of us just dive in and see what turns up; others study each option before choosing, while some people make choices based on what they like the look of. Then there are those of us that study all the options carefully, take into account all the information and ask the opinions of others before making a choice. The outcomes for each one of us will be different with varying degrees of uncertainty, excitement, trepidation and satisfaction, but because we have had some control over how our chocolates are chosen we also take responsibility for the outcome. For example, if we give someone the power to choose for us and what they choose is not what we want then it's probably fair to assume that we didn't give enough information about what we like, or perhaps we gave the chooser too much freedom in making the decision, or even that the person didn't listen to our instructions and therefore didn't fulfill their role effectively. However, the worst thing that can happen when choosing chocolates is that we get something unpleasant and unexpected and that it leaves a bad taste in our mouths.

If only the choices we had to make in life were as simple as choosing chocolates and the consequences of our choices had the same minor impact on us. This chapter is obviously not about choosing chocolates, but it is about the importance of making sure that the right people are involved in helping us make choices about how we live our lives and that we find the best ways in which to get the right information to those people.

How do we do this?

In every other aspect of our lives, the services we buy focus on what we – the customer – want and needs. If we are buying a car, a birthday cake, a new kitchen or a tailor-made suit, the seller's attention is always going to be focused on making sure that they are providing exactly what we want within the constraints of money and practicalities. In this commercial market there is an understanding that without your input, the seller will not have a clear understanding of your needs, and without this information they may provide the wrong product and they will subsequently lose your custom.

Historically, the services we have received from health and social care to assist us in living our day-to-day lives has been dramatically different to this. We have been asked what we need and then – providing we meet the required criteria – are offered a poor selection from a very small menu, which usually includes home care, day services, residential care, respite care and, if you are lucky tele care. It was rare that we were ever asked what was important to us, mostly the questions were about how many times we need to go to the toilet and what help do we need to get up in the morning. Whilst these things may be important, they are most definitely not what define us and they should not determine how we live our lives.

In addition to this, the services provided using this old model rarely took account of other things in our life or how the timings or the nature of the services impact on us as people – as workers, as parents, as marriage partners or as members of a faith community or whatever. For many people we had the distinct feeling that we were being 'done to' and that we had very little choice about the way in which our services were delivered or who delivered them, and we were given the clear message that the rest of life had to fit around these services.

Most disabled people just want to live their lives with as little intrusion as possible, we want to make choices about where we go, who we see, how our time is spent, and who comes into our homes. It should not be surprising that the things that disabled people want out of life are much the same as the rest of the general population, but for some reason it has been seen as acceptable that we don't have access to those same things, and many disabled people are made to feel grateful for the minimal, restrictive, inflexible support that has been historically provided.

What is important to disabled people is much the same as it is for the rest of the population and the key to ensuring that disabled people have an equal chance at achieving their aspirations is first and foremost to find out what those aspirations are. This sounds simple, so why, then is it that so many disabled people never achieve even the most simple goals that many non-disabled people take for granted? In my view the answer is that they are rarely asked and supported to explore what they want.

Learning how to take control

It is often said to me, 'Well it's ok for you, you are assertive, you know where to go for things and who to ask and what your rights are. What about those people who can't speak up for themselves or don't know where to go for help?' My answer is that I wasn't born with those skills and knowledge, it was acquired, and it was acquired in a range of different ways. I became assertive because of the encouragement and support of my family; I gained my knowledge about rights by creating a network of people around me who I could ask when I wasn't sure. I would draw on different people for different things at different stages of my life, and I am still doing that now. When I became a mum I talked to other mums, when I became disabled I talked to other disabled people; it's what we do mostly without realising; we create our own little support groups around us to help us get over those tricky moments that we haven't yet had experience of, where we need others' opinions and support to help us make our choices.

So is it reasonable to expect disabled people, after a lifetime of being told what they can and can't have and how they should live their lives suddenly to be expected to make lots of decisions and choices without those little support groups around them? It's no good simply asking someone who has needs to help them communicate what they would like to do with their day when up until now they have only known visits to the day centre or spent days with family. The right sort of support needs to be in place to ensure that the person can firstly express him or herself wherever possible, and secondly to ensure that they are enabled to explore different ideas and options that they have never previously considered. This can be a long process, and many of us – people with learning disabilities included – need to actually experience something before we can take a view to choose or not choose it. Where the 'capacity' of the individual is an issue, then it is even more important to create a circle of support around the individual. At this point it is important to say that there are disabled people, including people with learning disabilities who are out there and living their lives, asserting themselves, making choices and challenging the status quo but I think it is fair to say that they remain a minority (see Chapters 2 and 16 for more on this).

Opening the door to a new life

It is important to understand why 'the system' hasn't worked in the past before we can fix it. If you don't ask people what they want and need then you won't have the information you require and you can't deliver. Equally if people don't know what might be possible for them or what might be available to them to realise these hopes and dreams, and if they don't have the confidence, skills, tools and support to go and find what they need to make things happen, then how do they know what to ask for and how to make use of what's around?

Personalisation opens a door that can allow disabled people to start living their lives the way they want. What it doesn't do is *make it happen*, people do this for themselves. They are the ones with most to gain and this is the reason why they must be seen as the leaders of the process.

The processes, mechanisms and attitudes that need to be in place to achieve a route to full citizenship need to be enabling and empowering, not controlling and restrictive. Personalisation is about much more than developing new processes and policies, it is about a whole system change in mind-set, a transformation in the way we do things. A local authority can have what looks on paper to be an effective, empowering policy in relation to the implementation of self-directed support but if it isn't also in people's hearts and minds, and if we don't have effective checks in place to ask the right questions and make sure it is being done in a values-driven way, then nothing changes.

By far, the best way of doing this is to involve people on the receiving end. Again this sounds easy: if so, why doesn't this happen as a matter of course? It doesn't because it takes time, resources and careful planning at the beginning, and constant vigilance to keep things on track to ensure people remain genuinely involved.

If there is this type of investment from the start it will produce a much more effective result at the end. If we look at person-centred planning, when the process is followed correctly then the result is always effective, but it's no good skipping bits; and the reason it works is because if done properly the person is at the centre of the process from start to end. Even where that person is not able to use speech or other communication media, or finds it difficult to express their wishes and choices, the process requires understanding and knowledge that is gleaned from those who know and care about that person and who know them in different settings, and can say what is important to them (as opposed to what is important *for* them). Doing things in this way means that there is less chance of misunderstandings and a much higher likelihood of support being provided in a way that really suits the individual. These points are discussed in more detail on Chapter 6 on support planning.

There are numerous examples where services have been put in place and the individual has no interest in what is being provided, and this applies particularly for people with learning difficulties. The outcome is that they become bored, frustrated and angry, they find it difficult to express how they are feeling and as a result are labelled as 'challenging' when in actual fact nobody has taken the time to explore what is it that the person really wants, what makes them happy or sad and what excites them.

Jason's story

When it was identified that Jason's mum and dad needed a break, they were offered 'respite care'. Jason hated change but the only option offered was to send him to a respite centre 20 miles away. By law, the family should have been offered a direct payment so mum and dad could have a holiday while someone stayed at their home to support Jason. Jason would then have been able to stay in his own home and there would then have been an opportunity for the supporter to be introduced gradually and get to know Jason and what works for him; also the family could then get to choose who that person is. The first option, the respite centre, tries unsuccessfully to fit Jason into a service, whilst the latter takes account of what works for Jason and provides support that suits him. By doing it this way Jason remains reasonably settled, mum and dad get the chance for a break, while knowing Jason is safe and resources are being used in the most effective way – a 'win-win situation' – and all because Jason was placed at the centre of the planning.

Gemma's story

Gemma is 42 years old and has learning disabilities and some physical impairments, which mean she has high-level support needs. She doesn't use words but smiles and laughs when she is happy and scowls and cries when things aren't right. Gemma goes to day services three days a week and a sitting service comes and stays with Gemma one morning a week whilst mum goes and has her hair done. Gemma doesn't have a person-centred plan and her key worker at the day service has just gone on maternity leave.

She has recently been placed in emergency respite due to sudden illness of her elderly mum who has been her main carer for all of

Gemma's 42 years. With a bit of time and effort you can find out that Gemma loves pink and hates green, but so often when people with learning disabilities are 'placed' in residential care nobody bothers to find out any details about the individual apart from basic personal care needs. The result is that Gemma becomes labelled as problematic at bedtime, when the reality is that they are trying to get Gemma to go to bed in a room painted green, with green accessories. With mum being very poorly in hospital and with no one to really attend to her, and no person-centred plan or support plan available, it will be extremely difficult to establish Gemma's likes and dislikes. Not only will the problems at bedtime cause sleeplessness and stress for Gemma but they will also create more work for the staff trying to put her to bed.

The result is that Gemma is unhappy and the staff are stressed, and all because nobody has taken the time and seen the importance of recording what is important to Gemma, what makes her happy and sad, what works and what doesn't work in her life. When people aren't able to express easily what they want it is all the more important to make sure that there is a person-centred record of it.

Had Gemma had a support plan or a person-centred plan, staff at the respite centre would have known Gemma's likes and dislikes straight away, and they would have understood what works for her and how she likes things done. People around her are immediately more confident and happier about what could potentially be a very stressful situation. This obviously won't take away any upset that Gemma is feeling about being taken from her home, but the person-centred plan or support plan would also have directions in place should this situation arise and it may propose alternative (less 'service-based') approaches that mean that emergency respite is unnecessary. A few hours work putting together a support plan means that Gemma's choices, likes and dislikes are taken account of and Gemma herself is at the heart of thinking and planning from start to finish.

Gordon and Hazel's story

Gordon and Hazel live in a group home and want to get married. Currently they live in separate rooms but want to live together once they are married; they don't really want to live in a group home and would like to have their own place. Gordon's sister has concerns about them managing money and being taken advantage of and Hazel's mum is reluctant for them to move from the protective environment of the group home. The care manager is worried that Hazel and Gordon's caring and loving, but overprotective families may override the couple's dreams and aspirations. So with their permission, she organises an advocate who will help them to get their thoughts together and present them to their families in a way that instils confidence and also assists them to be more assertive about their decisions.

The care manager organises a family meeting with Gordon and Hazel's agreement and together they agree to develop a support plan that will help the couple to plan for their wedding, look for a new home, and organise support that will help them to manage their money and some of the daily tasks that they consider to be difficult. Hazel's cousin has just got married and she agrees to help plan the wedding, and in return, they use some of their personal budget to help her with the cost of petrol to visit and take them to places relating to the wedding planning. They also buy her a bouquet of flowers once everything is done as a thank you gesture. The local Disabled People's Organisation that runs the direct payments support service has agreed to support them to manage their budget and set up a holding account until the couple, the family and the care manager are confident that they can hold the money themselves.

With some planning and imagination Gordon and Hazel's dreams can become a reality, they have a circle of people around them who can help them with some of those tricky new things and an advocate to help them when they find it difficult to tell people what they really want to say.

The beauty of putting the individual at the centre in this way is that with a little bit of imagination, that person's life can become so much more interesting to them – rather than falling back on services that are designed primarily to keep people safe, secure and away from the risks of everyday life.

With each new challenge, confidence, knowledge, experience and fulfillment are gained by all parties. Sometimes things don't go to plan, but this is how we all learn and understand how to do things differently next time. For those that find this difficult then it is a great opportunity to put in those extra supports that will reduce the risk of that particular thing going wrong again.

Work with user-led organisations

From the perspective of the disabled person the majority of policies and processes are enabling; many are disabling; and most are simply ineffective. This is often because these policies and processes are dreamt up behind closed doors and implemented and monitored by the very people that have written and implemented them. How do you know you are getting it right when you don't involve people who are on the receiving end? You can make assumptions but will this give you a true picture? To get really good effective policies, procedures and strategies that actually do what is required they need to be *co-produced*.

Putting People First (Department of Health, 2007) discusses the need for 'co-production' and the importance of involving disabled people and carers from an early stage. This means active participation from the very start of the process, not once the document or service has been developed and a few disabled people are brought into rubber stamp it. The best and most straightforward way to do this is to involve your local user-led organisation.

Recommendation 4.3 of *Improving the Life Chances of Disabled People* (Cabinet Office, 2005) requires '*By 2010, each locality (defined as that area covered by a council with social services responsibilities) should have a user-led organisation modelled on existing centres for independent living.*' Therefore every local authority in England should now have a user-led organisation that you can go to, so no excuses!

User-led organisations by definition are what they say on the tin, organisations where decisions are made by a majority of those that are beneficiaries of whatever that organisation is providing. For too long disabled people have been represented by organisations made up of well meaning non-disabled people who were often under the impression that they knew what the disabled person wanted and needed. In no other minority group is that acceptable today. It would be inconceivable to set up a women's support service whose steering group or trustee board was made up of men; equally a charity that supports Asian elders would not hold any credibility in this day and age if its decision-making board was made up of non-Asian men and women. However, today there remain many 'disability organisations' around the country that still have decisions made exclusively by non-disabled people.

As a society we now seem ready to accept that we don't have the right to decide what is best for most minority groups and would not consider planning any work or events without their input as an integral part of the process. However, as disabled people we are really struggling to shake off the need by non-disabled people to make decisions for us. With the right support and guidance we are able to work through the tricky stuff and manage our own organisations. *Putting People First*, for example, has been successfully running their own organisation for many years and has made a huge impact on the way in which services are delivered to people with a learning difficulty.

You need user-led organisations, they have the knowledge, experience and expertise that will help you get it right. Without them you will waste time and money and continue to provide services in a way that may deliver some limited objectives, but which does not enable people to direct their own support and cannot meet the aspirations of disabled people to be included in society as equals.

Conclusion

There are a number of things you now need to consider when supporting me as a disabled person so that I can take control.

▶ Whatever your specific aims, find out what I need first. Without the input of the disabled person you are setting out on a journey that will take you to completely the wrong place.

▶ If it is difficult to find out what I want, then bring together a circle of people who have my best interests at heart and who know me best. Get them to work with me to paint a picture of me that I recognise and which helps you know what I want.

▶ Make sure that if I can say what I want and need but find it difficult to be heard, that I have the right sort of independent support so that I can express myself in ways that are clear for others who have a part to play in making things happen for me.

▶ Talk with those 'user-led organisations' who know from first-hand experience what disabled people need and want, and help you to write good quality, effective policies, procedures and strategies, and to implement them and check that they are working well and making a difference.

And finally, no matter how hard it is and how long it takes, you get a much better outcome for everyone if you remember *nothing about us without us.*

References

Cabinet Office (2005) *Improving the Life Chances of Disabled People.* London: The Prime Minister's Strategy Unit.

Department of Health (2007) *Putting People First: A shared vision and commitment to the transformation of adult social care.* London: Department of Health.

Chapter 6

What support planners need to know

Tony Bamforth

Tony Bamforth has worked in the social care field in a variety of settings, both statutory and voluntary for over 12 years and is currently the assistant director at The Elfrida Society, which is a small organisation based in Islington, North London. The Elfrida Society provides independent brokerage and advocacy support for people in Islington to get their personal budgets. Tony has led in developing this service and is currently working with 14 people who are at different stages in the process of getting 'choice and control'.

Introduction

In this chapter, I aim to provide insight into the process of support planning by describing some issues faced by Jenny, a woman I worked with who has learning disabilities. I then set out a support planners' toolkit – a set of key skills and tools to help people get the best from their work together. These skills and tools have their roots in an approach best described as 'person-centredness'. There is an art and a science to support planning, which incorporates this and more, and I conclude with some reflections on this 'art and science' and with some tips for support planners, before returning to Jenny who has the final words.

Everyone involved in creating a support plan is a support planner. Most often support planning is best done by someone close to the person at the centre. If this is not possible, then someone from their local community is the next best placed, and a professional 'support planner', broker or care manager after that. There is usually one person responsible for co-ordinating the process of planning and compiling the information into an actual plan.

Even when an individual has a clear-cut role, planning is always a collaboration; a democratic process with a clear aim to support an individual to make the best choices they can, using the resources available to them to get the best out of their life. When it is done right, support planning can be an incredibly empowering and satisfying experience for all involved. It can provide the key to self-determination.

The real learning for support planners come by reflecting on their own direct experience of the process. There is no substitute for that, but maybe the next best thing is to hear a story about support planning, so this is where I start. Here is Jenny's story.

Learning from experience

Jenny was fed up. After a lifetime of feeling let down by social services, she harboured a deep-seated distrust and contempt for social workers and for authority figures in general. She said, '*I don't like people in authority, they can take power away from you*'. As far as Jenny was concerned, social services failed her parents and failed to protect her when things started to fall apart at home. She had been passed from institution to institution as a child and young adult, and finally was 'allowed' at the age of 36 to live independently with outreach support.

She saw herself as a 'nuisance' and believed very strongly that it was only by being a 'nuisance' she would get any help at all, as this was her experience. But Jenny also had a wicked sense of humour and beneath all the cynicism and bitterness beat a heart of gold and a fiercely defiant independent spirit.

Jenny would continually retell key events from her life – the death of her parents, running away from the children's home, being run over by two cars in the street and surviving to tell the tale of how by forcing herself to stand up after being hit the first time, she avoided the full force of the second car. Although her mobility is permanently impaired by the accident, Jenny is still able to do most things for herself.

When invited to take part in the personal budgets pilot, Jenny chose me by name as she knew me quite well and felt I was someone she could trust. She was initially cynical about personalisation and its potential to make any difference to her life. At that time, she was neglecting her home environment to the extent that her tenancy was at risk. Her previous flat had to be regularly blitz-cleaned; she refused to allow support workers to clean her flat or even to help her, claiming that cleaning was a *'waste of my support workers' time'*. It got so bad sometimes that her support workers refused to go inside the flat. Jenny had then signed an agreement before moving flat that she would accept support to keep her flat clean and four months later, she once again refused almost all offers of support to do just that.

Despite initial doubts, support planning quickly became a positive process for Jenny simply by allowing her the time to tell the story and show her that she was being heard without being judged. The more exactly I recorded Jenny's verbatim, the less angry and antagonistic she seemed to become. She would read through the previous minutes and make amendments before moving on. Initial cynicism had transformed into enthusiasm, as Jenny seemed almost invigorated by the process and very much in control.

One of the first person-centred planning tools we used was *important to* and *important for*. I explained that *important to* is about things that make you feel happy in your life; *important for* relates to things you might need to stay safe. Sometimes these are things that other people see as being more important – people like social workers, for example.

The issue of keeping her flat clean, however, was still out of bounds and Jenny saw this as being something *'other people think is important for me'*. Reluctantly she added this to the *'important for'* column in her person-centred plan. What was really important to Jenny were her cats, keeping her flat (which she loved), her health and her work at the local city farm. I accepted this but asked Jenny to take some time to think how *important to* and *important for* might be linked.

When we next met, I suggested that keeping the flat clean was crucial if she really wanted to hang on to her flat and reminded her about the agreement she had signed, and also that if she had to move again she might not be able to take her cats with her. This seemed to hit home and Jenny was able possibly for the first time to appreciate how cleaning might actually be important. Jenny agreed to move 'keeping my flat clean' into the 'important to me' column of the plan. I was astonished, as a huge breakthrough had been made, and one that was later to transform Jenny's relationship with her support workers, neighbours and eventually herself as she began to take more care about her appearance and personal hygiene. This led to Jenny successfully applying for work in a local advocacy group and going back to college to improve her budgeting skills.

The support planners' toolkit

1. Person-centred planning

A support plan is a person-centred plan with a budget and a set of strict criteria to meet. Good support planners will be fluent in person-centred thinking and able to support people to make best use of the funds available to them.

Person-centred planning is a way of thinking and engaging pragmatically with a person, a conversation aiming to understand who the person is and what they need to become as fully self-determining as they want and are able to be. The tools now widely used in planning are used because they have been well tested, and they work. Make creative use of a range of tools and be bold enough to experiment and create new ones, according to the needs of the person as these needs arise through the process.

Support planners need to live and breathe person-centredness in their own lives and with their colleagues, as well as with the people they support. Person-centredness is in other words as much a way of seeing the world and working effectively with colleagues as it is an aid to service design. Tools such as '4 + 2 questions' (what have we tried, learned, what are we pleased about, concerned about, what will we do next and share) and 'working/not working' are excellent for team meetings, plans and appraisals. Embed the use of these tools at work to fully understand how to apply them. Do this well and it bears fruit as you demonstrate personal authenticity and consistency when using them in support planning.

Familiarity in using these tools prompts regular reflective practice, continuous professional development and helps stimulate a shared body of practice. The effectiveness of networks and peer support groups for family carers can be greatly enhanced by their use. Support planning will benefit participants having such an experience, generating enthusiasm and familiarity.

2. Taking risks

A person-centred positive approach to risk will help maximise effectiveness of the support plan.

'The purpose of any risk assessment is just as much about the happiness of the person, their family and the community as it is about their safety.'
(Neill *et al*, 2008)

The reality for many people with learning disabilities is very different; services tend to be traditionally risk averse, emphasising safety over happiness and personal choice. People with learning disabilities are also becoming more visible in society, and sometimes this provokes a backlash from those who harbour fear and resentment towards people because they are different.

'Hate crime' against people with learning disabilities is not a new phenomenon, but it is now part of the reality of life for many in our so-called 'inclusive' society, and is something that we must join together to defeat if we are to reach our goals. There is a real danger in our health and safety attuned times that the first response from some will be to keep so-called 'vulnerable people' completely away from what are seen as 'risky situations'. Support planning has a central part to play in challenging risks brought about by discrimination, negative attitudes and fear. It is aimed at helping people live fuller, more active lives, and every care must be taken that it is not used to justify risk-averse practice.

Be realistic though. Take into account the dangers in society; to and from the person, and develop creative solutions that allow the person to take risks in a way that enables them to grow and develop. Guard against 'risk averse' responses.

3. Capacity and informing decision-making

The ultimate purpose of your relationship with the person is to assist them to make decisions in a more informed way. If the person lacks capacity then you need to achieve this through the person's representative. This applies from the initial meeting where you explain what support planning is and what they can expect, to the final stages where you work with them to make specific decisions on what to spend the budget on.

Cultivate an evidence-based approach; demand evidence to back up why it's important that money is spent in this particular way. This is especially relevant with people who have communication difficulties or lack capacity to make their own decisions, and therefore rely on others to interpret what their wishes and decisions are, or might be.

People must be allowed to make their own choices *even if others consider them unwise*, as long as they are able to comprehend and accept the consequences. Enable people to understand what their options are, what the consequences of their choices may be, to reflect upon the risks involved and to think creatively about mitigating these.

The issue of capacity is likely to arise where an individual has communication difficulties. Lack of speech can often be mistaken for lack of capacity and many people have their decision-making rights denied on this basis. Everyone communicates in some way; take a 'total communication approach' to planning and enlist the help of specialist speech and language therapists to support individuals to develop communication methods and systems.

For many people with communication difficulties, their methods of communication are misunderstood, particularly where their only means of communication is through behaviour or use of gesture. Patience and understanding are required in such situations. Be realistic about the person's potential to be in control of their support and decision-making. You cannot fully know a person's potential to develop and use systems of communication, but you can recognise where there is capacity to improve. Judgments about capacity can never be absolute, they are always based on best available evidence. Be prepared for surprises.

4. Budgeting

Start planning only when you have a clear picture of how the whole budget is comprised: the indicative budget, any charge the person has to contribute towards it and any other funding streams such as independent living fund, disability living allowance and 'supporting people' funded services.

The more detailed the budget is the better, for example, about exactly how much a laptop will cost or at what times and days the person will do the shopping with their friend and how much the petrol they are paying for will cost. Exact detail can be adjusted at review but a realistic estimate based on objective data at the planning stage is helpful.

An indicative budget is an estimate and should be challenged if:

a. it is insufficient to keep the person safe

b. it is insufficient to prevent deterioration in the quality of the person's life

c. you can demonstrate that extra funding will lead in the longer term to a reduction in need, greater independence and a significantly better quality of life for the individual.

Be clear about how the budget will be managed and what the costs of this will be if:

▶ managed by a provider as an 'individual service fund' (ISF), what the management charges will be. (See proforma for an ISF from the in-control website. See Chapter 8 for more on the provider's role).

▶ the person is using the budget to employ staff then ensure an amount is set aside as a contingency to cover the costs of staff training, supervision, cover, insurance, recruitment.

5. Advocacy and complaints

'Advocacy is taking action to help people say what they want, secure their rights, represent their interests and obtain services they need.' (Action for Advocacy, 2010)

Advocacy is clearly a function of support planning. Most local authorities distinguish informal advocacy and formal advocacy, as formal advocacy has a different meaning where an individual wants to lodge a complaint or appeal against any involved support service, provider, council or professional support planners. This prevents planners getting embroiled in a formal dispute with professionals they need to collaborate with, and avoids a potential conflict of interest.

On the other hand, from the perspective of the person at the centre, having to involve another person in their planning further complicates and delays the process. Professional planners need to know whether they are expected to provide formal 'A'dvocacy or not in order to effectively signpost and manage the expectations of the person they are supporting. For example, if the person you support wants to challenge their indicative budget and you can demonstrate the need for additional funds, you need to be clear whether you can take up this challenge or whether you must refer the person to an independent advocate to carry out this role.

In either case, it is important that you are able to fully inform the person of their rights and to understand the process they will need to follow.

6. Challenging assumptions and thinking out of the box

Support planners can make a real difference to the way society functions by supporting individuals to challenge barriers based on discrimination and ignorance. Using social care resources to make changes, one person at a time, can transform society in much the same way as a single court judgment sets precedent.

Whenever we support someone to challenge and overcome a barrier we are moving one step closer to a more egalitarian society. When we fail to support someone to challenge, we collude with discriminatory attitudes in society; we miss the opportunity to make a difference. The real challenges are those that exist in the minds of the people we support and in our own minds. Accept the possibility that any of us may get in the way, even with the best of intentions.

Try to imagine a society where the gifts, viewpoints and differences made possible thanks to people with learning difficulties are welcomed, valued positively, and celebrated, not seen as a burden or a problem. What would this society look like? What would cease to happen? How would this affect you? If you find this hard to imagine, ask yourself why and ask yourself if this is fair.

7. Effective listening and vision

High-quality support planning requires the planner to combine effective listening with creative insight and the ability to envision what may be possible. Use the language the person uses, encourage reflection and insight by recording and reviewing the exact words and phrases used.

One of the most exciting parts about support planning is the moment of insight where suddenly a connection is made between some aspect of the planning work to make sense of the person's life with the things that are uppermost in the person's mind or which concern the person or people they care about most. This can lead to a profound breakthrough for the person, as in Jenny's example about keeping her flat clean. It can also lead to a sudden reassessment of risk as new information comes to light about the person's previously hidden informal support network.

The real skill in support planning is being able to get stuck into the detail without getting overwhelmed, distilling the reams of information and focusing in on key aspects of particular relevance. Seemingly peripheral information can take on central significance – stuff that people take for granted, like support provided by or to family and friends, unrecognised skills a person has, their gifts and qualities, their untapped potential.

8. Counselling skills

Telling the story of the person requires personal information to be shared. Sometimes this is difficult for the person or others to hear. A person can seem to be 'stuck', unable to see a brighter better future for themselves. They need help to 'un-stick' themselves; to deal positively with whatever is holding them back. This process is therapeutic in nature and requires a certain degree of sensitivity from the planner, together with a professional non-judgmental approach. This can be easier (or at least less complicated) to manage if the planner is standing outside the person's family or circle of support – so this is one of the instances when it is better sometimes to bring in a 'professional' support planner.

Key counselling skills planners need include: authenticity, congruence, empathy and unconditional positive regard. Employed effectively, these skills will enable planners to develop and earn the trust of people they plan with and to uncover any 'skeletons lingering in closets'. If you are lucky, the skeleton will leave of its own accord once it is discovered. Make sure you know how to refer for more formal therapeutic intervention from a psychologist or counsellor, and make sure you (the support planner) are well-supported and looked after.

9. Project planning – goals, outcomes, milestones

The more detail in support plans the better, particularly when it comes to the action planning section. Know the difference between an outcome, a goal and a milestone and be able to link them all together.

Outcome: why it's important (eg. in order for the person to stay healthy and well).
Goal: what the person wants to achieve overall (eg. to join a football team).
Milestones: how the person will take steps towards joining the team.

The plan needs to make sense and be SMART (Specific, Measurable, Achievable, Realistic and Time-bound).

10. Knowledge of how and when to apply legislative framework

Familiarity with the key concepts and implications of relevant legislation will mean you can make use of them in the person's best interests. Two key ones are:

▶ Mental Capacity Act (2005) – protects the rights of individuals to make their own decisions and also protects people who cannot make their own decisions about things – people who 'lack capacity'. Important because of the need for the support plan to show how the person will stay in control. If a person lacks capacity to make specific decisions, the plan should evidence that the decisions made on the person's behalf are *in the person's best interests*.

▶ Equalities Act (2010) – protects the rights of individuals not to suffer unfair discrimination on the basis of disability, age, ethnicity, gender, sexuality, belief or lack of belief. This act incorporates the Disability Discrimination Act – particularly relevant for people with learning disabilities. Bear in mind when supporting people to look at options available from the so called 'mainstream' of society ('non-specialist' services and organisations), use it to challenge assumptions and barriers to inclusion.

11. Mapping the territory

Investigate what the person and their circle of support already knows, uses and has tried. Knowing *how to find out* what's available is more important than simply 'knowing what's available'; know where to look, who to ask and what questions to ask. Cultivate an open mind willing to challenge, query and investigate possibilities. Seek out people who hold information about what's available by all means, but aim to break new ground and tap into new resources, not just existing ones.

12. Access to information

Gather as much information about the person you are supporting from as wide a range of sources as possible. Build a full unique picture, identify any apparent contradictions or sticking points, and avoid duplication. Avoid making assumptions about the individual based on prior information. Information is always an interpretation based on a particular person's viewpoint at a particular moment in time. Enable the person to tell their story and make decisions how to make the best of what's available to them.

Know how the local authority works; processes and systems used and how to negotiate them. Find out what types of things the local authority will agree to fund. Each local authority has their own rules but broadly they can fund anything legal apart from gambling and alcohol; provided it will result in positive outcomes for the person. But different local authorities have set their own rules, particularly around the use of *legal rewards*, and the employment of family members. You need to know about these and challenge them if necessary. Don't allow precedent to exclude possible options. Every individual is unique and what might not be an appropriate option for one person may well be just the thing for another. Knowledge of precedent is useful for giving advice, not necessarily for making final decisions.

Develop good relationships with key people, particularly care managers, direct payments officers, and speech and language therapists. Get to know them and develop an understanding of the constraints they have to work with.

The art and science of support planning

The art of support planning is in the approach employed by the planner and the values embodied in that approach. This requires a mindset which cultivates creative vision, maintains a strong belief in equality of opportunity and fundamental human rights. It is the aspirational 'humanising' element to the work. This art underpins listening and counselling skills and determines how effective the planner will be as an advocate. It also makes planning vital, creative and fun; tapping into resources, liberating the will and prompting reflective practice in the moment. This is, I believe, what Sam Newman meant when he talked about having '*No agenda*' when working with people, seeing the person and not just a stereotype or a mirror for ourselves (Newman, 2009). The ability to hear our own deeper thoughts by really listening, to be actively reflective, to become aware of how our role is developing and adapt our approach according to what would achieve the best outcome for the person. Avoid templates and embrace the blank canvas!

Be prepared for disclosures of past abuses and know that the way you respond to these is key to developing a trusting relationship. Quite often this is a pre-requisite to planning – you may be tested and evaluated, scrutinised and maybe even deceived. Be prepared for anger, impatience, frustration and short tempers. Be measured, balanced, rational and outcome focused in response. Remember it will be damaging to the person in the long run if you collude with any negativity they express – it will prevent movement from that place and hinder progress in planning.

The science of support planning is in the method and process you are required to follow to meet the criteria; the analysis of outcomes and presentation of argument. Be methodical, consistent and systematic as time is of the essence. You will be met with conflicting demands; the local authority will be interested more in numbers of people supported to implement their support plans; the individuals you work with may well have other agendas and will resent any pressure to restrict their planning time. Be consistent and effective in planning, be clear about your remit and any time limit imposed on you.

In practice, there is a marriage between the art and science; you need to be both consistent in your approach and creative in your use of method.

Support planning is a journey and each person has their own unique destination; your job as a support planner is to find out where it is they want to go, where they are now and how to get to the departure point. You need to find out what they need for their journey, what they have already and who the best people are to accompany them on their travel.

Tips for being an effective planner

▶ If there is a potential conflict of interest, get someone else in there to help you, preferably a professional advocate or care manager depending on the nature of the conflict of interest.

▶ Always get the charging assessment done before you start planning.

▶ Have a checklist with you of things you need to get done and questions you need to ask.

▶ Develop or obtain a folder of information handouts about key areas such as direct payments, examples of support plans, knowledge of what the council will and won't allow, questions to ask in planning, basic info such as 'what is a personal budget?' and update this regularly.

▶ Don't assume that 'professionals' know what they're talking about, if in doubt, check it out; trust your gut feelings and ask yourself if what they are saying fits with the spirit of personalisation.

▶ Do your very best to support people to get their budget as a direct payment but ensure they fully understand the implications and responsibilities of employing staff – this is the option which gives maximum choice and control to the person. Investigate fully what resources they have to hand, and their extended support network.

▶ Always get support when you are dealing with tricky issues, particularly involving people who misuse substances or have additional mental health needs where this has a significant impact on their capacity to make decisions; and people where there is a specific identifiable risk of financial abuse from someone in their life.

▶ Your aim is to *minimise the need for your involvement.* There is always a risk in the helping professions of creating dependency. Support planners need to be on guard against this and actively reflect on their own practice as well as that of others involved in the person's life to prevent development of behaviours or tendencies which serve to disempower the individual.

▶ Have fun but mind your language and know that attitude is infectious.

Jenny: the final words

As a 'trailblazer' for personal budgets, Jenny later gave a speech at the local Partnership Board meeting and this is an excerpt from her speech:

'Tony tried to write down exactly what I said so that it's in my words. This is very important because it's me saying it rather than them saying it for you or making assumptions about what you want.

I think the plan we came up with was sort of suitable to my needs, in my own words. Having a [personal budget] *is about having your own independence and choice. You are making decisions rather than other people doing it for you.*

The more independence you get, the more confident you get, it brings the confidence back because you're doing it and sort of know the reason why you're doing it. You can always read through your plan to remind yourself if you forget. You're doing it for yourself, making the choices and decisions for yourself.

The thing is, whatever the problem is in your life, if you're given enough time to think it through for yourself, you can always come up with some sort of solution.

I'm not saying that my plan is perfect, I'm not sure if my plan will work out for me or not, we'll have to wait and see what happens, it's a matter of waiting to see how it works. If it doesn't, then I will work out how to change it so that it suits me better.'

*Jenny (name changed to protect identity)

References

Action 4 Advocacy [online]. Available at: www.actionforadvocacy.org.uk/ (accessed November 2010).

Neill M, Allen J, Woodhead N, Reid S, Irwin L & Sanderson H (2008) *A Positive Approach To Risk Requires Person-Centred Thinking* [online]. Available at: www.puttingpeoplefirst.org.uk/_.../A_Person_Centred_ Approach_to_Risk.pdf (accessed November 2010).

Newman S (Ed) (2009) *Personalisation: Practical ideas from people making it happen*. Brighton: OLM-Pavilion.

Further reading

Bamforth T (2007) Everyone communicates in some way. *Community Living* **20** (4) 22–23.

Equalities Act (2010) [online]. Available at: www.equalities.gov.uk/ equality_act_2010.aspx (accessed November 2010).

In Control, for support planning and review [online]. Available at: www.supportplanning.org/ (accessed November 2010).

Mental Capacity Act (2005) [online]. Available at: www.webarchive.nationalarchives.gov.uk/+/www.direct.gov.uk/en/ disabledpeople/healthandsupport/yourrightsinhealth/dg_10016888 (accessed November 2010).

Zeedyk S (2008) *Promoting Social Interaction for Individuals with Communicative Impairment*. London: Jessica Kingsley.

Chapter 7

Support brokerage: how people can direct their own support and get help if they need it

Kate Fulton

Kate Fulton is a senior consultant for Paradigm, a national training and consultancy organisation. She has worked in a variety of settings supporting people with learning disabilities and people who experience mental ill health. Kate has led Paradigm's contribution to the learning, to date, around support brokerage.

Introduction

As self-directed support develops in England we are learning from people, families and practitioners about the kinds of assistance people require to be in control and to direct their own support. This chapter aims to explore what activities or assistance are included under the term 'support brokerage' and how we can best provide this assistance in ways that are empowering, useful to people and offer them real choice. This chapter advocates a community-based approach to providing support brokerage in the context of self-directed support.

Key points

▶ The nature of the assistance that people need to make best use of self-directed support differs. Approaches to 'support brokerage' need to differ to reflect this.

▶ We use In Control's Seven Step Model to define the sort of assistance that an individual may need.

▶ Many people make use of family and friends to help them. This is much easier if the process is simple and easy to navigate with good accessible information.

▶ We adopt a 'community-based perspective', which means that we look to a diversity of approaches to support.

▶ Every locality needs to have a range of approaches to assistance available for local people.

▶ The development of 'support brokerage' needs to be seen within the wider transformation towards self-direction. It is one of a number of important factors that need to be in place for success.

Support brokerage and self-directed support

What do we mean by support brokerage?

There is a variety of approaches to the provision of support brokerage in countries that now operate on a model of self-directed support (Duffy & Fulton, 2009). These approaches differ in what we mean by support brokerage and in who offers the assistance. Since the emergence of self-directed support in the UK, support brokerage has been defined both as the offer of a range of *informal* supports to the person; and as the provision of a *professional* service (Department of Health, 2008). A review of these various approaches teaches us that no one solution works for everyone. This is encouraging given that the premise of personalisation is the empowerment of individuals to shape their own lives and the services they receive, in their own ways. 'Support brokerage' is a term used to describe a range of tasks or functions with which people may require assistance when directing their own support. It is a part of the infrastructure that enables citizens to make use of the self-directed support processes which local authorities are now putting in place. To really understand this assistance it is important to look at In Control's Seven Step Model from an individual's perspective, and to make use of this to determine what we need to put in place so that different people succeed in directing their support using these new processes. See **Figure 1** below.

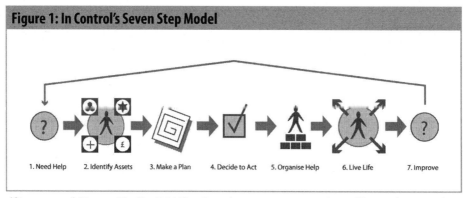

Figure 1: In Control's Seven Step Model

1. Need Help　2. Identify Assets　3. Make a Plan　4. Decide to Act　5. Organise Help　6. Live Life　7. Improve

(Courtesy of Simon Duffy (2010) taken from www.centreforwelfarereform.org)

Pam, a mum of two young people who both have learning disabilities explains the things her family had to do as they began to direct her son Andrew's support. (The list is not exhaustive but gives an indication of a typical 'customer journey'.)

▶ Complete an assessment which determined Andrew's indicative budget.

▶ Explore how Andrew wanted his life to be and what good support looked like for Andrew.

▶ Explore what was available locally that may suit Andrew and his chosen lifestyle.

▶ Develop and then submit Andrew's support plan that says clearly how Andrew wants to live his life and how he wants to spend his budget to help him meet his self-defined outcomes.

▶ Once the plan was approved – set up the support, which includes buying equipment, meeting local providers and interviewing supporters.

▶ Get it going – help new supporters to get to know Andrew and understand how best to support him.

▶ Manage the budget – this includes paying invoices and keeping an eye on the budget so that we know it is going to last the year, whilst being flexible to suit Andrew.

▶ Review the budget and support plan – sitting down with Andrew, supporters and the social worker to check that things are working, thinking about the changes we want to make and check that these are continuing to work for Andrew.

When we understand what people need to do as they direct their support in this way, we get an indication of the kinds of assistance they may require in designing and setting up their support arrangements. Before leaping into developing a variety of support services to offer assistance to people, we need to remember two things:

▶ many people can and do all of the above themselves with family and friends if the process is simple and easy to navigate with good accessible information

▶ there is a plethora of people and organisations who currently offer a range of assistance for people directing their support, albeit all may not define this assistance as 'support brokerage'.

'*It looked straightforward to me, we as a family know what's going to work for Stephen as he grows into an adult and as we worked through the process we discovered new ideas along the way, which ultimately led to one of the most creative support packages we have ever had – and we did it ourselves!*' (Family member)

As we develop the infrastructure to enable people to direct their support, we must then be acutely aware of people's capacity to do things for themselves and we must not assume that everyone will automatically require formal assistance. We must also be very conscious that assistance is made available for those people who want, need and choose to use it. It is with this in mind that we can think about the kinds of support that people are likely to need at each stage of the Seven Step Model, should they require it. The following diagram (**Figure 2**) shows this.

Support brokerage – a functional approach?

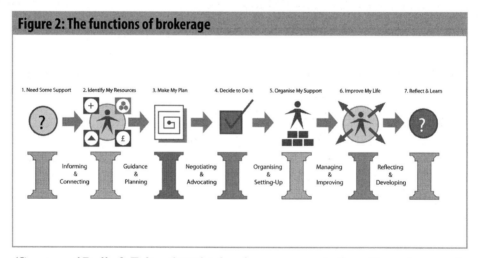

Figure 2: The functions of brokerage

(Courtesy of Duffy & Fulton (2010) taken from www.centreforwelfarereform.org)

Once we understand the kinds of support or assistance that people may require in this way, we can then think through what this may look like in practice – what exactly do we need to have available for people to draw on (should they want it) as they direct their support? (see **Table 1** opposite).

Table 1	
Function	**What does this look like in practice?**
Informing and connecting – helping people with good information about local resources and entitlements, researching new possibilities, offering advice around self-directed support, helping people to make useful connections.	▶ Good information, advice and signposting/facilitation connecting to networks and services ▶ Good information about local resources in the community ▶ Clear ways of connecting with others who have experience of directing their support
Guidance and planning – helping people to think through their needs and desired outcomes, helping people to develop their own support plan.	▶ Resources to assist people to think through their lives including their resources and needs ▶ Easy-to-use support planning resources or assistance to help develop a support plan ▶ Clear support planning criteria to explain approval process ▶ Clear accessible information about the approaches to managing a budget
Negotiating and advocating – helping people to negotiate contracts and agreements with others and to advocate their own needs and outcomes when necessary.	▶ Resources and information about the range of ways to manage the budget which may include budget management services ▶ Useful, accessible information about local support providers, their services and costs ▶ Accessible contracts and person-centred support agreements ▶ Advocacy support for people who need it

Function	What does this look like in practice?
Organising and setting up – helping people to organise their support systems, recruiting supporters and agreeing guidelines.	▶ Clear person-centred plans that outline how supporters are expected to best support people ▶ Resources that assist people to get their support set up ▶ Resources to assist recruitment and managing support systems ▶ Accessible information to assist in exploring and developing good support
Managing and improving – helping people to manage their funding, their supports and using expert advice to make improvements.	▶ Budget management services with clear costs and ease of use ▶ Quality monitoring resources ▶ Clear understanding of expertise available locally that people can draw on should they need it ie. occupational therapists, housing specialist etc.
Reflecting and developing – helping people to review their needs and their support arrangements and to initiate changes where necessary.	▶ Person-centred review processes and resources ▶ Assistance and resources to review and develop the support plan ▶ Assistance and resources to re-think if and where changes are needed

If we think about the kinds of support that people look for, and then about where in our local communities this support may be available, we can build up a comprehensive picture of what is available today, even before we actively stimulate something new that we call 'support brokerage'.

There are, in fact, many people, resources, services and networks that offer these types of assistance. The challenge is to ensure that all these people, resources and networks understand the model of self-directed support, how they can make a contribution to it and how important it is that people can easily access them, should they want to.

Approaches to providing support brokerage

Community-based support brokerage

So, there are many different people and organisations capable (and indeed currently offering) the assistance we are calling 'support brokerage'. It is very important that we do not ignore these already existing strengths and capacities. The more sources of support we have in a local community, the closer we get to offering all citizens a real choice about who they receive the assistance from – people and organisations that they believe best understand them and their situation. The community-based model acknowledges that people have unique needs and different networks – they therefore look to different people in their community to offer them assistance in directing their support. This model is based upon access to:

▶ information networks

▶ peer support

▶ mainstream community support and services

▶ service providers

▶ professional people.

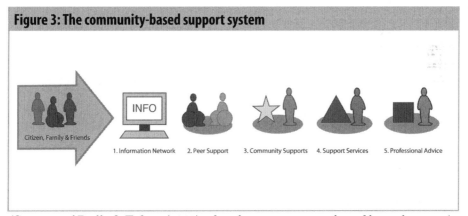

Figure 3: The community-based support system

(Courtesy of Duffy & Fulton (2009) taken from www.centreforwelfarereform.org)

Such a community-based model:

1. starts by assuming and encouraging the capacity of citizens and families by enabling access to a wide information network

2. facilitates the early use of peer support for everyone

3. ensures access to community supports from organisations and associations within their community

4. enables citizens to work with service providers directly and to explore with them what options are available

5. puts in place sufficient professional advisers, such as social workers or other specialists, so that everyone can get the help they need.

What does this look like in practice?

Information networks

It is vital that people can easily find accessible information about what is available and what they are entitled to. Relevant, up-to-date information which the person can make use of needs to be available at all stages of the process. For many people the chance to talk through this information with someone who has experience also helps. There are a variety of ways that information can be made available, including standard handbooks, websites, short films explaining the process from people's experiences and templates that people can work through themselves. There is a wide range of organisations both statutory and independent which are in a position to offer information, advice and guidance.

We need to empower everyone with the tools and knowledge necessary to begin directing their own support. It is important that information is available in places that make sense to citizens ie. schools, colleges, community centres, libraries, advice bureaux, service providers and local support networks. Developing and maintaining universal information, advice and guidance in this way is vital to this process.

Peer support

Time and time again people and families tell us that other people's experiences are invaluable and often one of their most useful sources of inspiration and support. This can be through a variety of routes, including simply talking through support ideas with someone with similar experiences to attending a formal mutual support group or network meeting. There are a variety of peer support networks now in place in many local communities, including centres for independent living, user-led organisations and self-advocacy groups. The ability to gain support and inspiration through networks of this kind is a vital element in the development of support brokerage.

Community supports

Many people get good support from a range of statutory, private and third sector community agencies and services. Many of these organisations not only offer assistance related to the more formal aspects of 'support brokerage' (as defined above), but also help to connect people with one another and with other local resources that can help.

Service providers

Many people can and do get good support and assistance from service providers (organisations which provide support services). As self-directed support becomes the approach of choice for all, these organisations need to work hard to ensure that the services they provide are right for each individual they support, whilst also being cost effective so that people get good value for their money. Organisations need to develop ways to enable providers to market, design and develop personalised services directly to people themselves (see Chapter 8 for more on this). People and families need to know that they have a choice and that they don't have to stick with that one provider. There are now many examples from across England of providers working hard to respond to people and families, developing creative support plans and designing support services alongside the person and their family, based upon what the person wants to achieve and within that person's budget.

Professionals

Some people will need or want professional advice or support in order to plan and develop their own support system. This small but important group of people may find that none of the other approaches work for them for a variety of reasons: they may be in crisis or a situation that is complex and requires significant time to work through and build what they need. It is important that all local authorities have the capacity to offer this assistance. Care managers or social workers in the local authority and care co-ordinators within health services can (and indeed in many places do) offer this. In some areas people are able to purchase the services of a private broker; or of a professional who offers specialist advice and support eg. specialist housing or employment brokerage. In these circumstances we need to be mindful of how people are enabled to purchase such services and how they sit alongside the universal services that everyone uses.

This range of approaches offers a diverse mix, building on local skills, knowledge and different experiences. No one approach is better than others, all having strengths and weaknesses (Duffy & Fulton, 2009); at the end of the day, they can only be judged by the people and families who choose to use one rather than another.

'I chose to use my adviser at my self-advocacy group, because I really like him and he knows me well. He helped me understand what getting a budget means and we worked out how I could get my flat and do things I like doing.' (Person with learning disabilities)

'I wanted some support from someone who knew my son who I felt was really on our side. I chose the advocacy organisation that has known me and my son for some time. Kellie was great, it was a fantastic way to think about what is going to work for my son.' (Parent)

Creating a community that works for everyone

Once all of these approaches are in place in local communities then people have a real choice over from whom they receive assistance and how they will direct their support. Co-ordinating this infrastructure can offer some challenges, and certainly requires a significant change from the way that local authorities have operated in the past.

The key point is the need to ensure that every locality offers a real choice of types of assistance. If this kind of community-based support brokerage is well developed with easily accessible options available to people, then we would expect that the numbers utilising the various approaches to be fairly evenly distributed across this range of options. However, early indicators based in one region in England (Duffy & Fulton, 2010; see **Figure 4** opposite) covering 14 local authorities suggests that most assistance is in fact given by professionals. We are still in the early years of self-directed support, so this may be understandable and may be in the process of changing. However, it is important that we keep this under review and over time that we develop and strengthen all approaches to ensure that there is choice for all.

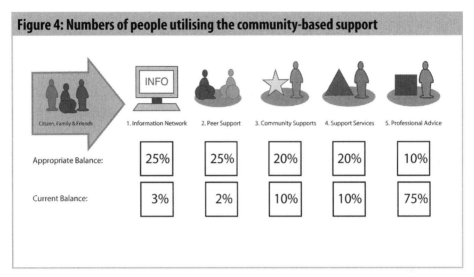

(Courtesy of Duffy & Fulton (2010) taken from www.centreforwelfarereform.org)

If we are to stimulate and develop all of the community options to offer a robust supportive infrastructure, then the people and organisations involved will need to grow and maintain understanding, skills and resources in the following areas:

Informing and connecting – helping people with good information about local resources and entitlements, researching new possibilities, offering advice around self-directed support, helping people to make helpful connections.

Guidance and planning – helping people to think through their needs and desired outcomes, helping people to develop their own support plan.

Negotiating and advocating – helping people to negotiate contracts and agreements with others and to advocate for their own needs when necessary.

Organising, designing and setting up – helping people to organise their support systems, recruiting supporters and agreeing guidelines.

Managing and improving – helping people to manage their funding, their supports and using expert advice to make improvements.

Reflecting and developing – helping people to review their needs and their support arrangements and to initiate changes where necessary.

As is clear from other chapters, support brokerage is one of a number of elements that are needed if we are to genuinely empower people and their families. If we were to ignore this and focus our efforts exclusively on getting the perfect resource allocation system or on developing the community of provider services whilst doing little about the way people navigate and negotiate their way through the system, then the risk will be that we continue to frustrate people. Currently we have a cumbersome and complex system which costs far more than it needs to do, and without this kind of direct help for ordinary people, things won't change. For these reasons, it is important to pay attention to each of the following three strands of work.

1. Invest in community-based support – a universal, enabling and flexible support system that is rooted in the local community.

2. Reform care management – a system for ensuring people get their entitlements, the right support and an appropriate level of monitoring.

3. Refocus commissioning – organisational systems which are able to invest directly in citizens and communities.

These themes are all addressed in different ways through this book.

Conclusion

When considering support brokerage in the context of self-directed support, we need to ensure there is a range of options available for people and families to choose from – to decide the right assistance for them, assistance that is available as and when they want it. The community approach to support brokerage described in this chapter builds on the strengths of local people, ultimately creating stronger communities.

As support brokerage continues to develop across the UK, and the range of options begins to increase, we are learning that the following areas need attention.

▶ Community leadership – create a real partnership with all local stakeholders including people and families to develop local assistance that works for everyone.

▶ Make self-directed support easy to understand from the beginning. Support options will then make sense and will be meaningful to all.

▶ Provide information for all – as social care changes and self-directed support becomes a reality for more and more people, we need to make sure that there is information, advice and guidance that is free, understandable and available to all.

▶ Create an inclusive environment where organisations can learn and develop in response to changing needs.

In these economically challenging times the belief in and commitment to ensuring that people and communities play a key role in the development of support brokerage is crucial. The community approach to providing support brokerage builds on local strengths, and therefore ultimately offers a range of choice and assistance for all citizens.

Thanks to Simon Duffy (The Centre for Welfare Reform) and the Yorkshire and Humber region for their determination to develop an infrastructure that is empowering and meaningful for all citizens.

References

Department of Health (2008) *Good Practice in Support Planning*. London: Department of Health.

Duffy S & Fulton K (2009) *Should We Ban Brokerage*. London: Centre for Welfare Reform.

Duffy S & Fulton K (2010) *Architecture for Personalisation*. London: Centre for Welfare Reform.

Further reading and resources

Department of Health (2010) *Support Planning and Brokerage with Older People and People with Mental Health Difficulties*. London: Department of Health.

Paradigm continues to develop their thinking and share their learning on their website [online]. Available at: www.paradigm-uk.org (accessed November 2010).

Scown S & Sanderson H (2010) *Making it Personal*. Stockport: Dimensions and HSA Press.

Chapter 8

Providers: what we need from them and what they need from others

Aideen Jones

Aideen Jones has spent over 35 years working in the independent social care sector, with the first 16 years working with young people in therapeutic settings in Wales and Sussex. She has worked for Southdown Housing Association since 1989, becoming the chief executive in 2001.

Introduction

Are the ideas and practices of personalisation new to service providers, or are they things that good providers have been doing over the years? This chapter suggests that the answer to this is a bit of both: good providers have always worked with the person at the centre of their practice, but some of the ideas from personalisation and self-directed support help them to take this further. We have a mission to ensure that everyone receives the most personalised support possible, and this chapter explores the important contribution that providers can make to achieving that mission.

Key points

▶ Providers have a key role to play in a personalised system.

▶ It is critical that we listen to what individuals tell us they want.

▶ In Control's Seven-Step Model is helpful in making the required changes.

▶ The system needs to develop in ways that give 'safety' for the individual and for the provider.

▶ We need to think through how to personalise our existing services.

▶ Local authority commissioners need to be clear about how they view personalisation, how they allocate resources and what they expect from providers. This is particularly important whilst many people still do not have an individual budget.

▶ If all this happens, then providers have nothing to fear from personalisation.

Personalisation and providers

There is no doubt that personalisation, individual budgets and self-directed support bring radical change. Providers struggle with how to play an active part in these radical changes, and this chapter will explore a number of strategies and remedies.

Until the late 1980s, many people with learning disabilities lived in hospitals, NHS campuses, and other large institutions or with their families. Then a wave of influential people, including Wolfensberger (1972; 1998) and John O'Brien (1989) suggested there were other ways to support people, the institutions started to empty and the group home and staffed house were born.

Wolfensberger provided a theoretical framework around concepts of self-actualisation, normalisation and social role valorisation (SRV). These were certainly progressive ideas at a time when people had been locked away in institutions, but they were not particularly accessible ones for people providing these new services. Unfortunately, the concepts were easily distorted and misused and they came to play a part in the creation of a new wave of institutions, where people were physically present in communities, but were not really *members* of those communities.

I remember once in the early 1990s being asked by a manager from a local authority if Southdown Housing were 'into SRV'. After taking a few moments to remember what SRV meant, I said we were 'into' listening to people with learning disabilities and providing the support they wanted. I think I failed the test as a provider who was involved in the latest thinking.

Wolfsenberger's approach was often misinterpreted and providers got tied up setting up elaborate systems to guide the work that they did.

What he and colleagues like Bengt Nirje were actually saying was, 'The normalisation principle means making available to all people with disabilities patterns of life and conditions of everyday living, which are as close as possible to the regular circumstances and ways of life or society'. (Nirje, 1969)

John O'Brien gave us the framework of the 'five accomplishments' to guide us on this journey. He suggested that positive experiences for people with learning disabilities would follow if providers were able to ensure that choice, community presence, relationships, respect and 'competence' were all in place or were attainable for the people using the service. Most good service providers used (and many still use) the five accomplishments as the value framework that underpins their work. This framework has helped shape induction training, NVQs for staff, and individual plans for people with learning disabilities.

There is no doubt that in the 20 years following the closure of many large institutions, the life experiences for people with learning disabilities have improved. People generally came to live in surroundings that are more comfortable; they have access to many more opportunities for choice and community involvement; and they are supported by people who are well-trained, and have values that ensure that people are treated with dignity and respect.

However, services are not consistently good in all areas and many people with learning disabilities have been badly let down and even abused by some services. There have been scandals that have led to major enquiries such as those in Cornwall (Health Care Commission, 2006); Merton & Sutton (Health Care Commission, 2007) and the others reported by Mencap (2008) into the deaths of people in hospital. These have led to a strong belief that if services were really personalised and if individuals were really in charge, then these abuses simply could not happen.

In 2008, Eric Emerson and Chris Hatton researched the future need for adult social care for people with learning disabilities. They found that:

▶ the majority of people with learning disabilities had no choice about where they lived or who they lived with

▶ a minority did not have acceptable levels of privacy

▶ 83 percent of people had no employment

► significant numbers of people lived in households and areas with high levels of deprivation

► many people had no contact with friends and family

► one in three people had experienced bullying and rudeness from the public

► one in 12 people were likely to be a victim of crime, against one in 26 of the general population

► only 28% were involved in self-advocacy

► only one in three people voted.

These are not findings that any provider will want to see. They suggest that truly personalised services for all are still some way off.

Providers and the Seven Step Model

► What do providers think about the Seven Step Model?

► What can providers do now to ensure their services can deliver this model?

Government policy in the last 10 years has been largely very positive. With the launch of *Valuing People* in 2002, *Putting People First* in 2007 and *Valuing People Now* in 2009 by the Department of Health, it should have become clear to providers that they could not stand still and continue to provide the traditional services that they had been delivering for the last 20 years. As a result, many providers have begun to remodel what they do and to offer a much more flexible range of services, based on what individuals tell them they want. However, there remain a number of difficulties.

The biggest stumbling blocks for providers, which we will address in the remainder of this chapter, are as follows:

► the potential loss of certainty when services are block commissioned no longer

► how to offer job security to workers when the purchasing of services may prove to be erratic

► how to fulfil employment law requirements

► how to ensure the quality of potentially fragmented services

► how to ensure the vulnerable people are safeguarded from risk and potential abuse

▶ what to do with the existing services, especially if they have long-term capital invested in them

▶ worries about individual services and their sustainability

▶ how to be able to provide affordable hourly rates that include management overheads.

Some providers are of course resistant to change of any sort, but these are real and genuine concerns. The list above is from providers who are already engaged in reshaping their services and who are keen to embrace personalisation, so we must take it seriously.

Many providers will work across local authority areas and a further difficulty arises when there is no consistency between authorities in the interpretation of:

▶ the underlying model of personalisation

▶ the *resource allocation system*, how money is allocated to individuals

▶ what people are allowed to buy with their individual budgets

▶ what is meant by 'individual service funds' or individual service budgets

▶ eligibility criteria

▶ support brokerage

▶ approaches to care management

▶ commissioning.

Many of these issues are addressed elsewhere in this book and the point here is the difficulty that these discrepancies make for providers.

In the Seven Step Model (developed by In Control, see Chapters 2 and 7) the key feature is that the individual controls the funds and therefore has the power to purchase support that suits them best.

What can providers do now to ensure their services can deliver this model?

Providers are generally resilient and many of us have lived with constant change over the last 20 years. If providers wait for a perfectly formed new system to come from the local commissioning authorities it will be too late.

Providers need to:

▶ ensure that they understand the strategic intentions of their local authorities. For example, do not set up registered care homes if the local authority has stated that they will not use them in the future

▶ assess their services against the Progress for Providers Tool version two (available on the In Control website www.in-control.org.uk) and draw up an action plan for change

▶ think about how they will provide new services that individuals really want to buy

▶ explore what they can do with existing services to ensure that they are as personalised as possible.

The Progress for Providers Tool developed by In Control with providers themselves enables organisations to assess how they can respond to the personalisation agenda. It covers eight key areas:

▶ leadership and strategy

▶ creating a person-centred culture

▶ community focus

▶ support planning and review

▶ finance

▶ human resources

▶ marketing

▶ reviewing and improving the services offered.

Under each heading there are five levels. If a provider is at the start of the journey of change, they will grade themselves one or two; if they have moved a significant distance on that journey they will score five. Very few providers are yet at this level in all eight areas, but this approach provides clear guidance on where to focus. The tool is not designed to show that a provider is *failing* but rather to *encourage action planning* and further work towards personalisation.

Providers and personalisation

Individual customers

Providers need to be able to break down what they have to offer to individuals in terms of a menu of services. Individuals may want to purchase a whole variety of services from a complete managed package, to a few hours of support a week.

Providers will need to make a major mind shift and view people with individual budgets as customers. Thinking of your own experience as a customer is really helpful in formulating a new approach to the services we offer.

Menus of services can include the following elements:

▶ supporting an individual to advertise and recruit their own personal assistants (PAs)

▶ buying hours of support worker time from the provider

▶ providing payroll support to the individual to employ their own staff

▶ support with managing money and setting up invoicing and payments

▶ cover for PAs sickness or annual leave

▶ training for PAs

▶ supervision for PAs

▶ management of PAs

▶ buying into existing classes/courses/clubs

▶ help to find employment

▶ support to manage property/cleaning/gardening/decorating

▶ vetting and Criminal Records Bureau (CRB) checking PAs

The providers will need to be clear about the cost of all these elements and then market these products in places where the customer can easily access them, including:

▶ individual living centres

▶ through social workers/care managers

▶ new consumer websites like Shop4Support (www.shop4support.com) and The Big Bridge (www.thebigbridge.org)

▶ through advocacy and self-advocacy groups

▶ via support brokers.

Charles' story

Charles is a young man who moved into his own flat and was able to secure his own individual budget to employ personal assistants, enabling him to live the life he wants. He was not able to manage the money himself so his parents do this for him and support him to make as many decisions for himself as possible. Mrs B, Charles' mother, took on the responsibility of making sure that his PAs knew what they needed to do and when they needed to support Charles. Mr B dealt with all the paperwork including contracts of employment, payroll and insurance. The first six months went well; Charles chose to spend £40 of his budget a week on a personal trainer; he became fitter and started to exercise daily. Even though he had been involved in recruiting his PAs he decided he didn't always want them around, which meant Mr and Mrs B often needed to cover. They both worked full time and were finding this very difficult. They decided that they would take their first holiday without Charles as he seemed settled with his PA's support. They were checking in at the airport when they were called to say that one of the PAs had gone off sick and Charles was without support. They had to cancel their holiday.

Mr and Mrs B realised that Charles' support was not sustainable without more back up so they approached a local provider who was able to offer training and supervision for the PAs; and to work alongside Charles to draw up guidelines on how he wants his support delivered. The local provider also aided the management of the PAs, working to make sure that there was always cover and back up support workers (interviewed by Charles) who could cover when PAs were away.

The provider had a menu of options that Charles and his parents could choose from and had already set up systems to be able to invoice individual customers. Mr and Mrs B have just had their first holiday free from worries about Charles and his support.

This example illustrates the importance of using a variety of different approaches and agencies to support someone with an individual budget, which still allows them to maintain control and self-direct their package of support in a way that is sustainable in the long term.

Remodelling existing services

The section above deals with how to respond to customers with their own individual budget, but individual budgets are still very new and many providers will not yet be supporting many people in this situation. This should not stop providers making considerable changes to the support they offer to make it as personalised as possible.

The Social Care Institute for Excellence (SCIE) suggests that personalisation for providers means:

▶ building open, productive relationships with people using services, along with commissioners, local authority care managers and the wider community

▶ being clear about what personalisation means so that everyone involved has a shared understanding of principles, practice and outcomes

▶ agreeing a 'personalisation statement' for the service with everyone's involvement, including frontline staff, people who use services and carers

▶ ensuring that all staff training and development is informed by the principles of personalisation and promotes person-centred and relationship-based working.

To address these issues, many provider organisations have found it useful to adopt three parallel work streams:

▶ developing person-centred thinking and approaches throughout the entire organisation to ensure that all people in all situations feel increasingly in control of their support

▶ transforming outdated, failing and unviable services into services that people will want in the future

▶ creating new types of service for self-funders or for people with personal budgets.

What needs to be done?

Providers should consider the following.

▶ What are the culture and values of your organisation and staff?

▶ How are people with learning disabilities viewed? As passive recipients of care or co-producers of the support they need?

▶ Do staff view where they provide support as *their workplace* or *the individual's home* to be respected at all times?

▶ How open are staff to encouraging parental and family involvement; advocacy and self-advocacy and friendships?

▶ If providers have set rotas for staff, consider scrapping them as people's support needs are not uniform. Staff hours can only be worked out after an individual has set up their own personalised support plan, and even then it might change as they grow and develop.

▶ Introduce flexibility in staff employment contracts. Make sure staff are available to support people to stay up late (see www.stayuplate.org).

▶ Providers may be paid by commissioners by a block or spot contract. Divide this up so that you know how much of the money and time relates to an individual (this is what is sometimes referred to as an *Individual Service Fund*).

▶ How much of this money can you make available for the individual to choose how to spend?

▶ How do you engage with mainstream services such as colleges, libraries, public transport, leisure centres and groups, neighbourhood watch, environmental and faith groups?

▶ How will policies and procedures and governance structures be put in place that support and enable a move towards personalisation?

▶ Above all: *listen to what people with learning disabilities are saying.*

What do providers need?

Most providers will have central or back office services that back up the frontline support services. This area will require the big changes in order to be able to deliver personalised services.

These changes will include:

▶ finance systems that can produce individual statements for customers on what they have spent and what they owe

▶ individual invoicing systems

▶ adjustments to recruitment processes to ensure people with learning disabilities are fully involved, from writing job descriptions to interviewing and appointing their support workers or personal assistants

▶ discussion with insurance companies about the new style of service

▶ changes to contracts of employment to allow maximum flexibility

▶ good relationships with local authority finance department especially where they take responsibility for administering an individual's funds.

Good contact with people with learning disabilities, partnership boards, advocacy groups and carers will all be important in terms of being able to gauge what people want and how they want their support to be provided.

All over the country, local authorities, partnership boards, local Mencap groups and other organisations and representative groups have been consulting with people with learning disabilities in the design and evaluation of services. Local authority commissioners are setting up systems to find out more clearly what it is people want and need. Providers need to be involved in all these discussions, otherwise they will be in danger of developing services that people don't want to buy.

Providers need to set up mechanisms that continually evaluate and elicit feedback from people with learning disabilities themselves about how to develop and respond to changing needs. As people with learning disabilities have a greater say in how they want to be supported, their aspirations are likely to change and to increase, and providers need to be in a position to respond.

What can local authorities do to help providers?

Unless providers know what the size and the shape of the potential market is, it will be difficult for them to respond quickly to individuals. Local commissioners need to work with providers to identify this.

In many cases, providers need greater clarity about the mechanisms that local authorities use when deciding on resource allocation. Some local authority resource allocations are being capped or banded, something which undermines the basic principle of personalisation.

Individual intensive services, especially where someone needs overnight support, are expensive. Commissioners need to discuss how to get the 'best of both worlds' so people live together and share support, whilst still maintaining a personalised approach.

Example

Southdown Housing Association had a property in West Sussex that they refurbished to provide individual flats and bedsits for people with learning disabilities. The local authority wanted the people who chose to live there to have individual service funds. Most of the people had high support needs, including the need for staff to be in the building 24 hours a day. The association was able to develop a model where individuals bought into the core service but then had a percentage of their resource allocation left over to buy their individual support.

For the *individual* this means that they can purchase support from other providers; they can buy into college courses; go horse riding; buy the support of employment services etc. It also means they have the flexibility to cease an activity and purchase something else. From the perspective of the *provider*, this means that they are able to provide a safe service, whilst meeting their overhead costs.

The tenants interview and recruit staff for the service and so they are able to exercise maximum choice about the people who will support them.

Given that not all people in the service have their own individual budget, the local authority funders need to pay more attention to the quality of the services that they are paying for. They need to insist that providers demonstrate that the services are personalised and that people with learning disabilities have a voice in shaping them. If this does not happen then there will be a danger of developing a two tier system for those with and without individual budgets.

Local authority commissioners need to be careful that the new rhetoric that sometimes sounds like 'registered bad/supported living good' does not alienate good providers. Across the country there are some great examples of personalised registered care and some dreadful supported living that does not even attempt to provide personalised services.

Conclusion

Providers have nothing to fear from personalisation. If providers supply good-quality support that individuals want to buy then they will always be in business. If they also do everything they can to modernise existing services and really listen and involve people with learning disabilities then they will be able to provide a rich range of services, and the depressing statistics cited by Eric Emerson and Chris Hatton in 2008 will be relegated to history.

When this happens, people with learning disabilities will have 'a life not a service'.

References

Department of Health (2002) *Valuing People: A new strategy for learning disability for the 21st century* [online]. Available at: www.dh.gov.uk (accessed July 2010).

Department of Health (2007) *Putting People First* [online]. Available at: www.dh.gov.uk (accessed July 2010).

Department of Health (2009) *Valuing People Now: A new three year strategy for people with learning disabilities* [online]. Available at: www.dh.gov.uk (accessed July 2010).

Emerson E & Hatton C (2008) *Estimating Future Need for Adult Social Care Services for People with Learning Disabilities in England*. Lancaster: Centre of Disability Research.

Health Care Commission (2006) *Joint Investigation into Services for People with Learning Disabilities at Cornwall Partnership NHS Trust* [online]. Available at: www.cqc.org.uk (accessed July 2010).

Health Care Commission (2007) *Investigation into Services for People with Learning Disabilities Provided by Sutton & Merton Primary Care Trust* [online]. Available at: www.cqc.org.uk (accessed July 2010).

In Control (2010) *Progress for Providers Tool* [online]. Available at: www.in-control.org.uk (accessed July 2010).

Mencap (2008) *Death by Indifference* [online]. Available at: www.mencap.org.uk (accessed July 2010).

Nirje B (1969) In: RJ Flynn & RA Lemay (1999) *A Quarter of a Century of Normalisation and Social Role Valorisation*. Ottawa, Ontario: University of Ottawa Press.

O'Brien J (1989) *What's Worth Working For?*. Georgia: Responsive Systems Associates.

Wolfenseberger W (Ed) (1972) *The Principle of Normalization in Human Services*. Toronto: National Institute on Mental Retardation.

Wolfensberger W (1998) *A Brief Introduction to Social Role Valorisation*. New York: Syracuse University.

Further reading

Department of Health (2010) *Personalisation Through Person-Centred Planning*. London: Department of Health.

Department of Health (2010) *Person-centred Planning – Advice for providers* [online]. Available at: www.dh.gov.uk (accessed July 2010).

Chapter 9

Commissioners – developing the new relationship with people and providers

Clive Miller

Clive Miller is a principal consultant for social care at OPM. His work on personalisation covers both children and adult services and is particularly focused on the implications for commissioners.

Commissioners are responsible for understanding and describing people's needs and wishes and trying to ensure that the right kinds of support are available locally at prices people can afford. This chapter provides an introduction to some of the changes that commissioners need to make as 'personalisation' gathers momentum. Commissioning uses tools derived from economics, demography and social science, which means that some of the language in this chapter is more technical than that in the rest of the book.

Introduction

Personal budgets are the main means by which 'personalisation' will happen in social and health care, but equal attention needs to be given to enabling people to develop their own social capital and to ensuring that targeted and universal services funded outside of personal budgets are also personalised (OPM, 2009a; Department of Health and OPM, 2009b).

By 'social capital' we mean the networks between people and the shared values which these networks give rise to. There are two aspects to this: an individual's social networks – family, friends, workmates etc. and secondly, neighbourhood relationships and community associations, 'the feel on the street' self-help networks and clubs. Understood in this way, 'social capital' is a critical element in making a success of personalisation: it is the stuff which people bring with them as a contribution – personally and collectively – and it is the fundamental reason why personalisation (if done properly) is affordable, in that it brings into play a wealth of additional resources.

What should social care commissioners do and which other commissioners should they collaborate with to achieve this wider transformation? The shift from contracting services, where all transactions are mediated by commissioners and the formal contracts and agreements they negotiate to a retail market, where there is a direct economic relationship between service provider and the person needing support, is fundamental to the success of personal budgets. What should commissioners do to ensure that the personalised services that budget holders require will be available for them to purchase? Both the wider scope of commissioning and the shift to a retail market will fundamentally change the relationship between people, commissioners and providers. How will this change the roles of care managers, contract managers and strategic commissioners?

There are now some great opportunities available for commissioners to play a leading role in the transformation that we are calling 'personalisation'. This chapter tries to give preliminary answers to the questions set out above and also to describe some of the things that commissioners can do to help create the conditions now needed.

Key points

▶ Commissioners must enable people to build and make best use of their social capital that includes their informal social networks and the formal organisations and clubs in their locality. They need to ensure support plans include reference to people's social capital.

▶ It is essential that commissioners work with providers to make services more 'user-friendly' and accessible. We need to secure a wide range of personalised services that people are happy to use and that give them a range of real choices. This applies to services purchased through personal budgets, and to other services.

▶ We need to explore ways to create a smooth transition to a retail market. Commissioners and providers need to work together to build a personalised market for services that really respond to people's expressed needs, rather than to what they think they want or what they have always done.

▶ There is an important role for joint commissioning arrangements (across social care and health care) to assist people to use their individual budgets to buy a variety of types of service to meet a given need.

▶ The commissioning role is changing away from direct contracting for services to one which is more focused upon market management and setting the conditions for personalisation.

Personalisation in the round

The impact of personal budgets in enabling people with learning disabilities to take control of the support they require is undeniable. However, as **Figure 1** shows individualised purchasing is only one part of the jigsaw that must be in place if the full potential of personalisation is to be realised. Alongside enabling effective individual purchasing, personalisation requires three other major transitions:

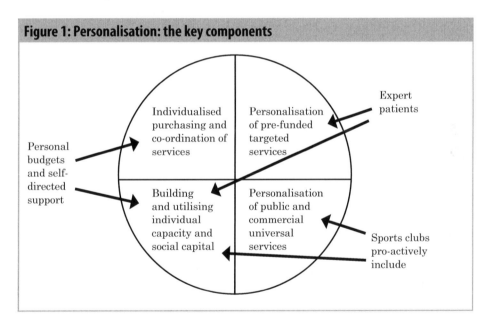

Figure 1: Personalisation: the key components

Pre-funded targeted services

Targeted services are those which people use to meet particular needs which they have, and which are not shared by everyone – for example, the extra help some people need to communicate, to learn or get a job. Many of these targeted services on which budget holders draw, for example, in education, health and employment, are provided outside of social care and therefore outside of the funding provided for personal budgets. But these services do need to be personalised, that is to say, they need to be made more flexible and responsive to the very particular requirements of individuals. Some of this will be achieved through extending the use of personal budgets into these areas.

There is still much to be done to personalise these services. For example, some of the moves to bring health and social services together for the benefit of those who use both, so-called 'integrated service pathways' although an important step forward, are still essentially designed largely to increase efficient running of services (not a bad thing in itself, of course) rather than to directly meet the particular needs of individuals. Hence the experience of citizens is of being more a 'well serviced bundle of needs' rather than people who are in control and supported by a well-connected set of service providers.

An example of the personalisation of existing targeted health services is the development of self-managed support to enable people with long-term conditions to better manage their health. Central to this approach is a change in the relationship between clinician and patient (see **Table 1**).

Table 1: Changing the clinician/patient relationship	
Traditional interactions	**Collaborative interactions**
Information and skills are taught based on the clinician's agenda	Patient and clinician share their agendas and collaboratively decide what information and skills are taught
There is a belief that knowledge creates behaviour change	There is a belief that one's confidence in the ability to change ('self-efficacy') together with knowledge, creates behaviour change
The patient believes it is the clinician's role to improve health	The patient believes that they have an active role to play in changing their own behaviours to improve their own health

Personalisation and Learning Disabilities: A handbook © Pavilion Publishing (Brighton) Ltd 2011

Traditional interactions	Collaborative interactions
Goals are set by the clinician and success is measured by compliance with them	The patient is supported by the clinician in defining their own goals. Success is measured by an ability to attain those goals
Decisions are made by the clinician	Decisions are made as a patient–clinician partnership

Commissioners in social care need to actively engage with those in other sectors who are involved in commissioning pre-funded, targeted services to both extend the range of personal budgets to those services and to redesign those that are directly commissioned. Redesign should start from the position that people can and do make positive contributions to improving *their own* lives. Services can be redesigned to support and help people do this more effectively. This must be accompanied by a change in the relationship between people and professionals, so that power, responsibility and accountability are all shared. Professionals and people must, in other words, work together to 'co-produce' the outcomes people set out in their support plans.

Universal services

Universal services are those which everyone is able to use at certain points in their life, for example, schools, GP surgeries and public transport. More is spent on universal services than on targeted services, but universal services are often designed for the 'average customer'. This means that special arrangements have to be made for many people so they are able to access these services – or they have to do without. Personalisation seeks to address this both by opening up universal services to all and by ensuring that services cater for a wider range of needs.

Many universal services have already made big improvements, for example, technical improvements have meant that it is now much easier for people with physical or sensory impairments to use bus services in many places. The problem is that it is very rare for these improvements to be all brought together and implemented as part of a cross-sector approach to personalisation.

Recent work on the personalisation of bus travel (Miller 2010a; 2010b) and library services identified an initial set of features that characterise a personalised universal service, and these are as follows.

▶ **Individually driven** – the individual service user can choose from a wide range of services to use and to vary the nature of the service provided to better meet their own requirements. For example, First Bus has produced flash cards that travellers can use to signal to the bus driver, for example, to allow them time to reach their seat before the bus starts to move again.

▶ **Person-centred** – the range of services, styles and providers enables everyone to be able to either make use of similar services or access one that best meets their requirements. For example, Bradford's library services 'changing places' where changing and feeding people with profound learning disabilities can be facilitated so that they too can make use of the library.

▶ **Safe and accessible services** – people are enabled to use services because they are both physically accessible and people feel safe getting to and from them, and when using them. For example, in Warrington, bus shelters were redesigned so the people can see buses coming without having to continually get up and down from the bench. They were also located away from the alleyways in order to make it difficult for thieves to surprise people.

▶ **Building individual and community capacity** – the service helps people develop new or existing skills; get to know other people and be part of the local community. For example, Enfield's It's My Life story book project enabled people with learning disabilities to not only tell their story but also learn the IT skills required to do so.

▶ **Active service user involvement** – service users take 'ownership' of, and actively participate in the planning and delivery of the service, such as the Nightlink Travel Club in Manchester, which enabled evening bus services to be restored to a perimeter housing estate. People can only use the service if they become club members. Club members help ensure good behaviour on the buses and those who break the club rules are excluded from membership and use of the bus.

▶ **Commissioners** in social care now need to make links with commissioners of universal services that are critical to the lives of people who have social care support needs and establish their right to universal services. Universal services must be redesigned so that they better reflect the needs of all members of the local community including those people with social care support needs. To achieve this, targeted services, which support specific groups of people with very particular needs may need to think much more carefully about how they are structured and how they work with and influence universal services. They may have to work much more closely with voluntary and community groups and to think about establishing themselves as social enterprises, becoming visible and drawing in and influencing local people.

Individual capacity and social capital

As we say above, it is useful to think of social capital as comprising **individual's social networks** – notably family, friends and neighbours:

▶ **neighbourhood relationships and community associations** – the people a person meets when they are out and about, the feel on the street, and the local and other associations that exist.

Social capital is an important resource on which people can draw alongside their own capacities and economic resources and local services (see **Figure 2**).

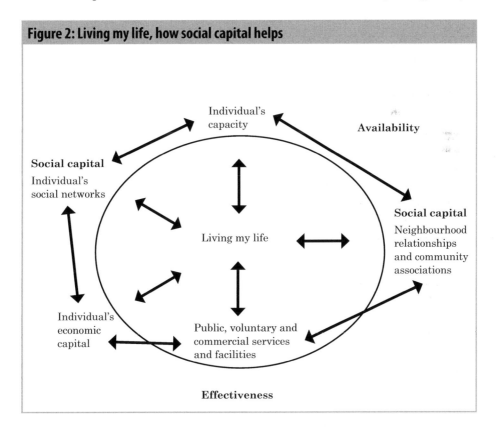

Figure 2: Living my life, how social capital helps

Self-directed support enables people to look at how they would like to live their lives and what they and others can do to realise their ambitions, and then to consider what support, delivered in which ways might add to and reinforce their own efforts. **Figure 2** on page 153 shows how social capital forms an integral part of the range of resources on which people will draw. The availability of these resources may vary; some may be in good supply, others may be scarce or non existent. In the case of social capital some people may have very dense social networks (ie. know lots of people) whilst others may be very isolated with few or no friends or neighbours.

Figure 2 also reminds us that whilst all resources can have a positive effect on people's lives, they can also undermine people's well-being. Research into disabled people's experiences of targeted violence and hostility ('hate crime') has shown that we need to be aware that streets are sometimes dangerous and community groups sometimes exclude people. Targeted bullying can cause huge distress, it stops people having friends and can cause social isolation or make it worse.

Examples of ways that people can be enabled to develop and make best use of their social capital (Chih Hoong Sin *et al*, 2009) are as follows.

Individual's social networks

▶ The Keyring Network, in which people with learning disabilities who live independently in their own homes in the community join together to form a mutual support network with one another, and with assistance from a part-time volunteer who is usually not disabled. People become friends and help one another with the challenges of day-to-day life. They regard Keyring as a club, with other members who they can turn to when they need to do so. Examples of mutal support are: '*Vic gave up his Christmas day plans to look after another member who was sick. Members gathered every night at the house of a fellow network member who had been burgled*' (community living volunteer). Members treat each local keyring cluster as a club.

▶ Time banks help people build up networks: '*Stephen has learning disabilities but is a big strong man so he is much in demand at his local time bank, which he views as his workplace. He earns hundreds of time credits and uses them to pay for help for himself and his mother, for example, for the labour and transport costs in time credits when he moved house* (Time bank facilitator).' (Simon, 2009, in Poll *et al*, 2009)

Neighbourhood relations and community associations

John, a local area co-ordinator in South Ayrshire approached the local bowling club as part of his work to help people connect to the local community. The club was reluctant to admit people with learning disabilities as regular members and John reminded the club of their legal requirements about equal access and encouraged the organisers to think of the financial benefits of including people with learning disabilities. Three individuals with learning disabilities now play regularly twice a week during the summer. They get support from other club members (Poll *et al*, 2009).

Small Sparks is a scheme that provides small grants to individuals and groups that have innovative ideas for a project to build on a person's particular enthusiasms to make a contribution to community. It originated in Seattle and aims to strengthen links within neighbourhoods. All projects submitted by local people must be completed within six weeks or less and completed for $250 or less; they must also be based on the organiser's passions or interests, and reach out and involve new people as well as benefit the neighbourhood.

'*Julie purchased a large bright red trolley with Small Sparks money and filled it with neatly organised magazines that she got from the local dentist's office and from other neighbours. She and her young son, who has learning disabilities, walked the wagon around the neighbourhood stopping at neighbours' houses. The wagon also included a bulletin board where neighbours could post announcements of events and activities of interest to others. Julie and her son got to know a lot of their neighbours while spreading good news. Eventually other neighbours took turns walking the wagon with her son.*' (Carlson, 2009 in Poll *et al* 2009)

There are many opportunities for commissioners in these sorts of areas. Commissioners need to ensure that all support plans include a thorough appreciation of an individual's social capital and how its use can be supported and further developed. They must assess the extent and effectiveness of voluntary and community sector organisations in enabling people to develop their social networks; community associations to open up to people with social care support needs; and communities to be inclusive. Where necessary, organisations can be contracted to work alongside specific personal budget holders to ensure they are directly benefitting.

From commissioning to market management

We do not yet know exactly how the 'retail market' that personal budget holders will require is looking. **Box 1** brings together some of the early indications from both health and social care.

Box 1: An effective personalised services market

▶ **Range** – the range of different types of services that budget holders may wish to purchase is available

▶ **Price and quality** – the services are of a quality and a price that budget holders can afford

▶ **Personalised** – the available services are personalised

▶ **Volume** – the volume of services available is sufficient to meet demand

▶ **Providers** – the degree of choice between different types and sizes of providers meets budget holder requirements for choice

---

Both local authorities and, in the case of personal health budgets, Primary Care Trusts are still at an early stage in making the transition from wholesale to retail provision of services. However, studies of leading edge practice (Department of Health and OPM, 2009; OPM, 2010) suggest that this will be best achieved if we are also able to make a number of further changes (see **Figure 4**). These include:

▶ the development and management of a market that affords a choice of providers of personalised services selling their services directly to people who need support

▶ providing support to budget holders in choosing services

▶ ensuring that services that are funded outside of personal budgets are also personalised.

Joint commissioning both across health and social care and with other local authorities has a key role to play in orchestrating these changes.

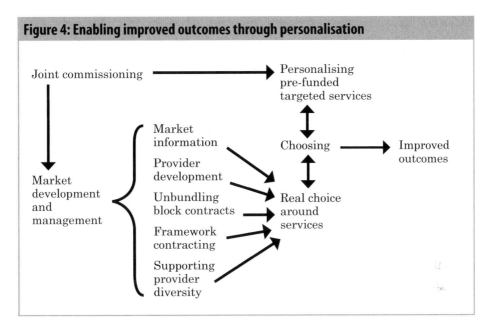

Figure 4: Enabling improved outcomes through personalisation

(Adapted from Department on Health (2010) Contracting and Market Development to Support the Use of Personal Health Budgets: OPM report for the Department on Health Personal Health Budgets Team).

Market management and development

There is a number of developments needed here.

▶ **Market information** – the provision of information that helps both commissioners and providers understand who is providing what types of personalised services to whom, their quality and pricing, how this pattern is changing and what further developments in service personalisation are now required.

Commissioners can enable this through aggregating demand based on reviews of support plans; signalling to providers that personalisation is 'here to stay' and working with budget holders on how best they can be supported in the future and sharing this with providers; and ensuring budget holders and providers are kept in touch with leading edge developments both locally and elsewhere.

▶ **Provider development** – at the current stage of market development few providers have personalised their services, some understand the need to do so but many have either not heard of personalisation or will need help to both understand the concept and transform their services and organisations to deliver it.

Commissioners can support provider development through: providing developmental workshops to introduce providers to personalisation and to help them get to grips with the range of changes it will require them to make; enabling groups of providers to work together, for example, in sharing development costs through providing common staff training programmes or developing new personalised billing systems; and the formation of provider development agencies to take on back-office functions that smaller providers may struggle to develop for themselves.

▶ Unbundling block contracts – the money that is used to fund personal budgets will come from that which is currently tied up in block contracts with providers. There is also money tied up in traditional 'spot contracts' managed by care managers. This money must be freed up in a way that both enables personal budgets to be funded but does not take income from providers overnight and destabilise continuing provision.

Commissioners can enable this transition by developing stepping stone changes such as moving from block to spot contracting and a planned phasing out of block contracts that enable providers to plan for the transition.

▶ **Framework contracting** – these arrangements are attractive to providers because they signal to personal budget holders that framework contracted providers have been quality assured and therefore provide 'good' services. They also assure people that they provide good value for money for their services and that the providers are also willing to support budget holders in managing their personal budgets through use of Individual Service Funds.

Commissioners can use framework contracting as a way of smoothing the transition from a block contracted to a retail market. The process of framework contracting is useful in assisting providers to grasp the realities of what it will mean to both provide personalised services and on a 'retail' basis.

▶ **Supporting provider diversity** – many personal budget holders express a preference for having some of their services provided by small, local providers with whom they can develop a close personal relationship. However, current contracting relationships and new approaches such as framework contracting are often too onerous for small and micro providers and hence it is much more difficult for them to market their services.

Commissioners must now make sure that personal budget holders know they have a right to purchase services from providers who are not included in the new framework agreements, develop 'light touch' approaches to quality assurance enabling small providers to use this in their marketing, and encourage framework contracting bids from larger providers that incorporate sub-contracting with small providers.

Choosing

If personal budget holders are to make best use of the emerging market of personalised services they need to know that, within their budget, they have the right to choose the services that best fit with their agreed support plan; have access to the information they need to be able to make informed choices; and where required, have the support to purchase the services they require.

Commissioners must now support personal budget holders in making choices through ensuring that high-quality information on types, quality and process of services are available in formats that are easy to use. They need to ensure that where they require it, people have the support to plan and get what is in their plan (whether through peer-support or some other form of 'brokered' assistance); and they need to arrange joint events with budget holders and providers, where providers can showcase their services and get feedback.

Joint commissioning

In the future, many social care budget holders will also hold personal budgets funded by health and other sectors. These budgets may or may not be pooled but there will need to be joint agreement about how they can be used. We now see personal health budget holders demanding 'non-health' services, for example, physical activities and support in daily living that impact on their health status. These are also the services that social care personal budget holders require hence it makes sense for heath and social care commissioners to collaborate in developing and managing this market.

Many of the providers of personalised services will operate in more than one local authority area. Having to bid for inclusion in many different framework contracts and other forms of local infrastructure is wasteful of resources – both those of the provider and those of the local authority.

Commissioners can use joint commissioning to:

▶ develop collaborations both with social care commissioners in other local authorities and those in health and other sectors

▶ develop common framework contracting processes and get information from online resources such as Shop4Support (see Chapter 2 for more on this)

▶ build on existing integrated case management and self-directed support processes to enable single support plans for people who are eligible for personal budget from more than one source; who have a personal health budget as well as a social care budget for example.

New roles for commissioners

In the past, whilst some commissioning has focused on understanding overall population needs and the reshaping of services to meet them, most of the action has revolved around contracting and recontracting for services. Whilst people with learning disabilities have had an increasing say in service planning, it is often difficult to see how people's views have then been translated into actual service changes.

The relationship with providers has mostly been 'arms length' and centred on the tendering and contract management process. This has restricted the opportunity for providers to be part of the process of suggesting and developing new types of services.

Personal budgets put people in the driving seat, allowing them to be able to choose both the services and the providers that they want. They will dramatically change relationships between people, commissioners and providers. What should be the new relationship if it is to enable people to self-direct their support? How will this change the roles that commissioners play and what support will they need to do so?

Figure 5: The new style market management relationship

People

Networking and self-organisation

Negotiate PBs; enable choice

Market research and development

Market and develop services

Negotiate and purchase individual support

Joint commissioning

Innovate and collaborate

Quality assured

Commissioners

Analyse market and enable provider development

Providers

'Collaborative relationship between commissioners and providers'

The experience of local authorities at the leading edge of personalisation is that they are switching their approach to commissioning from one that focuses on contracting and contract management to market development and management. This has also been accompanied by a change in their relationship with providers moving away from the previous arms length adversarial style to a new collaborative relationship. Key features of the new relationship (see **Figure 5,** OPM, 2009a) are:

▶ **A three way relationship** – between budget holders, providers and commissioners that replaces the previous two way relationships between commissioners and service users on the one hand and commissioners and providers on the other. The new three way relationship is characterised by:

  ▶ *Budget holders and providers* – budget holders commissioning, at an individual level, their support packages directly from providers. Providers also directly market their services to budget holders and work with them to decide how best to develop services.

  ▶ *Budget holders and commissioners* – at an individual level budget holders negotiate their personal budgets and support plans with local authorities. Local authority commissioners need to keep track of both what service people are purchasing and how well they meet their needs and to work with budget holders to identify unmet needs and service developments.

▶ *Commissioners and providers* – need to work together to pool information on market trends and budget holder requirements. Commissioners need to work with providers to enable the development of new personalised services. The quality assurance of services forms a key aspect of the market management relationship: commissioners and providers need to work together to make a success of this.

▶ **Collaborative self-help** – the new approach to commissioning also requires greater trust and collaboration within each of the key groups of stakeholders: budget holders; commissioners; and providers. It is now very clear that more can be achieved through collaboration rather than leaving it to a series of individual market interactions:

▶ *Budget holders* – can share information about what works for them; new services they have heard of, their experiences of existing providers and what they are paying for their services. This can be supported through face-to-face networks and the use of web-based information systems such as Shop4Support. People can also come together to design new types of service; get a better deal from a provider; or simply to support one another.

▶ Commissioners – can collaborate with others in neighbouring authorities and in health and other sectors to reduce the costs of collecting and analysing market information; creating and maintaining web-based information platforms; sharing common approaches to framework contracting and quality assurance; and in supporting provider development.

▶ *Providers* – may want to sub-contract, or develop partnership relationships that enable them to provide wider and more integrated packages of support. They may also wish to reduce their development costs by collaborating in the provision of staff training and the development of the new back office functions required to support personalisation.

The change in focus from contracting to personal budget holder support and market development, and management and the consequent shift in relationships with budget holders and providers, will require changes in the commissioning roles at all levels; that is to say the individual, operational and strategic levels **Table 2**, based on exploratory work with commissioners and providers (OPM, 2010) outlines some of the expected changes.

Table 2: The impact of personalisation on commissioning roles		
Commissioning role	**Current role**	**Personalised role**
Care managers	Working mostly from a menu of pre-contracted social care services. Professional assessment, service procurement and review	Enabling access to the full range of supports within and outside of social care. Negotiating, enabling and reviewing self-directed support plans and budgets
Care management team managers	Procuring the best response mostly within contracted services	Little involvement in strategic commissioning beyond periodic planning exercises
Maximising choice, self-care and community participation	Key source of market intelligence	Contracts managers
Contracts most focus on cost and volume	Block and spot contracting and management	Phasing out existing contracts
Introducing outcomes into contracts and framework agreements. Strategic commissioners	Securing a range of social care provision integrated mostly with health	Strategic planning and contracting
Personalising all services, including social care, to meet individuals' support requirements in the round	Strategic planning, market development and management and some contracting	

Commissioners now have the opportunity to work with providers of both universal and targeted services to build a more detailed picture of what personalised services will look like and how they will be commissioned; to use this to identify the changes required in the commissioning workforce;

and to develop the staff training and development programmes required to support change. This is a huge opportunity for commissioners to play a critical part in the change process.

References

Carlson C (2009) In: C Poll, J Kennedy & H Sanderson (Eds) In Community: Practical lessons in supporting isolated people to be part of the community. Stockport: Carl Poll, Helen Sanderson Associates and In Control.

Chih Hoong Sin, Hedges A, Cook C, Mguni N & Comber N (2009) *Disabled People's Experiences of Targeted Violence and Hostility*. London: Equalities and Human Rights Commission.

Department of Health & OPM (2009) *Contracting for Personalised Outcomes* [online]. Available at: www.opm.co.uk (accessed November 2010).

Miller C (2010a) *Personalisation of Universal Services 1: Bus travel* [online]. Available at: www.opm.co.uk (accessed November 2010).

Miller C (2010b) *Personalisation of Universal Services 2: Library and information services* (accessed November 2010).

OPM (2009a) *Personalisation*, OPM Public Interest Briefing [online]. Available at: www.opm.co.uk (accessed November 2010).

OPM (2009b) *Contracting and Market Development to Support the Use of Personal Health Budgets*. London: Department of Health.

OPM (2010) *Putting People First: The workforce implications. What do commissioners and providers need to do?* London: OPM.

Poll C, Kennedy J & Sanderson H (Eds) (2009) *In Community: Practical lessons in supporting isolated people to be part of the community*. Stockport: Carl Poll, Helen Sanderson Associates and In Control.

Simon M (2009) In: C Poll, J Kennedy & H Sanderson (Eds) (2009) *In: Community: Practical lessons in supporting isolated people to be part of the community*. Stockport: Carl Poll, Helen Sanderson Associates and In Control.

Further reading

Chartered Institute of Library Information Professionals (2011) [online]. Available at: www.cilip.org.uk/about-us/medalsandawards/libraries-change-lives/pages/iclafinalists05.aspx#life (accessed January 2011).

Community Catalysts, for information on micro provision [online]. Available at: www.communitycatalysts.co.uk (accessed January 2011).

Office for Public Management (OPM) is an independent, not for profit employee-owned centre for the development of public services. OPM provides consultancy, coaching and research to organisations that want to improve social outcomes, meet the needs of their communities and respond to change [online]. Available at: www.opm.co.uk.

Naaps, for information on micro-provision [online]. Available at: www.naaps.org.uk (accessed January 2011).

Chapter 10

What do we need from social workers – and what do they need from others?

Andrew Tyson

'I feel that I am doing holistic social work: making a difference. I feel that service users have more say, that they are empowered, being independent and being valued. Some people say that social workers are no longer required, however we feel that it is now that social workers are really required because we now empower clients; before it was mechanical in the way that a comprehensive assessment was completed and a care plan drawn up.' (Social worker in the London Borough of Newham)

Introduction

When many people think of 'social work' they think of it as compassion in action, and of social workers as committed, hard working, caring individuals. However, professional social work in local authorities has had a troubled history: it has been attacked in the media on a variety of grounds; it has struggled to assert a place as an equal with its sister professions in the health service and beyond, and it has failed to find many friends among those disempowered citizens whose cause it has championed. Some local authority managers view the salaries of qualified professional social workers as unaffordable in the harsh new economic world, and some cite critiques of 'the professional gift model' (Duffy, 2006) as an indication that the new 'personalised' system is better off without this 'professional expertise'. Duffy's proposed alternative model – the citizenship model – does not do away with professionals. In fact, Simon Duffy sees professionals as valuable members of society with skills, passion and a positive professional value-base. On his alternative model, professionals are not removed nor are the old power systems simply reversed, but instead he proposes that professionals form equal and mutually beneficial partnerships with citizens.

But the question needs to be asked: do people with learning disabilities and other disabled people *need* social workers, and if they do, what is it that they need *from* them? If the answers to these questions are positive, then a second set of questions arise – what is it that social workers themselves need from their managers and employers to make a success of their role in the new personalised support system?

Key points

▶ The General Social Care Council views social work as being committed to personalisation.

▶ We need to ask whether we really need social workers if we have a personalised system. We believe that we do and we can make sense of this by looking at social the worker's role in relation to the Seven Step Model of self-directed support.

▶ We also need to ask how social workers' contributions fit with the contribution others make.

▶ We then need to ask, what are the specific things that social workers can contribute to a personalised system?

▶ We need to consider what is it that local authorities need to do to transform the 'whole system' so that it is personalised, and how might social work find a place in a 'transformed workforce'.

Social work and personalisation

The General Social Care Council, the body that regulates social work says that, '*Social work is committed to enabling every child and adult to fulfil their potential, achieve and maintain independence and self-direction, make choices, take control of their own lives and support arrangements, and exercise their civil and human rights. It looks at people's lives and circumstances in the round, and works with them to personalise social care responses to fit their own individual situations. Its approaches and working methods aim to promote empowerment and creativity.* (General Social Care Council, 2008)

This could hardly be a more powerful assertion of how social work *should* serve a personalised system, but is this sort of assertion simply the profession protecting its own interest?

This chapter suggests not. It makes the case that if personalisation is to work well, then many citizens and families will continue at their times of the greatest difficulty and distress to need skilled helpers to listen to their troubles and to take action on their behalf; for some people social workers are best placed (and sometimes the only) candidates for this role. To make a success of the new challenging role, then professional social workers need to hear that they are valued by their employers and colleagues; and they need to be given the tools they need to do what is asked of them.

It is important to add that, in fact, the skilled help people need may come from a variety of people with varied backgrounds, with a wide range of experiences. As other chapters in this book clearly show, for many people the best helpers are very often those who know and love the person concerned, close friends and family. Such people understand and care in ways which no outsider can and they are very often by far the best placed to advise, guide and make plans with them. Sadly, many people with learning disabilities do not have strong relationships of this kind; or their interests differ or they have lost connection with their family. This often results from living away from home and living in institutional care over many years.

In some cases, other members of their own community can then be found to step in and help fulfil this role, such as advocates, brokers or people from a local citizen's group. Often, and perhaps especially for those with the greatest needs and who are the most troubled and isolated, there is no one there for them. In those circumstances their need is for a person who has the skills to get alongside them to help them make sense of and work with the system, which is designed to 'gate keep' paid support (whether that system is old care management or the new one of supported self-assessment, resource allocation and personal budgets) and who can support them on the road to choice, control and a better life.

▶ Some people will need further help as they move along this road to think about and design the set of support arrangements that suits their personal needs and wishes to begin to put these arrangements in place and then at the appropriate time to step back to review what is working, what is not working and what changes to make. The 'traditional social work role' as defined and described with variations several decades ago, now by Felix Biestek (1957), Florence Hollis (1964) and others, and adapted by English local authorities following the Seebohm report (1968) has always had to assimilate this most difficult of tasks: the support and guidance of citizens in their times of trouble as they seek to make best use of scarce public funded support services, or (since the Direct Payments Act) in the direct personal use of public funds (see Tyson & Williams, 2010, for a short discussion of this history).

▶ How might we think about this role now under a transformed system, one that has important structural differences from the pre-existing approach and which has the citizen and his or her needs and preferences truly at its heart?

▶ And as we do so, can we really justify the continuation and sustainability of the role in times of economic austerity?

Social work and the Seven Step Model

'I sometimes felt that I was limited in what I could do to bring about the desired change in vulnerable people's lives by resource-driven service provision and delivery (managers have become more like finance controllers). I was therefore thrilled by the introduction of self-directed support/individual budgets as a more flexible alternative ... especially in leaving users in control of how services are delivered and in the assessment of their own needs.' (Social worker in the London Borough of Newham)

'When I first met Nan a 94-year-old lady ... I was struck by how determined she was to stay as independent as possible and in her own home. She knew exactly what she wanted and how she wanted her support to be organised. Having choice and being in control was crucial to her as was being able to continue living at home and in the community she had known since she was a child. What was also clear was that the 'traditional' approach to social care would have found it difficult to meet her needs in a way that made sense to her. Nan became her own assessor and planner with appropriate support from friends, family and myself as her social worker. The more Nan was involved in the process the more her confidence grew.

This approach certainly fits well with the ethics and values of social work ... as a social worker I have really enjoyed working with Nan and her family, I have seen the positive impact this has had on both Nan and her daughter and her husband. All this without it costing the department any more money than the traditional system would have done.' (Social worker in Sheffield City Council)

Many social workers make comments similar to these as they begin to work with self-directed support. In Control's local evaluations of the implementation of self-directed support repeat the message. To take just one example, in Barnsley in South Yorkshire, 35 staff were asked to complete a questionnaire covering all aspects of their working lives. The results are shown in **Figure 1**.

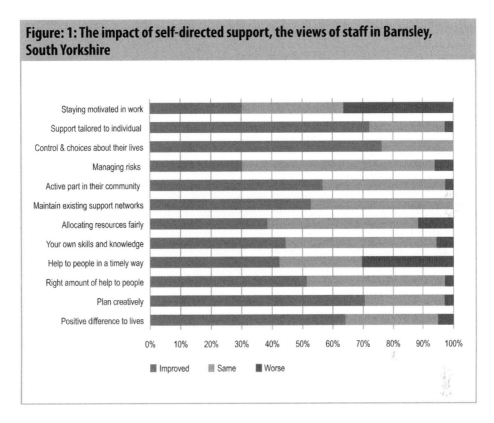

Figure: 1: The impact of self-directed support, the views of staff in Barnsley, South Yorkshire

(From Tyson *et al* (2010) *A Report on In Control's Third Phase* [online]. Available at: http://www.in-control.org.uk/phase3report (accessed November 2010).

Similar examples from across the country can be found in the reports which can be downloaded from the Evaluation page of In Control's website (www.in-control.org.uk).

What is it that social workers actually do in terms of the new system which is now coming into use in local authorities across the country?
To answer this we need to turn to the model of the seven steps of self-directed support. The seven steps are illustrated in **Figure 2** opposite.

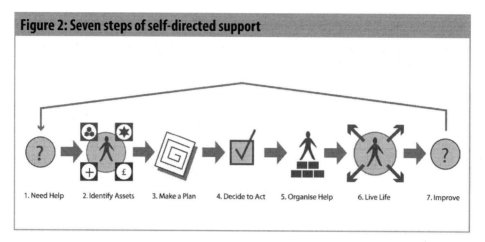

Figure 2: Seven steps of self-directed support

1. Need Help 2. Identify Assets 3. Make a Plan 4. Decide to Act 5. Organise Help 6. Live Life 7. Improve

(Courtesy of Simon Duffy (2010) taken from www.centreforwelfarereform.org)

In 2008 social workers and social work managers from eight local authorities across England came together for a series of meetings to think about this model and to consider how social workers can and should work with it. Their conclusions (Tyson *et al*, 2009) were expanded in the form of a guidance document for local authorities (Tyson, 2010). These conclusions are summarised below in **Table 1**.

Table 1: Conclusions	
Step	**The social work role**
Step one: my money, finding out how much	Professional social workers have a role in helping some people understand and complete the supported self-assessment process; and in coming to terms with the emotional impact of life changes and their need for support. Social work training encourages a holistic view of the person in their social and economic environment, and this perspective is often crucial at this stage.
Step two: making my plan	The skills and focus of many professional social workers are well suited to support planning, and sometimes the social worker will be the best person to do this alongside the person. Social workers are trained to help people to assess, manage and take appropriate risks, and as we move away from an overly risk-averse approach, social workers are well-placed to assist with more person-centred ways of managing risk.

Step	The social work role
Step three: getting my plan agreed	In agreeing someone's plan the local authority social worker will need to 'think outcomes'. Social work skills are of great relevance and social workers should be effective and experienced in challenging support plans when these are not completely fit for purpose. In doing this they will help people to make real, informed choices.
Step four: organising my money	Social work skills will be highly relevant for many of the decisions required here. They are in a good position to advise and assist people about the different 'management options' for their personal budget, and about where to turn for specialist support to make use of each of these. Social workers are often in a good position to mediate between the person at the centre and the local authority as commissioner. Social workers may have important specific roles in relation to arrangements such as individual service funds, where there may be a need to advocate on behalf of the person, and to work alongside providers to help them change the ways they deliver support.
Step five: organising my support	Professional social workers are trained to think about both the individual and system, and link the two together. This may be especially important where someone has no one else in their life to provide help. They are trained to think broadly: the old care management system did not always make use of these skills, but doing so is critical to the success of self-directed support.
Step six: living life	Under self-directed support, people are fundamentally citizens within a wider community. Social workers are well placed to provide information about what is available and to help people to restore connections and build new relationships. They are also in a good position to provide an on-going 'quality check' on what is in place.

Step	The social work role
Step seven: seeing how it has worked	The journey to make effective use of a personal budget over time concerns life changes, some of which are very positive in terms of finding ways to come to terms with disability or old age. Social workers are well placed to guide people through such changes; they have the training and professional orientation to assist people to take stock of their progress on these journeys, and to advocate on their behalf if necessary where changes are indicated.

What do social workers need?

This suggests then that social work skills *can* help to make support more personalised and there are now many examples where local authorities are making use of their professional social work employees in just these ways. But this analysis and observation does not deal with all of the challenges thrown up by social work's troubled history and poor public image. Many local authorities remain unconvinced that ordinary citizens are the best custodians of public money in the form of strings-free personal budgets, and many continue to commission large block-contracted services under the impression that this will save them money. They continue to pursue risk-averse policies and procedures believing that these will help people to stay safe, and they ask their social work staff to implement these approaches, sometimes claiming that this is the local approach to personalised support. In these circumstances, no amount of anti-oppressive practice or person-centred planning by social workers will be sufficient to enable people to find the wherewithal for a good life. What is needed, in fact, is local leadership with vision, that is to say, a measure of political will to make things happen in a clear ethically determined manner. This needs to come from political leaders, community leaders and from senior managers in the local authority and in the third sector.

So, in favourable circumstances of this kind, what is it that social workers themselves need in order to play their part in building a successful local system for self-directed support?

▶ Firstly, they need the right **policies and procedures** to enable them to deliver. Crucially, what it is that people can use their personal budget for needs to be liberally defined – the summary formulation is that people should be allowed to use their budget for *anything that is legal*.

▶ Secondly, social workers also tell us that they need a similarly clear but liberal definition of their role as *professionals* assisting people to access and make use of these budgets. So there needs to be strong but permissive **local practice guidance**. For some examples and templates, go to the In Control website at http://www.in-control.org.uk/site/INCO/Templates/General.aspx?pageid=1508&cc=GB

▶ Thirdly, social workers need really good **induction, training and support** from their managers. These things need to be more than *technically* helpful; even more important, they need to sustain social workers in the difficult emotional work of engaging with people at times of trouble and trauma in their lives and enabling those people to move on from these times to take control.

▶ Fourthly, social workers need to be part of a **local system that is actively supportive of personalisation**. This means that policies across the local authority and across agencies must reflect the values and the imperatives of the transformed relationship we have been talking about. This applies in terms of the provision of important public goods such as health, housing, leisure, libraries, community transport and education. These services need to be welcoming and accessible to all, and they need to be held to account where they fail to welcome people with learning disabilities and others. Having said this, we are beginning to increasingly appreciate that much of what we do in our day-to-day life has little or nothing to do with these 'public services', hence we also need to find ways to engage with commercial and 'universal' services, community and faith groups and those based around ethnicity and culture, and to work with them to welcome citizens using their personal budgets.

▶ Finally, no citizen, family member or social worker will make a success of personalisation without good **'personalised' support services** and **simple** accessible information about what these services can and cannot offer, together with a clear easy-to-use **process for using a personal budget** to make the purchase. We need a much wider range of services in most localities – more social enterprises and micro-services in order to respond to the needs of local people with specific local concerns. The Shop4Support system does all of this well: providing information, facilitating the purchasing process, and making the 'commissioning' and de-commissioning of services more natural and less painful. However, local authorities have not been quick off the mark to invest in this technology and in many places citizens and social workers continue to struggle with outdated information systems and unresponsive markets for support services.

What can local authorities do to help their social workers?

In June 2009, Bronwen Williams and I spent a day with a group of social workers in the London Borough of Newham, talking with them about their sense of self-directed support in practice and trying to learn what it is that they need from their local authority employers to make a success of it. It was a fascinating and rather humbling experience, listening to the reflections of a group of highly motivated, thoughtful people striving to make the most of self-directed support and to enable the people they support to make the most of their lives. By most measures, the local authority in Newham is doing very well indeed, and as the quotes used in this chapter demonstrate, the practitioners shared not only evidence of considerable 'technical progress', but also of their sense of rediscovering real professional pride in their work as they saw themselves as starting to engage with people's deep needs for community, connection and affirmation. This is why the majority of professional social workers say that they join the profession for – to help people, and particularly to work with people so that they acquire the means to help themselves.

But with a little reflection upon the very largely positive experiences of our Newham social worker group and upon feedback from elsewhere in the country, it becomes clear that the creation of truly personalised local authority social services departments is still some way off. The challenges are many and various, but here are some of the key messages that impact in particular on the professional social work role, as we have tried to capture it above, and the capacity of local authorities to respond to the emotional needs that we all have at times of trouble.

▶ If local authority staff are to empower the citizens they work with then those staff themselves need to feel that they are well-respected, valued members of the workforce. Social workers have struggled with this for many years. Local authorities now need to take a clear, hard look at what it is they ask of their staff, at the emotional as well as the technical demands of the roles and tasks involved, and make some clear statements about how their professionally qualified staff should conduct themselves, and about the support they are entitled to receive.

▶ Social workers (and their colleagues) need the tools to do their job: this includes access to good information to inform their practice, information that is also available to those they work with. The information needs to cover the 'what' (what services, what opportunities) and the 'how' (how the system works and how individuals access support). The era of 'exclusive, professional information' is over and the new contract between citizen and state will only work if people are informed.

▶ A related requirement is that the local personal budget processes work well. This means that there needs to be simple, streamlined, clear systems for resource allocation, assessment, support planning, service design, and for review. No one should find these processes bureaucratic or confusing, or have problems identifying local people who have personal experience of the processes to help them. This will mean that professional social work time can be used to good effect, where it is really needed.

▶ Social workers need to be part of a 'whole system' which is focused on the needs of the individual citizen. It is not acceptable for other council departments or other local agencies to be allowed to block the path to personalised support: go vernment policy is clear, and has been since the *Putting People First* concordat (Department of Health, 2007) (across government departments), and this was reinforced and restated through the coalition agreement after the election in May, 2010. It is the responsibility of leaders from across the spectrum of local civic society to make this a reality.

▶ In line with this approach, social workers and those they support need to see their role as members of a transformed workforce. In early 2010, In Control published a workforce framework document on its website and we conclude this chapter with a summary of that document.

  ▶ Workforce transformation must extend beyond the local authority, and indeed beyond social care. It needs to include staff in 'universal services'.

  ▶ All staff need to understand and really believe that the 'real experts' are those who are closest to the person. The professional role is largely about supporting and facilitating these relationships.

  ▶ Social workers and others need a deep understanding of how the self-directed support process works: what a person-centred approach involves, what are the full range of funding streams a person can access; and perhaps especially about what is meant by an outcome.

  ▶ There needs to be a transparent local information system in place, and this system needs to be open to professionals, non-professionals and ordinary citizens.

▶ Social workers and other staff need to be skilled in helping people complete the self-assessment process.

▶ Social workers and others need to be skilled in helping people write a support plan and to get what is in that support plan. They also need to have skills in service design and in co-ordination.

▶ Social workers and their managers need to be skilled in scrutinising plans, ensuring that these plans help people stay safe, and then in signing them off. Social workers need a good understanding of risk enablement and safeguarding issues.

▶ Social workers and others need a strong, broad-based understanding of what is available in specific communities and localities to provide the full range of support to people.

▶ Social workers need to have an awareness of all the issues associated with employing personal assistants (tax, insurance, employment law etc) and they need to know where people can go to get specialist help with these issues. Social workers and others need to understand the importance of reflection and review as a critical element for people in them achieving real choice and control over the longer term.

▶ Social workers need an awareness of broader issues in their local communities, and to link with colleagues who are building community capacity – for all ages and across all areas of life.

References

Biestek F (1957) The Casework: A Psychosocial Therapy. New York: Random House.

Duffy S (2006) *Keys to Citizenship*. Birkenhead: Paradigm.

General Social Care Council (2008) *Social Work at its Best: A statement of roles and tasks for the 21st Century* [online]. Available at: www.gscc.org.uk (accessed November 2010).

Hollis P (1964) Social Casework: A Psychosocial theory. New York: Random House.

Putting People First, Toolkit [online]. Available at: www.puttingpeoplefirst. org.uk (accessed November 2010).

Seebohn F (1968) *Report on the Committee on Local Authority and Allied Personal Social Services*. London: HMSO.

Tyson A, Brewis R, Crosby N, Hatton C, Stansfield J, Tomlinson C, Waters J & Wood A (2010) *A Report of In Control's Third Phase*. London: In Control.

Tyson A, Thompson J & Waters J (2009) *Self-directed Support, Social Workers Contribution* [online]. Available at: www.in-control.org.uk (accessed November 2010).

Tyson A & Williams B (2010) Self-direction, place and community, re-discovering the emotional depths: A conversation with social workers in a London Borough. *Journal of Social Work Practice* **20** (3).

Tyson A & Williams B *et al* (2010) *Systems, Practice and Support of Professional Social Work under Social Work: A resource for local authorities* [online]. Available at: www.in-control.org.uk (accessed November 2010).

Further reading

In Control [online]. Available at: www.in-control.org.uk (accessed November 2010).

Chapter 11

How local authorities can help to create the right conditions for personalisation

Andrew Tyson

Andrew Tyson is a social worker living in Brighton, East Sussex. He has worked for the social services in East and West Sussex for the last 28 years.

From 1999 to 2006 he had responsibility for commissioning services for adults with learning difficulties and for leading on *Valuing People* implementation in West Sussex. In June 2006 he began work as a member of the In Control core team.

Introduction

Local authorities in England play a key role in our social care system and increasingly in that of health care. One hundred and fifty English local authorities have 'social services responsibility' that is to say they are required to ensure that when asked to do so they carry out assessments to determine an individual's 'needs' and 'eligibility' for certain statutory services, services which they are then responsible for arranging. Local authorities play key roles in supporting families where a member has a learning disability, providing help in the home, day services, sheltered employment and funding residential homes and supported living. In many parts of the country they were also instrumental in the 'resettlement' programme from long stay hospitals as these institutions closed over the last couple of decades. In 2010, local authorities are taking on responsibility for the 'commissioning' of all specialist health and social care services for people with learning disabilities, and they have a number of other functions in relation to public health and the quality assurance of health services.

Local authorities have been largely responsible then for managing the 'old system' of care for people with learning disabilities – the system which we now see as failing. However, it is also the case that many of the people most closely associated with the reform of that system and developing its replacement, self-directed support, are local authority employees – managers, social workers and support staff. The first testing of self-directed support in six English pilot areas in 2004–2005 was led by local authorities. Local authorities remain central to the success of personalisation, and for this reason this chapter looks at what it is they need to do to help to create the conditions for its success.

This chapter draws heavily on a programme of work undertaken in the years 2006–2008, which was known as the In Control Total Transformation programme. This was a programme involving adult services in 20 local authorities who elected to change their culture, systems and process quickly. The chapter draws in particular on an evaluation of work in Hartlepool in northeast England. Hartlepool Borough Council was a member of the programme and was one of the group of authorities that embraced the self-directed support model most wholeheartedly (for a full account of this work, see Tyson, 2009).

Key points

▶ Local authorities have a key role to play in creating the conditions for the success of personalisation.

▶ *A road map of the change process* is important. We call this our critical path to transformation.

▶ The quality of the leadership is the single most important factor in success or failure.

▶ There are a number of important 'minimum necessary tools' including economic systems to ensure personalisation is cost-effective.

▶ Local authority culture and practices need to support personalisation for people with high support needs, just as for others.

▶ The fundamental shift needed is in the 'culture' of organisations, so that the person at the centre *really* is at the centre.

A critical path to transformation

All or almost all local authorities working to introduce personalisation adopt a project management approach. In Control is not opposed to such an approach, in fact, we support and recommend it but we are not project managers, and we leave the detail of project dependencies and accountability arrangements to the specialists in this field. We are clear, however, that we need a road-map of the change process, and this is something we have developed over the years and which we drew on through our Total Transformation programme. This 'critical path to total transformation' is illustrated below in **Figure 1**.

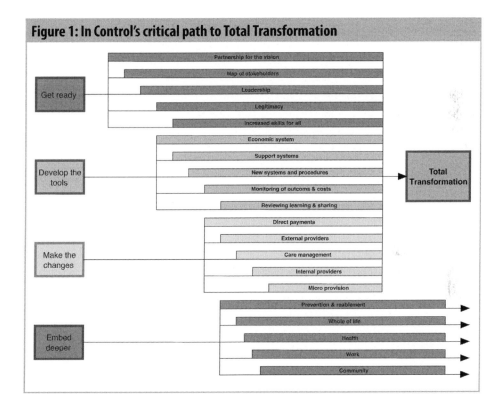

Figure 1: In Control's critical path to Total Transformation

Preparing for self-directed support

What are the most important things for local authorities to think about and pay attention to when preparing for self-directed support?

In Control suggests that there are four areas which must be addressed in the early days: **leadership; legitimacy** (shared understanding and ownership); a system for **resource allocation**; and a system for **support planning and brokerage** for citizens. In November 2006, In Control led a workshop with senior managers in Hartlepool to self-assess where they were with each of these four elements, based on their views about the state of a number of components which contributed to the four areas. The aggregated scores for the elements which make up these four areas were 9.0, 5.5, 6.9 and 4.6 respectively – where 10 represents completely ready, 5.0 is just ready and 0 is completely unready. The picture in Hartlepool in 2006 then was of a department with strong leadership, a moderate degree of shared legitimacy or understanding across the piece, some adequate financial systems but barely adequate support systems for citizens. Digging a bit deeper, there were particular concerns about fair access to care criteria, about charging, support planning, and especially about support brokerage (helping people get what is in their plan). On the other side of the coin, there were many good and important things in place – not least the system to interrogate the costs of the components of a support package, detailed to each individual person; and some very positive work over the preceding year on direct payments and support systems for direct payment users. Most striking in 2006 was the universally positive approach of the department's leadership, an observation recorded at the time reads: '*It is very apparent that there is whole-hearted commitment from senior managers responsible for social care in the Borough. This has been the most important single factor in those authorities which have become the leaders of the self-directed support movement and it augurs well.*'

Each local authority is different with different history, different strengths and different local issues. Cultural and ethnic diversity matters; the state of the local economy, and how equal or unequal the area is matters; and the state of the relationship with other key players, health, housing other public services also makes a big difference. However, the single most important factor in Hartlepool and elsewhere is the quality of the leadership in place and the ways in which the leaders work with their staff and with elected members, and the extent to which they are able to seek out and use opportunities to make transformational changes.

In Hartlepool the director of social services, Nicola Bailey described how she had seen the need to shape her role following her appointment in October 2005. 'In the beginning, my role was to be very directive; I told them what was to be done. People hated it... I gave them a hard time if they were not at the meetings. I was the project leader initially. Later, I was more supportive when the going was tough for people. Recently I've stepped right back to see how others take up the challenge, but now I see the need for a bit more direction again.' She went on to describe how important she sees managing staff to be: '*Early on I saw that the staff were great but were very traditional. I spent some time in my early days getting to know people, spotting who were the rising stars, and who were able to manoeuvre and those who weren't.*'

The key opportunity in the early days in Hartlepool was presented by the existing direct payments scheme in the Borough. It was this scheme that provided the means to break the mould and move the culture in the department and in the wider council to the next level. Nicola spoke about 'taking up the DP cudgel'. Most of the proposals in the early days were to buy personal care, she says, and in some cases these plans seemed to lack ambition – hence she took the decision to start monthly steering groups, take the chair and sign off each direct payment personally. She also sought out opportunities to show the potential of direct payments: one example was an approach from the Blind Welfare organisation who wanted to change how they made use of a small grant so that it was of greater direct benefit to their members – Nicola's advice was to take the grant as a series of direct payments, then individuals could use the money as they saw fit, rather than for some pre-determined purpose.

So leadership is critical, but as we have noted, this is far from the whole story. 'Legitimacy' or 'shared leadership' involving key staff was a difficult issue in the early days in Hartlepool and one which took significant time through active membership of In Control, with staff exposed to good practice elsewhere and then bringing this back home and spreading the word further in a series of workshops over a considerable period of time. And other areas are important too: it is critical that there is a system to allocate resources to individuals (as a personal budget) and that there are strong arrangements for people to think about and draw up their support plans, and then to make those plans happen.

To be clear: the message is that if these things are not in place, then they need to be given priority. None of them are complex or difficult, but the arrangements need to be substantial and robust and more than mere ticked boxes. They are the foundations on which self-directed support stands or falls. At their heart is the 'organisational culture', the response to the question 'how do we do things round here?' If the answer to this question is that we do things in a way which combines a relentless focus on the needs and wishes of ordinary people to live decent lives with a positive, professional approach to deep system transformation, then the rest will follow.

The tools for transformation

The second section of In Control's sketch map of the critical path to transformation focuses on the tools required. These are perhaps best thought of as the 'minimum necessary' tools. Other things may be necessary in some places as well, depending on local circumstances. However, we look at it, whatever words we use to describe these systems and processes, this is the engine room of the new vessel, the machine code that specifies and configures the new operating system.

Economic systems are critical in this and self-directed support needs to be cost-effective. Indeed in the current climate, it probably needs to be seen to be contributing to savings in the local authority budget. Paradoxically, it can only achieve such savings by doing what many would see as loosening its grip on resources and taking what could be seen as big financial risks through allocating money directly to people and families. If authorities are to do this then they need to have the best possible systems to monitor how this money is disbursed, and indeed, how the new system is performing in terms of outcomes. This is not the same as saying that they need systems to account for every penny that is spent by an individual or family, or to prohibit expenditure on certain things.

In Hartlepool what this meant was that the authority put time and effort into developing excellent systems for recording spend to the level of individuals and personal budgets (ie. they were interested in who got how much, but were less interested in the sense of what they spent it on), and for producing and interrogating reports. When combined with a prudent approach to the allocation of resources – the resource allocation system – this provided reassurance that the new system was robust and financially sustainable. All of this did not mean that self-directed support in Hartlepool was designed for the over-riding purpose of containing costs (the director and several other senior managers state very clearly that this was not the case), but it did mean that the monitoring and profiling of spend could be achieved relatively straightforwardly, and there was early warning of any financial problems.

Many of the other tools are discussed in other chapters in this section. We have already noted that support systems are crucial and that these systems need to include options to guide and support people so that they can spend their personal budgets in ways which suit them. This is particularly an issue for someone when they wish to employ staff directly, usually in the form of a team of personal assistants, and they are confronted by all the issues of staff recruitment, employment law, national insurance, taxation and so on. In Control's advice to local authorities is that they need to ensure that assistance with these issues is readily available, in forms that ordinary people can easily access and use across the whole locality; note that this is not the same as saying that local authorities necessarily need to provide this information themselves. One very good example is the booklet produced in another of the 'total transformation' authorities, Newham (Newham Coalition, 2009).

Many people will not want to employ staff in this way, and it is unhelpful to equate self-directed support with 'employing staff'. Employing staff is easier in some places than others (depending on the state of the local job market in particular) – so in order to make this a genuine option for people, local authorities need to make an assessment of what is needed locally and what they can do to help.

Local authorities also need to support people in terms of making available the full range of management options for personal budgets, as illustrated here. These are described in other chapters in this section.

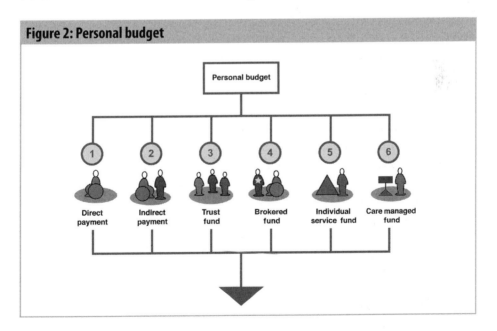

Figure 2: Personal budget

'Review' is the final tool in the list in this section and it is particularly important. As noted in the chapter on social work, making effective use of a personal budget over time concerns *life changes*, some very positive and others are a means to come to terms with the challenges posed by disability or old age. Local authorities need to ensure that their systems for review are strong; too often in the past they have been tick boxes or phone reviews. Self-directed support is a *process* whereby people learn by doing. Reflection and review is the means by which this can happen and local authorities have a key responsibility in enabling this to happen.

In Control has worked with local authorities on developing these tools for a number of years now and has a good knowledge of best practice in terms of the 'minimum necessary tools'. Examples can be accessed on the In Control website.

Changes in the way support is provided

The way most people experience the social care system is through the support that they or their families receive. In some ways, the biggest change which self-directed support brings is in terms of the nature of that support and the way in which people are able to take control of it. Local authorities retain the ultimate responsibility for commissioning support. Chapter 9 explains some of the changes needed in these commissioning arrangements as we move forward. Provider organisations, themselves need to change and these changes are addressed in Chapter 8; professional social work needs to change as well, as discussed Chapter 10.

The central point about all of these changes is that they need to focus upon the expressed needs and wishes of local people, and they need to do this in ways which 'give permission' for innovation to flourish, and for imagination to be freed so that new social enterprises and small-scale providers get off the ground; where appropriate these providers must bring people together to use (pool) their budgets on things that engage and interest them; and they must be supported to spot niches in the market and opportunities to make a living, with the end result that people use their personal budgets for the benefit of the whole community.

To foster this sort of environment the local authority needs to develop a 'can do culture' which is responsive to individuals, but which is shaped by the principles set out by the government nearly a decade ago in *Valuing People* (Department of Health, 2003): rights, independence, choice and inclusion.

The local culture needs to be just as responsive to individuals and the families of people with high support needs (those sometimes described as having profound and multiple learning disabilities) as it is to those with fewer or lesser impairments. In many ways, more (not less) imagination is required when working with people whose needs are greater. The shaping and design of services for this group requires, firstly, great powers of attention to hear what the person at the centre is telling us about their wants and preferences (not just their needs); secondly, skilful multi-professional work to design the response that suits the person; and thirdly almost invariably some work across agencies to access multiple funding streams to pay for housing, personal care, education and support at different points in the week and in different environments. This is a complex set of tasks, but it is one that good local authorities are practiced in, and it is the key to a good life for those with high levels of need – surely a key indicator of the success of personalisation. (For more information on working with people with high support needs, see the work of Phoebe Caldwell, listed under further reading on page 192).

The fundamental shift needed, as has already been hinted at a number of times, is in the mindset of all concerned and in the *culture* of organisations, so that 'the person at the centre' really is at the centre; so that professionals, while continuing to do their professional job – are accountable to that person; and so that families, friends and other community members receive the respect that they are due.

Embedding deeper

It should now be clear that self-directed support and personalisation are about much more than personal budgets for adults with 'social care needs'. They are about *individual* budgets, that is to say budgets from a range of funding streams (social care, health, housing, education, the independent living fund, welfare benefits); they are about a *whole life approach* that starts in childhood and extends into old age and which covers the full range of activities; and fundamentally they are about a whole different way of seeing the world and of operating, with the person needing support at its centre. What is the local authority role in leading and facilitating these broader, deeper changes?

▶ An individual budget is a single sum of money that someone controls, from various sources within the public purse to meet a defined set of needs. When personalisation was first seriously discussed in the middle 2000s, there were great ambitions to 'braid' a number of funding streams. The individual budget pilot programme (Glendinning *et al*, 2008) ran between November 2005 and December 2007 and covered funding for adult social care, the independent living fund, access to work, supporting people, community equipment and the disabled facilities grant. Although there were positive results in terms of some of the self-reported changes in people's lives, when it came to the process of integrating the funding streams, '*staff experienced numerous legal and accountability barriers*' (Glendinning *et al*, 2008). This was sad, but fortunately is not the end of the story. As we move into an era of significant real reductions in all public sector budgets, the imperative to find economies by aligning or combining budgets in different ways becomes stronger, and personalisation makes it clearer that the acid test of public services is how things look, feel and taste for the individual – not how easy they are to manage for the public servant. Several of the key funding streams are in the control of the local authorities, and this issue is one many are now revisiting.

▶ A whole life approach: local authorities are well placed to lead the transformation process in a way which involves all aspects of someone's life. They are responsible for planning, commissioning and sometimes for providing services which cross the age range and which include education, youth services, leisure, libraries, community transport and economic regeneration, as well as social care services for children and adults, and the interest in health we have already noted. The difficulty is that these different aspects have tended to be planned, managed and delivered in silos – that is to say clusters of 'similar services' rather than around the requirements of an individual with a range of needs. The model has been that the individual needs to navigate the system, rather than that the system flexes around the individual. Whilst turning this on its head may seem difficult, some of the ideas about 'personalising universal services', which Clive Miller describes in his chapter as well as some of the experiments in the *Total Place* pilots, suggest that given the will there is a way.

▶ A different way of seeing the world and operating: self-directed support has actually found its feet and become mainstream in adult social care incredibly quickly. This, it can be argued is because it actually does what it says on the tin – it enables people to take control of their money and their support and to get a better life as a result. *Putting People First* reflected that fact and made it official policy but In Control and its allies have from the start had wider and deeper ambitions for social change. These ambitions are for a more compassionate society, where '*people are interested in and really concerned for others, where people's gifts, talents and passions and contributions are valued, encouraged and respected ... a society in which, if people get ill, lonely, confused or disabled, they will still be counted and their community will look out for and support them and where we see this as an ordinary part of everyday life'* (In Control, 2010). This is not a society where local authorities cease to exist, but it is one where their role is radically changed; where their primary function is no longer as holder of the public purse strings but is much more as champion, facilitator and enabler of local people's rights to the opportunity for a decent life, as they themselves define it. This becomes possible if and only if systems for 'resource allocation' become much more transparent and equitable and local authorities are freed of some of the responsibility for making invidious decisions about how to allocate resources and who therefore is 'more or less eligible'.

Conclusion

Local authorities have a massively important part to play in determining whether people with learning disabilities (and others) get the pay off from personalisation that many of us dream of. Some local authority staff remain anxious and unconvinced and still cling onto the old way of doing things, finding numerous ways to hang onto control.

Others, however, can see the positive changes that have happened for many, and are slowly and cautiously working to put the building blocks for the new system into place. A few visionaries and transformative leaders can see to the far horizon and are leading the charge. It is important that we remain open-minded, pragmatic and responsive to criticism, and do our best to bring all these different people and perspectives with us as we work to meet the challenges ahead.

References

Department of Health (2003) *Valuing People: A new strategy for learning disability in the 21st century.* London: Department of Health.

Glendinning C, Challis D, Fernandez J-L, Jacobs S, Jones K, Knapp M, Manthorpe J, Moran N, Netten A, Steven M & Wilberforce M (2008) *Evaluation of the Individual Budgets Pilots Programme.* York: SPRU, University of York.

In Control (2010) [online]. Available at: www.in-control.org.uk (accessed November 2010).

Newham Coalition (2009) *Every Adult Matters: Employing your own staff.* London: The Language Shop.

Putting People First, toolkit [online]. Available at: www.puttingpeoplefirst. org.uk (accessed November 2010).

Tyson A (2009) *Self-directed Support in Hartlepool, 2006–9* [online]. Available at: www.in-control.org.uk (accessed November 2010).

Further reading

Phoebe Caldwell's website gives a lot of helpful information about working with people with high support needs [online]. Available at: www. phoebecaldwell.co.uk/ (accessed November 2010).

Social Care Institute for Excellence has also produced useful material for local authorities and their staff [online]. Available at: www.scie.org.uk/ (accessed November 2010).

Chapter 12

Learning through supporting the delivery of *Putting People First*

Sam Bennett

Introduction

In December 2007 the *Putting People First* (PPF) concordat set the direction for the transformation of adult social care in England through personalisation, prevention and early intervention. Alongside this, the last government confirmed the social care reform grant of 520 million pounds over three years to support councils with the work of transforming their systems and processes and initiating a huge cultural shift across the sector in the way that care and support is organised and provided for older people and people with disabilities. In November 2010, the coalition government confirmed the direction of travel for social care in a document entitled, *A Vision for Social Care, Capable Communities and Active Citezens.* (Department of Health, 2010).

In order to help councils and others do what is required and to help to turn this policy into real change for real people, the Department of Health's PPF delivery programme has worked to provide advice and support regionally and locally. This chapter does not concern policy issues as such, except insofar as they set the context for and shape how change is delivered. Rather, it draws on learning from the first two years of the PPF delivery programme, describes the range of activity undertaken at national level during this period and draws some conclusions from this work. Reflecting and learning in this way will help us to understand the change process better, and will therefore influence the way we provide support of this kind in the future.

The chapter begins with a general exploration of the purpose and value of 'delivery support' and an overview of the PPF delivery programme. It then outlines three different components of the delivery programme and how these were developed to fit within this particular context. The chapter concludes with some reflections on how future delivery support to personalisation in learning difficulties might be undertaken most successfully.

Key points

▶ Delivery support is help from specialist staff in government departments for people whose job is to implement national policy in their area.

▶ Delivery support involves creating the right environment for change, connecting people and committing time and resources.

▶ Change happens from the ground up, not top down. *Putting People First* talks about this as co-production; and 'delivery support' itself needs to be co-produced.

▶ *Putting People First* was radical, partly because it said that everyone with ongoing care and support needs should have these met through a personal budget.

▶ The programme is arranged as a partnership between a wide range of stakeholders. Service providers are critical to its success.

▶ The programme is not yet complete and its success is not yet assured. Budget restraint brings new challenges.

▶ There are many important lessons we can learn for the future, including the importance of practical support for people working locally.

What is delivery support?

Before we get into it, it is probably worth reflecting on what we actually mean by 'delivery support'. Put simply, delivery support is a catchall phrase used to describe a range of often quite different activities, which share the common thread of supporting the implementation of a particular policy objective, or set of objectives.

Policy only gets you so far and may not materialise as changed practice on the ground if not supported by people whose job it is to help everyone else to 'operationalise the vision'. This doesn't of course mean actually doing all the work, which would be impossible and unnecessary given the number of passionate, committed people that exist within organisations and who are responsible for getting things done in their locality.

The role of delivery support is, as far as possible, to:

▶ **create a conducive environment** – providing clarity or reassurance where it is asked for and smoothing the way where blockages occur or where further information is needed

▶ **connect people together** – arguably the most important task is to prevent the invention of hundreds of different wheels where one (or two or three at most!) would do just fine. This means helping people from different organisations and different places to share what has worked for them as well as what has not

▶ **commit time and resource** – to make progress where it is most needed, whether in relation to a particularly challenging aspect of implementation (how do we make this work for people with complex learning difficulties) or a specific geographical area? (How can we make this work for us in People's Borough?).

Having described the accepted logic and the general set of tasks involved, it is now worth pausing to question whether this actually makes any sense!

Does it work?

Transformational change in public services does not happen from the top down because government says it should. Most often, it happens through a fortuitous combination of strong local leadership, the tireless hard work of inspirational individuals and community groups, and the willingness of people and organisations to do things differently because of a shared vision or conviction that it is the right thing to do. It is hard to create these kinds of conditions locally (Chapter 11 gives examples of what local authorities can do). These things are rare and cannot be imposed; and since one place is only superficially like another, there can be huge variances in the experience of implementing change from one part of the country to the next.

This is the joy (and the frustration) of local democratic processes and accountability. Accepting this view, it is reasonable to question the logic behind and efficacy of any support for transformational change that emanates from a national delivery programme. How can it possibly be effective when so far removed from the day-to-day reality of making things happen? This certainly appears to be an important question when we look at PPF in social care.

Within the pages of the PPF document itself (a 'concordat' between local government, the sector and six government departments) it becomes abundantly clear that this is no regular policy. Rather, the *transformation of social care* positively sets itself apart as unique and as intended to happen as a result of its collaborative approach: '*It seeks to be the first public service reform programme which is co-produced, co-developed, co-evaluated and recognises that real change will only be achieved through the participation of users and carers at every stage. It recognises that sustainable and meaningful change depends on our capacity to empower people who use services and to win the hearts and minds of all stakeholders.* (Department of Health, 2007)

This is about local ownership and about government working with local communities as active and equal partners in shaping the changes they want to see. So PPF itself explicitly recognises the issue that we noted above, in that change does not and cannot happen from the top down. Yet I do not think this makes delivery support unnecessary and I do not feel I've been doing a pointless job for the last three years. What I *do* believe is that a 'co-produced' reform programme deserves co-produced delivery support; that the balance of activity must reflect the particular nature of the challenge and that the range of people 'supported' becomes much broader. So, let's look at what this has meant in practice.

The PPF delivery programme

We can observe the following characteristics of the PPF delivery programme:

▶ PPF was a pleasant surprise
▶ PPF is a vehicle for getting the best expertise out there from trailblazers outside government
▶ PPF is a collaboration between citizens, families, different partner agencies and people in government
▶ PPF in fact potentially involves everyone in the community. 'Service providers' have a particularly critical role to play.

A surprising opportunity

Putting People First was radical and far reaching, and included an element of the unexpected. These facts naturally had a significant impact on the nature of the delivery support that was needed. At the time, personal budgets had been piloted by only 13 councils (and tested independently by a handful more) and the full evaluation of this experience was still some 10 months away from publication (Glendinning *et al*, 2008).

PPF states that *'everyone with ongoing care and support needs should have this through a personal budget'*. This has very wide-ranging implications, and its inclusion came as a surprise – a welcomed surprise but a surprise nonetheless.

This chapter is not about the reasons for this policy decision, but we must at this stage touch upon the implications. Any strategy involving the incremental expansion of self-directed support through further and wider piloting suddenly became impossible. This is not to say that more pilots would have been preferable or more effective – indeed, such a strategy may not have led to full scale rollout at all, which would have been infinitely worse. However, this radical approach did create real challenges for the delivery support programme who were trying to help council staff to implement personal budgets locally. This led to the development of the personalisation toolkit that was launched through DH Care Networks in summer 2008.

Putting People First toolkit case study

With the evaluation of the pilots still some time away and its content stopping short of offering best practice advice and practical tools (which was never the expectation), the formative delivery programme began the work of very quickly building a body of useful materials to support local implementation. This became what at the time was called the 'personalisation toolkit' and has since become the 'PPF toolkit', a wider set of resources that accommodates other aspects of the transformation agenda. This is a web-based resource consisting of an ever-growing collection of case study materials, examples, protocols, policies etc. drawn initially from the practical experience of the individual budget pilots.

In addition, the team quickly began the work of developing guidance documentation for each key element of the new operating model as well as papers on some of the wider strategic implications. In practice, this was an opportunity to draw in the experience and expertise of trailblazers from outside government whose passion and commitment had shaped the agenda for years previously, giving a fair wind to their ideas and bringing them to the widest possible audience. This meant working with In Control on the self-directed support process and resource allocation, with Helen Sanderson Associates and Paradigm on support planning and brokerage and with the National Centre for Independent Living on disability issues. The toolkit remains the single most accessed resource for information and advice on personalisation and has played a pivotal role in supporting the free exchange of information between networks for the last two years.

Partnerships and co-production

Once established, the PPF delivery programme quickly became much more than a central government initiative. This reflected both the 'co-productive' aspirations of the reform programme (see Chapter 9 for more on 'co-production') and the wide set of signatories to the concordat, each with a stake in its successful implementation. The list of those involved in the delivery programme now includes:

▶ the Local Government Association (LGA)

▶ the Improvement and Development Agency for Local Government (IDeA)

▶ the Association of Directors of Adults Services (ADASS)

▶ the Social Care Institute of Excellence (SCIE)

▶ Skills for Care.

The work is overseen by a delivery co-ordination group (DCG) beneath the Transforming Adult Social Care (TASC) Programme board, where the resources of a wide range of partners have been brought together and a more coherent programme of activity established.

The DCG has also had consistent representation from several key provider organisations and the Care Providers Alliance, a consortium of umbrella associations within social care whose combined membership spans two thirds of the independent and community and voluntary sectors. This 'broad church' approach has helped to maintain momentum and ownership across the whole social care system. It has also helped to focus effort and resources in ways that have the widest possible impact. It has also been like knitting treacle at times, the inevitable consequence of trying to bring so many parties along with such a wide range of views and priorities.

More important than these partnerships between agencies and across the sector have been efforts to ensure that the delivery programme is co-produced with people with support needs, their carers and families. This is critical, both for setting an example for local authorities to follow and for protecting the credibility of the reforms associated with PPF – *'this is the direction we are headed because disability groups and older people's organisations have said this is what they want and have led the way.'*

In practical terms, this has meant the establishment of a 'transforming adult social care co-production group', which meets regularly and makes recommendations into both the DCG and TASC board. This really works and is an extremely valued and valuable part of the programme.

Another important example of the centrality of co-production in everything we do is the work of the user-led organisations (ULO) programme over the last three years.

User-led organisations programme case study

Though predating *Putting People First*, emanating from the commitment the government made in article 4.3 of Improving Life Chances for Disabled People in 2005, the ULO programme became part of the PPF delivery programme in 2008. The programme supported the development of two waves of ULOs in local authority areas across England as part of the aspiration that every council area should have an active ULO modelled on centres for independent living by 2010. While the TASC co-production group has ensured co-production of the programme at national level, the ULO programme and associated development fund has committed to supporting local organisations with the aim of promoting independent living within their areas. Some 28 organisations have been involved in this work, resulting in a wealth of learning and useful resources now available through the website of the National Centre for Independent Living.

A wider set of stakeholders

As well as being represented in the governance arrangements (as detailed above), service providers have a critical role to play in the actual delivery of the programme. In any £24 billion industry, suppliers would be a powerful constituency with an awful lot of expertise to offer. When we are talking about transforming the relationship between citizens and the state and a fundamental reshaping of the social care market, it is even more important that providers are seen as key partners. After all, who is it that most people with support needs see most often in their experience of social care if not care workers? And how can anything be truly different for people if the nature of these relationships and experiences does not change? This kind of change cannot be imposed from the outside, it has to be owned, felt and acted out by the thousands of organisations actually out there doing the work (Chapter 8 discusses what this means in reality for providers).

However, strong collaborative relationships between local government and providers are not always the norm, especially when poor commissioning and the 'us and them' of contractual negotiations gets in the way. The delivery programme has therefore committed time and resources to fostering strong partnerships between people with support needs, providers and commissioners and to supporting providers to make changes to their services in response to personalisation. This has happened nationally through the national market development forum, where a group of leaders from across the sector have met regularly throughout 2010 to address key challenges and propose solutions for the development of a diverse market of high quality, personalised services. It has also happened locally through the work of the national provider development programme.

National provider development programme case study

The PPF delivery programme worked with a group of councils, providers, community organisations and people using services to test and refine a method for collating and analysing person-centred information from people's outcomes-focused reviews for use in commissioning and service development. We called this process working together for change. Using working together for change, the provider development programme has been working with more than 30 providers from all around the country to adapt what they do in response to the things people say are important to them, now and in the future. These have ranged from small social enterprises with only a handful of staff, to user-led organisations developing their role, to national coverage providers with multi-million pound turnovers. Each of the providers engaged with the programme is responding to priorities for service redesign and development identified by the people using their services, with an emphasis on improving choice and control and embedding person-centred practices. We hope that this learning will lead to meaningful change in each locality as well as being helpful to other providers across the sector who are looking at how they might need to adapt in response to personalisation. The products from the programme will be published later in the year through the PPF website.

What can we learn for the future?

The above sections illustrate several aspects of the PPF delivery programme that were considered valuable by a range of different stakeholders. This is not to say they couldn't have been done better or that all aspects of the programme have been equally successful. The changes happening in social care are so significant that there are bound to be some false starts along the way and we have all been learning as we go along. There is still a huge amount to do; we are not yet at tipping point where the changes are inevitable, and new challenges now present themselves as budgets get tighter and services are cut. This will not be an easy task.

If there is a continuing role for delivery support (which may not in future be through central government) then there may be some value in reflecting on learning from the first three years of the PPF delivery programme. The following list is a personal top five offered in humble suggestion to whoever does this work.

▶ Build a broad base – establishing and maintaining a wide set of partnerships can be onerous but you do need to do it. Everyone needs to own this change to keep up the momentum as things get tough.

▶ Connecting people will always be important – if we're to avoid wasting time and effort recreating the wheel many times over, then we have to keep funding effective ways of sharing ideas and bringing people together. They will have the answers.

▶ Co-production must be integral – this is not an optional extra: you may not like the word but it describes something crucially important. Make sure you build it into everything that you do.

▶ Don't neglect providers – the balance of innovation that has occurred in support services over the past few years has come from passionate, committed provider organisations who have striven to put the people they support in control of their lives. Harnessing this innovation and wealth of experience is going to be increasingly important if we are to succeed in making personalisation a reality for everybody.

▶ Make sure it is practical – delivery support can be rather impersonal when it consists of closed discussion groups and results in wordy think pieces that nobody has the time to read. Make sure that everything you do is intensely practical and try to spend time on-site with people understanding their problems and working through to solutions.

References

Department of Health (2007) *Putting People First: A shared vision and commitment to the transformation of adult social care.* London: Department of Health.

Department of Health (2010) *A Vision for Social Care, Capable Communities and Active Citizens.* London: Department of Health.

Glendinning C, Challis C, Fernandez JL, Jacobs S, Jones K, Knapp M, Manthorpe J, Moran N, Netten A, Stevens M & Wilberforce M (2008) *Evaluation of the Individual Budgets Pilot Programme: Final report.* London: Department of Health.

Further reading

The National Centre for Independent Living [online]. Available at: www.ncil.org.uk/categoryid22.html (accessed November 2010).

Putting People First, toolkit [online]. Available at: www.puttingpeoplefirst.org.uk (accessed November 2010).

Chapter 13

Thinking about outcomes: a framework for citizenship?

John Waters

Introduction

The great Indian political leader, Mohandas Gandhi (1869–1948) is believed to have said that you can measure the greatness of a nation by how it treats its weakest citizens. When asked what he thought of Western civilisation, he is reputed to have replied that he thought '*it would be a very good idea*'.

Key points

▶ Despite devoting significant resources to the provision of community services we have lacked any meaningful measures of the performance of these services.

▶ With the introduction of personal budgets, community services for people with learning disabilities are set to undergo a bigger transformation than the closure of the long-stay hospitals.

▶ Meaningful measures can only be arrived at by asking people using personal budgets what difference they have made. We have developed and tested a framework to do this.

▶ When we have used this to ask people about whether or not personal budgets have helped, the results have been very positive.

▶ We can see this as the beginnings of a 'framework for citizenship' – part of a process to enable people to become full and active citizens.

Leaving institutions behind

Gandhi was speaking in the post-war period at a time when the lives of people with learning disabilities in England were very different from now. Very few people with learning disabilities at the time would have received any formal schooling, and they would have spent their lives hidden away from the mainstream of society, either incarcerated in a long-stay hospital or held at the heart of a close-knit family unit. Independent living and inclusion as we know them today were yet to be born.

The institutionalised social exclusion of the long-stay hospitals was motivated by fear, fear of people who are different, who don't communicate in the same way as everyone else and who find it difficult to fit into modern, industrial society. This fear was fed by the eugenics movement of the early 20th century, which advocated compulsory sterilisation – and sometimes worse (there are many chilling quotes from the advocates of eugenics recorded now on websites, see the resources listed below for examples). The policy of incarceration was unashamedly designed to segregate those with disabilities from the mainstream of society: it ruled the lives of hundreds of thousands of learning disabled people throughout the 20th century and caused great misery and waste of human potential. The numbers in long-stay 'mental handicap hospitals' reached their peak in 1968 when 65,000 people were incarcerated. Simon Duffy has written about this history (see Duffy, 1996, for a brief introduction).

Judged by the standards of today or by those of Gandhi, England in the mid-20th century would have failed the test of civilisation, certainly in regard to the lives of people with learning disabilities. Regardless of what views we may have today of such policies, their purpose was clear and the implementation effective, and the policies were for a time at least affordable.

The purpose and effectiveness of what followed is less clear. In the last third of the 20th century the policy of segregation began to be reversed. Policy makers at the time were faced with two irresistible forces, one social and one financial. Social pressures for change grew from the discrediting of the eugenics movement and the horrors of the Second World War. This was followed quickly by a series of scandals caused by the abuse and neglect rife in the long-stay hospitals, which led to public outcry and calls for their closure. At the same time commissioners were faced with the need for large scale capital investment in the ageing asylum infrastructure; and the costs of rebuilding or refurbishing large long-stay hospital buildings to modern standards was quickly seen to be prohibitive.

Set against this history, the purpose and effectiveness of the community care reforms of the last 30 years or so are perhaps best defined by what they are *not* ('asylums') rather than what they are (real homes for people, who have the same rights and responsibilities as their fellow citizens). Emerging from the shadow of the segregation policies of the 20th century it was perhaps understandable that services were judged as 'good' merely because they were something other than large institutions. It rapidly became clear that 'not being a hospital' was in fact not nearly good enough. Indeed it has been strongly argued that the hostels and day centres that comprised the services that came to make up the community care infrastructure were the 'new institutions' within our communities (see Extended case study 1: Home, on page 11 for more on this).

The community care reforms changed services beyond recognition and there are many examples now of good 'person-centred' support arrangements for people with learning disabilities across the country. But if we take a step back and apply Gandhi's test of 'civilisation' to the society, which emerged from these reforms to the way most learning disabled people experience school; to their housing and homes; to their experiences of friendship and romantic love; to their use of the health service; to how they spend their 'working days' and make a contribution; to their opportunities to have fun; and finally to their experiences in retirement – how would we fare? Can we honestly say that people with learning disabilities are now equal citizens, with all the rights and responsibilities that go with that position? And if not, what does that say about our society in Britain today?

Judging today's services

Gandhi's test comprises a deceptively simple question, one that will certainly be of great personal interest to us if we ourselves need additional support with day-to-day life, or if someone we love or care about is in this situation. The question gains an interest beyond the personal, however, when we appreciate that councils and the NHS in England together spend around £5 billion on care and support for people with learning disabilities, around £80 million more than is budgeted each year, with spending rising year on year faster than inflation (Cattermole, 2007). Martin Cattermole's study also notes that despite drives towards community services, more than two-thirds of this money is spent on *buildings-based services*; and over half on residential or nursing care homes.

Cattermole goes on to say that that whilst these are the hard facts, *'there is limited information available about customer satisfaction and the outcomes being achieved'*. In fact, we currently lack any framework that is routinely used to measure how well these services are performing in any way that is truly meaningful. Hence, it is impossible to say with any confidence how the five billion pounds is being spent and to what effect. What we can do is to take the aspects of daily life that most of us would judge as important – where we live, opportunities to work, our health and well-being – and make some general observations from the data that is available.

▶ 122,000 adults with learning disabilities were receiving support from services in 2007 and about a third were living in residential or nursing care with 11,000 of these people living 'out of area' that is away from their home area (Department of Health, 2007).

▶ Only about one in 10 people with learning disabilities who are in touch with services are doing any form of paid work (Department of Health, 2007).

▶ Four times as many people with learning disabilities die of preventable causes than people in the general population (Disability Rights Commission, 2006).

▶ People with learning disabilities are 58 times more likely to die before the age of 50 than the general population (Disability Rights Commission, 2006).

Looking at these figures and reflecting on Martin Cattermole's commentary, it would seem that pressure for change is again growing as the same two irresistible forces build once more, one force is financial and the other social and moral.

The transformation from asylum to community that led to our current service infrastructure began in the early 1970s and it is only very recently that the last of the long-stay hospitals closed. As the earlier chapters in this book show, a further transformation is now underway and one that may take a similar length of time to come to fruition, but one that holds equivalent or greater significance. Concerned about the growing cost and poor outcomes of social care services, successive governments have over recent years committed to a radical reform programme to replace the provision of pre-commissioned community care services with a system based on the allocation of resources to individuals – that is to say *personalisation*.

The thinking behind this new system and the ways ordinary people are shaping it are described in the chapters in part one of this book. The roles of different stakeholders in creating the conditions for its success are in part two. The chapter by Caroline Tomlinson explains how this new system of support was developed by In Control from 2003. Many of those driving the transformation to self-directed support began with a vision of how the future might look, and in the final chapter, Julie Stansfield, In Control's chief executive, reflects on how that vision has evolved over the last couple of years.

Just as important as the wider vision, In Control's work has been shaped by a perspective on what the system needs to achieve for *individuals* who crave a decent life. This perspective has meant that we have needed to introduce a completely new and revolutionary approach to measuring the effectiveness of the system in delivering change for one person at a time. We do this by aiming to show the extent to which support arrangements have a *positive impact upon the lives of people using them*. By doing this, we measure how well each local authority is succeeding in making good the original values and vision.

We observed that the old approaches that were used to monitor the performance of social care services had focused on activity happening within the system itself. These traditional performance management systems looked at how many people were being served and the type of service they received. Some measures captured the cost or length of time it took to deliver a particular activity.

The measures attempted to understand what was happening in the various parts of a complex system by identifying and measuring a small number of 'key components' as proxies for other things. The intention was to provide a simple set of numbers to indicate the overall performance of the wider system. In the early 1990s this methodology became established and is by now embedded in the day-to-day work of social services departments. Approaches of this kind measure *what the system does*, they set benchmarks for performance and provide management information helpful to those charged with managing the system.

The thinking behind these old approaches is based upon an established view of what a good social care system looks likes. All 150 of the English local authorities measure and report in detail the activity they undertake and the time taken for 'key tasks'. For example, local authorities are required to report the number of people who have their support arrangements reviewed each year, and the average length of time between referral and services being put in place.

Performance is also measured by counting how many people receive services in a particular way; the number of people who have a direct payment; the number of 'carers' who have an assessment of their needs; and the number of times authorities carry out certain listed tasks.

This 'industrial quality control' is fundamentally flawed. It is based on an assumption that it is possible to define proxies for what is 'good'. The length of time from referral to service delivery can, it is argued, for example be used as a proxy to show whether the system is operating at an appropriate speed: if it is quicker than 28 days the system is performing well; if it is slower than 28 days it is failing.

However, when we apply such a quality control measure to a truly *personalised* system we see no meaningful results. Who decides that 28 days is a desirable timeframe; and even if so, is 28 days always an appropriate measure in all circumstances? An individual thinking about their life as they approach school leaving age may wish to plan their support over an extended period, whilst someone suffering the loss of an immediate family member may need a very rapid support plan to be developed. In the first scenario 28 months may be appropriate, whilst 28 hours may be the required response in the second.

Approaches based on absolute standards are unhelpful for two essential reasons.

1. They push the local authority in a direction directly contrary to the policy of personalised support, increased choice and control.

2. They do nothing to encourage (or measure) individual efficiency (people using their own resources) or indeed the use made of the community's social capital to multiply the resources of the state.

A new approach to evaluation

When In Control came to develop its approach to evaluation it rejected these systemic approaches, criticising them as costly to operate and often unhelpfully linked to public judgments on *local authority performance*. They do nothing to measure actual impact on the lives of real people. An important unintended consequence of the use of 'proxy measures' is that the system itself can become distorted (emphasising 'measured things' and ignoring 'unmeasured things') as the evaluators focus on the proxies rather than of that which is really important. The system responds by putting more time, effort and resources into the privileged 'proxy' aspects of the system.

In addition, when we looked at the old performance regime we struggled to see how approaches that rely on measuring tasks and activity could offer anything other than a very partial account of performance. We came to see therefore, that there was a real need to develop new and better ways of measuring effectiveness. What we felt was required was a series of much more direct measurements of the impact of the system on the lives of the disabled and older people and families for whom that system was designed.

To this end, John Waters from In Control and Professor Chris Hatton of Lancaster University set about working with people who need support together with their families and with local authorities, with the aim of developing a new way to think about and recording *outcomes*.

The work was underpinned by a series of aspirations, such as:

▶ the evaluation methods should be low cost (including the cost of the measures themselves, the cost of collecting information and the cost of analysing the information)

▶ the questions being asked in the evaluation should be recognised as important by every group involved in the evaluation

▶ the evaluation methods should impose a minimal burden in terms of time on the people being asked to provide information

▶ the information provided should be analysed and reported in ways that can be used by the groups of people taking part and others interested in self-directed support

▶ the evaluation methods should be freely available for use by others.

The evaluation framework that emerged has enabled In Control to offer an informed commentary on the current shift towards personalised social care services, and to report the views and experiences of people taking control of personal budgets.

In Control's evaluation framework

In Control's evaluation framework comprises a series of simple questionnaires designed to gather views and experiences of people who are taking control of a personal budget, together with the views of their families and of the staff who support them. Each of the questionnaires captures information in three core areas:

▶ demographic information (age, gender, ethnicity etc.)

▶ process information (the experience of taking control of a personal budget)

▶ outcomes (the effect of the personal budget on the person's life).

The questionnaires simply ask people to identify how their life (or for staff, their work role) has changed in a number of domains since they have had a personal budget, using a simple three point scale. This allows people to report whether things were *worse, the same or better*, following the introduction of the personal budget.

Use of the framework

The framework has been used by a number of local authorities who have written accounts of their work to implement self-directed support and focus explicitly on the experience of people with learning disabilities. In Control has aggregated the data from this work; reports are published at www.in-control.org.uk/evaluationreports.

The exact wording of the scale is sensitive to the context of each question and has in some cases changed slightly as the framework has been adopted in different local authority areas. This has resulted in some variation to the precise wording of each question. In some questions 'more' was used to indicate a better outcome and 'less' or 'fewer' to indicate a worse outcome. As the questionnaire for personal budget recipients was implemented locally, some of the domains were omitted and replaced with other domains.

An informed commentary

Despite these local variations it has been possible for us to identify a set of domains that have emerged as *core*. These have been included consistently when the framework has been applied in local evaluations.

Data from these local evaluations show that depending on the precise definition, a population of between 385 and 522 people using personal budgets have been given the opportunity to say whether their lives improved, stayed the same or worsened since the introduction of a personal budget across eight domains of their lives:

▶ health

▶ being with people they want

▶ quality of life

▶ taking part in their communities

▶ control over the support they use

▶ feeling safe both inside and outside their home

▶ feeling that they are supported in ways that maintain their dignity

▶ standard of living.

More than two-thirds of people using personal budgets reported that the control they had over their support (66%) and their overall quality of life (68%) had improved since they took up a personal budget. A majority of people reported spending more time with people they wanted to (58%), taking a more active role in their local community (58%), feeling that they were supported with more dignity (55%), and feeling in better health (51%) since they took up a personal budget. In the domains of feeling safe (58%) and standard of living (52%), more than half of people reported no change after they took up a personal budget. In all domains, less than 10% of people reported any domain of their life getting worse after they took up a personal budget.

Looking at these findings there seems little doubt that personal budgets are working well; and that people are reporting significantly improved outcomes.

A framework for citizenship?

Something more than this is happening though: our very way of understanding *what 'good' looks* like is changing. When we come to consider whether our social care system is working well, we no longer have to rely on the industrial system measures that dominated the community care years. We have instead started to understand and report people's own accounts of their *lived experience*.

We have begun to create a framework for citizenship, one that is developing as the social care system changes. We can claim this because we are beginning to measure what is working well in terms of how the social care system is helping people to be full and active citizens, to be part of their society and to lead active social lives. It would probably be too bold a claim to say we have passed Gandhi's test, but we have perhaps now at least understood the question.

References

Cattermole M (2007) *Getting to Grips with Commissioning for People with Learning Disabilities* [online]. Available at: www.icn.csip.org.uk/_library/Getting_to_grips_with_commissioning_for_LDs.pdf (accessed November 2010).

Department of Health (2007) *Valuing People Now*. London: Department of Health.

Disability Rights Commission (2006) *Equal Treatment: Closing the gap*. London: Disability Rights Commission.

Duffy S (1996) *Unlocking the Imagination. Strategies for purchasing services for people with learning difficulties* [online]. Available at: www.in-control.org.uk (accessed November 2010).

In Control (2010) [online]. Available at: www.in-control.org.uk (accessed November 2010).

Further reading

Prisonplanet.com [online]. Available at: www.forum.prisonplanet.com/index.php?topic=57446.0;wap2 (accessed January 2011).

Harmlesswise.com [online]. Available at: www.harmlesswise.com/conspiracy/quotes/eugenics (accessed January 2011).

Section three:
The broader picture
– what next for personalisation?

The final section of the book broadens the focus to ask what needs to happen *next* to make a success of personalisation.

In reality, the things we describe here need to happen *now* and happily, many are beginning in some places. In a sense, these are not 'optional extras', it is just as important to define outcomes and to 'think community' as it is to have good arrangements for support planning or commissioning, but the difference is that these three chapters show us some of the ways to take personalisation to the next level. That is not, as Julie Stansfield makes clear in her final chapter, to some sort of mythic utopia, but to a place where we have arrangements to support people with learning disabilities (and others) that are effective, efficient and which build upon the struggles for rights, independence, choice and inclusion which were at the heart of *Valuing People* a decade ago.

In Control has set out its vision for 2020:

'Our members and supporters are passionate about striving for a better tomorrow. Learning lessons from the past, we have a vision of a freer, fairer society with people at its very heart. It's a place where everyone takes part and everyone's contribution is truly valued. What's more everyone who needs extra help has the right and responsibility to choose and control that support – whatever their personal circumstances. We believe in a society where people are interested in, engaged with and compassionate about others. Not only are individual talents, passions and contributions encouraged and respected, but if people fall ill, become lonely, confused, or are disabled, they are still valued and their community supports them. Businesses are part of and contribute to local communities, while government services help communities to support themselves. This is a society which doesn't try and divide people's lives into "health", "social care", "education" and "welfare benefits". Instead it sees the

whole of life and recognises that children, adults and older people all require different kinds of targeted support at different times.

In some ways our vision echoes the community care of the 1980s, when the inclusion and independent living movements began. But although community care did free people from long-stay institutions, the reality for many was that they were transferred to smaller local homes – they were 'in' the community but not 'part of' the community.... And so, our vision for 2020 is more far-reaching than just 'community care'. Our vision is about building a society where compassion, mutual respect and equality form the foundations of our everyday relationships – and are seen as the norm, not the exception.' (In Control, 2010)

The third and final part of this book then looks to the road ahead, not in some 'misty eyed' way that wishes away people's struggles and impairments but in the same practical and pragmatic terms as do the earlier chapters, to guide people, to provide them with inspiration and leadership with the aim that people with learning disabilities, their families and supporters will one day soon be truly 'in control'.

References

In Control (2010) *Vision 2010: Real impact, real change.* Wythall: In Control.

Chapter 14

Thinking whole life

Nic Crosby

Nic Crosby joined In Control in 2007 and his current work as a member of In Control's core team includes supporting a number of adult social care departments, alongside leadership of the children's programme. This has led to an increasing focus on developing our understanding of a truly 'whole life approach' to personalisation across the age range and the 'domains' of people's life.

Before this, Nic worked as a consultant at Paradigm, leading work on individual budgets for young people moving into the adult world. Previously he worked at the Foundation for People with Learning Disabilities and the Institute for Applied Health and Social Policy.

Key Points

▶ A whole life approach unites all work on personalisation with a focus on the person, their life, the resources they have to draw on and the support they need.

▶ The resources we all draw on we refer to as our 'real wealth' and relate to all the resources we use to live, plan for the future and contribute to our community and the wider society.

Real wealth is:

▶ **Connections** – the important people in a person's life, people who love, respect and care for the child or adult.

▶ **Access** – being able to get out and about, use cars and public transport, being able to access information and knowledge.

▶ **Capacities** – skills, abilities, knowledge, learning and work.

▶ **Control** – the assets under the control of the person, including capital goods such as a house or flat and maybe an individual or personal budget.

▶ **Resilience** – physical and mental health, emotional well-being, inner strength, faith or belief system.

Everyone should be able to self-direct their life, regardless of any additional support needs. To make this a reality the government must invest in the real wealth of all.

Introduction

A whole life approach starts with the individual, with how we all live our lives and what resources we draw on to live the life we choose.

This perspective sets the context for state funding: to support people with or without additional support needs to live a safe and healthy life, to work, learn, to have relationships and to play. 'Whole life' extends from conception through to the end of a person's life; it unites ages and all parts of our lives. The approach is based upon understanding how the government and its agents act to support people in self-directing their lives and those of the people they love and care for.

The drive to personalisation has seen most action within the world of 'adult social care' and is now starting in the worlds of health and employment. There is a growing body of work within the 'children's world', which will soon be added to by the publication of the evaluation of the individual budgets pilots in six children's services, funded by the Department for Education. We should now see all of this work as part of one agenda, as opposed to many different programmes headed in a similar direction. The phrase 'whole life' encapsulates this.

Most if not all of the energy has been focused on process and system design and misses the underpinning values which In Control sees as so important. It also tends to miss the fact that all our efforts must lead to *improved outcomes* – that is to say better lives for children, young people, older people, disabled adults and families.

This chapter stands back from work on systems and processes and shows how, if we do have a relentless focus on the individual in this way, self-directed support has the potential to make lasting change to the lives of people of all ages. What we need is a single, co-ordinated and efficient approach to supporting the 'whole life' of a person.

There is much discussion about 'rights and responsibilities'; in terms of personalisation this refers to the 'deal' or 'contract' between the government and the citizen. This 'deal' is one of 'we will support you … and you will be expected to make a contribution'. To make such a contribution, people need to be able to participate, need to be able to hold down a job, pay tax and give of their time and energy to the communities they are part of whether those communities are geographic or virtual.

What does 'whole life' mean?

We will start from the position of thinking about how most of us live our lives, and in doing this we will aim to establish a *standard* or *expectation*. The task of the government agency, local authority, health trust etc. is to ensure that its activity enables all those it is involved in supporting are able to live a life like all others, to self-direct their lives, to reach this standard or meet this normal expectation.

Everyday living for most of us of all ages means making best use of the resources we have at our disposal to live, work, learn, play, take risks and build relationships. To understand these resources In Control created a model in 2008 called 'Real Wealth' (Crosby & Duffy, 2008). This model has been refined over the past two years by In Control and the Centre for Welfare Reform and now offers a useful way of thinking about where we all start from when we think about how we live our lives.

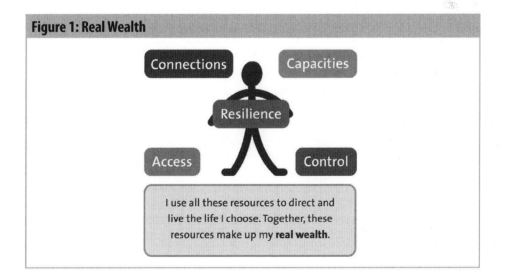

Figure 1: Real Wealth

Connections   Capacities

Resilience

Access   Control

I use all these resources to direct and live the life I choose. Together, these resources make up my **real wealth**.

This graphic displays the resources we all use to self-direct our lives; how we make decisions about what we do, with whom, when, how we contribute to our communities, support our friends and families and make plans for the future.

Connections – the important people in a person's life, people who love, respect and care for the child or adult.

Access – being able to get out and about, use cars and public transport, being able to access information and knowledge.

Capacities – skills, abilities, knowledge, learning and work.

Control – the assets under the control of the person, including capital goods such as a house and maybe including an individual or personal budget.

Resilience – physical and mental health, emotional well-being, inner strength, faith or belief system.

Together these elements represent our *real wealth*. Thinking 'whole life' means thinking through the ways the government and others invest in these resources, so empowering us all to control our own lives. All the solutions to a person's needs for support are parts of their *real wealth*.

Connections

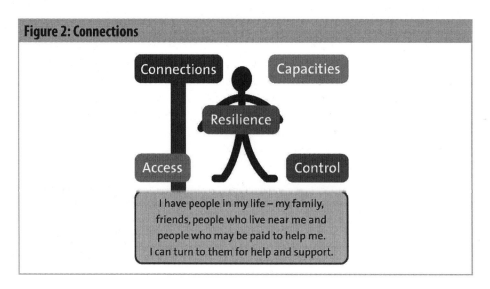

Figure 2: Connections

The networks of people involved in our lives, the people we turn to when things get difficult and in return the help that we are able to give to these people are central to how we live, who we socialise with, how we spend our time and what knowledge or expertise we may be able to draw on as and when we need it.

The support planning process starts by thinking about who is most important in a person's life, who loves, cares and respects the person, and then about the wider network of people involved in the person's life. For some people this network is a formal 'circle of support'. Being part of a network of people, being able to support and in return be supported by people and being able to access expertise from sources within the network are important to us all. Many people with learning disabilities can be isolated and their only contact is with people paid to support them, for many young people with learning disabilities opportunities to build these networks, to socialise with people of the same age, to share in activities and build lasting friendships are very restricted. My Fantastic Life youth club in Cambridgeshire addresses this issue.

My Fantastic Life

My Fantastic Life is a small organisation in Cambridgeshire set up five years ago to support young people with learning disabilities and their families to move into the adult world.

They have been running youth clubs and other projects such as peer mentorships in primary and secondary schools in Cambridgeshire for some time and have recently started five new youth clubs across the county. The youth clubs meet once a week, do lots of different activities; and currently are planning a short break with a difference, an inclusive youth camp in early September. Alongside this they support young people to work on issues of self-advocacy, person-centred planning and have recently become a partner working with Cambridgeshire County Council, young people and their families on personal budgets.

The Ely group recently took part in some consultation with In Control. One view echoed by all its members was the importance of My Fantastic Life to them, the friendships they now have and the new things they have done together.

Youth clubs such as these are not specifically linked to personal budgets, yet they are great examples of how investment in building connections can have a lasting impact on people's lives, build relationships, combat isolation and hence impact on the whole of life. As we know, isolation is a major contributor to difficulties with emotional well-being and mental health.

The Partners in Policymaking programme has developed a nationwide network of disabled people, carers, parents and families who now support each other via email, social networking and telephone. People find they are able to turn to many different people who understand exactly what they are going through, not only for advice or information but for emotional support at times of crisis or difficulty. (There is more about Partners in Policymaking in the Chapters by 2 and 16.)

There are many examples where creative use of personal budgets has been supported by local authorities. People have found ways to use part of their money to meet friends, to go to the cinema, to meet at the pub, to organise an activity that interests them, etc. Such use of public money delivers outcomes that ultimately save public money: socialising promotes positive mental health, can contribute to physical health, and continues to build friendships and relationships.

Access

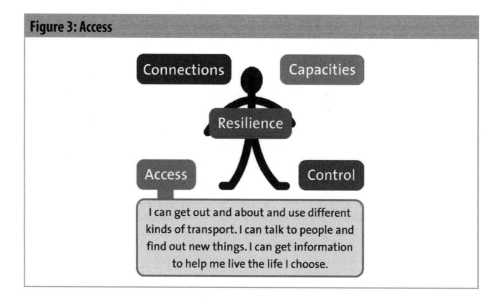

Figure 3: Access

Connections

Capacities

Resilience

Access

Control

I can get out and about and use different kinds of transport. I can talk to people and find out new things. I can get information to help me live the life I choose.

Our lives are profoundly affected by our ability to negotiate the physical world around us – to get where we want to go without too much bother – and by the extent and the ways in which we are able to access, understand and make use of knowledge and information – in whatever form. Government initiatives to introduce accessible public transport and free bus travel are straightforward instances of initiatives that improve our 'access wealth'. How might a local authority take a lead in making life easier in these ways for local people with learning disabilities?

Changing places in Plymouth

Plymouth Learning Disability Partnership through Plymouth City Council has been championing the development of accessible toilets and changing facilities for people with complex physical care needs across the city. They have a strong commitment to developing better facilities so everyone can take their rightful place in the community and use shopping centres, leisure facilities and community spaces that are properly equipped. This plan was started with a successful negotiation with Drakes Circus Shopping Centre that delivered the first 'changing places' toilet in Plymouth.

The Plymouth Learning Disability Partnership submitted a successful bid for learning disability development capital funding which was used to develop accessible facilities across the city. Not all the facilities have been designated as 'changing places' toilets due to the size of the existing spaces, but all are being used successfully by members of the community. The venues include community centres, a library, swimming pool and church.

Adaptations of this sort open up the 'universal world' of sport, shopping and leisure that most of us take for granted. For a person with a personal budget this means being able to plan a day in town with a personal assistant and being able to stay out for a whole day, as opposed to having to be home after a couple of hours. Similar works have featured in the Aiming High for Disabled Children programme in some areas, where money has been invested in making leisure centres more accessible and in equipment and hoists which mean disabled children can use swimming facilities alongside their peers.

Capacities

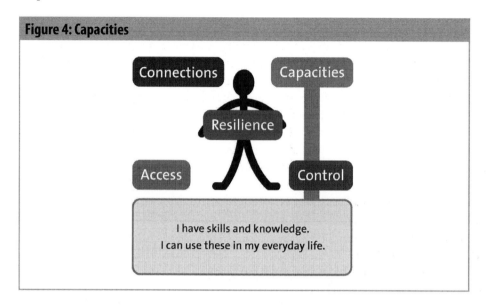

Figure 4: Capacities

Connections · Capacities · Resilience · Access · Control

I have skills and knowledge.
I can use these in my everyday life.

Any activity in life requires certain skills and knowledge. Whether it concerns getting a paid job, volunteering, following a hobby, or managing your affairs at home, the skills and knowledge you have at your disposal is hugely significant. For many people with learning disabilities being able to learn work skills is a challenge, not because of their learning difficulty as such, but because they are not allowed the opportunity or time to develop skills, or to participate in work experience and training.

Most people attend college to learn skills which will prepare them for a career. People with learning disabilities attend college to learn 'independent living skills' and very often this means that they miss out on the chance to acquire any skills which will help them to find and keep a job. Work in Sheffield over the past three years sets out how this could be radically different; it shows how by developing local opportunities many young people on leaving school no longer need to be looking at residential college as their next step. This story first appeared in *A Whole Life Approach to Personalisation: Children and young people* (Crosby & Duffy, 2008).

Joined-up support

Jonathan is a disabled teenager and his quality of life has been transformed since he left school in July 2008 with an individual budget. Now he and his mum decide what he should do, when he should do it and who should support him. Jonathan's complex health condition means he receives funding through continuing health care, and he was fortunate to be part of a pilot run by the Learning and Skills Council where he was allocated an individual learning support fund. Putting the different budgets together has enabled Jonathan to employ one full-time personal assistant (PA) and two part-time PAs for activities in the evenings and weekends.

Jonathan's mum reports that there has been an, '*amazing improvement in his quality of life. It has given him so much more freedom to explore life. Without this individual budget he would not have been able to do anything like the things he can do now. I would have had difficulty taking him to these things. It is encouraging Jonathan to have a bit of an independent lifestyle and with Jonathan having his PAs, I have more time to spend with my other two sons who both have learning difficulties, and Jonathan can't stop smiling!*'

In addition to enjoyment and happiness, Jonathan's learning needs are fully met. His week – tailor-made for him – allows many opportunities for developing his independent life skills, his special interest in computers and multi-media, and for individual tuition.

If the same approach of personalised funding in other sectors is taken up across sectors in this way, then here is a clear example of the impact. Not only is there a vast improvement in outcomes for the young person and their family but there are clear efficiencies generated for both the adult social care department, the health trust and the Learning and Skills Council through the elimination of duplication. This approach demonstrates a very creative way of investing in a person's skills and knowledge: young people are able to develop skills in preparation for work or everyday life by accessing particular opportunities which meet their *individual* needs.

Control

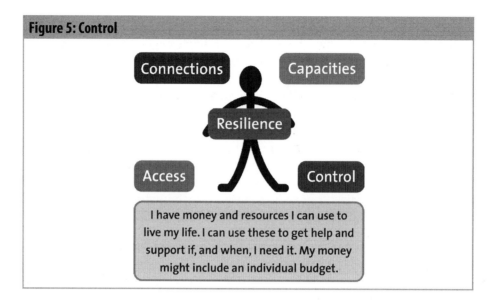

Figure 5: Control

Connections · Capacities · Resilience · Access · Control

I have money and resources I can use to live my life. I can use these to get help and support if, and when, I need it. My money might include an individual budget.

Control means much more than having an individual budget: it concerns all the money and capital resources which we control, so in some cases it will include a house, other property, investments and so on.

As the introduction makes clear, *personalisation* is often seen to focus on personal budgets, rightly in some respects as they challenge statutory agencies to deliver support in a radically different way. However, this focus can lead us to see personal budgets as the beginning and end of personalisation, which they most certainly are not. What they do represent for many is a vital element of the resources a person can control, but there is much else which we all draw on to access opportunities and to self-direct one's life. A personal budget can be most useful, in fact, in helping a person make good use of other parts of their wealth: it can help a person attend a club, take part in activities with friends and peers, get a job, learn new skills, get out and about, and keep fit. Chapter 9 makes it clear that what he calls the 'personalisation of universal services' is critical to the success of this whole process.

There are many stories about how people have used their personal budgets to get the support they need or to build relationships and participate in the local community. One taken from an edition of *In Control Now!* in 2009 tells the story of an older man who used to rely on a meals on wheels service. He spoke about eating on his own, often the food wasn't very hot and it wasn't great quality. He used his personal budget to set up an arrangement with a local pub, which meant he had his lunch there every day. Not only did he have a cooked meal but he also built up and maintained a circle of people at the pub, he was less isolated and more involved in local life.

Evaluation work undertaken by In Control (2010) with its members clearly identifies the fact that when given control of their personal budgets, people are far more likely to choose local activities, and more ordinary ways of spending their money than they are special services; they themselves are investing in their own wealth, they are developing circles of friends and supporters, keeping fit, getting out and about and developing new skills.

Resilience

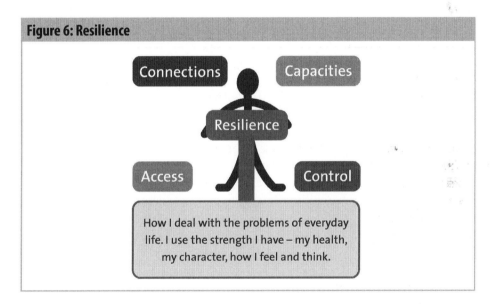

Figure 6: Resilience

Connections Capacities

Resilience

Access Control

How I deal with the problems of everyday life. I use the strength I have – my health, my character, how I feel and think.

This is well summed up by one parent as, '*the bit that gets you up in the morning after you've been up all night with your child, the bit that gets you up even after 10 years of being up all night*'. Resilience can apply to our physical and mental health, our emotional well-being and for many their faith and beliefs about the world they live in. Our resilience is central to all our wealth, and is dependent upon the other aspects. The underlying assumption here is that the stronger we are, the more resilient we are and then the more able we are to self-direct our lives.

Children are part of and clearly reliant upon the wealth of their family. Many families involved in piloting individual budgets for their children speak of the impact of this on their family life, how they feel more like a family, how their other children begin to get on better with their disabled sister or brother. In Halton, children's services built a strong relationship with their local Barnardos Children's Centre (Murray, 2010). Along with support from Halton Speak Out, Barnardos staff supported families in developing support plans using small individual budgets. Here are some of the comments and feedback from families:

'We can very rarely go on long holidays as a family because it all depends on David's health and arrangements with doctors and nurses. Now that we have an individual budget, we just wake up on a weekend and if David is well and happy, we pack up and go find a campsite somewhere for the weekend. It's all very spur of the moment, but this way we can make the most of things and my other children love it too.' (Parent)

'Having an individual budget has affected the whole family. We have had a summer like no other – we are a lot less stressed out and we have a much healthier relationship with each other. All our children are happy. They are allowed to be just kids who are having fun together.' (Parent)

'I would absolutely recommend this programme to other families. It allowed us as a family to do things we would have never been able to do before. It truly enriched our summer.' (Parent)

For a child, a healthy home life is of paramount importance; the ability of a personal budget to invest in building up a family's resilience cannot be underestimated.

A whole life approach

Thinking whole life means dropping the old philosophy of seeing people in segments: learning, health, social, work. It means thinking from the very start about the child's life and what lies ahead for both child and family.

Adopting a whole life approach means beginning with the individual and understanding how investment in a person's real wealth will enable them to self-direct their life, and to play their own part in the local community in a way that suits them as an individual. The pre-occupation of statutory services with changing systems and processes takes away from the central values underpinning this change, that is to say: supporting people to be people.

Simply put, a whole life approach sees people as whole from their birth through to the end of their life. The approach unites all activities with the single focus on investment in an individual person or a family's *real wealth*, in the way we have described in this chapter. Through this investment, not only do people find the capacity to self-direct, but they also find that they can make a real contribution to their community and society. A whole life approach brings an inclusive society because it aims for 'a life like all others'. This is not about extraordinary lives; instead it's about an 'ordinary life' as a reasonable expectation for all.

Whole life thinking is common sense thinking; the way we organise our services at present is anything but common sense. Most of our services have various assessments and thresholds, often duplicate work by others and are a confusing and frustrating experience for anyone needing to access information, advice, guidance and support. Such a system simply perpetuates the 'gift' or 'power over' relationship between government and its public. This chapter has used a simple way of thinking about how we all self-direct our lives and how to make best use of the resources we have available to us; unless the government tackles the plethora of initiatives, of pilots, of disparate and unlinked work then the simple focus of people's day-to-day lives will be lost. A whole life approach is one which invests in the *real* wealth of the nation.

References

Crosby N & Duffy S (2008) *A Whole Life Approach to Personalisation: Children and young people*. London: In Control.

In Control (2010) *A Report on In Control's Third Phase*. London: In Control.

InControl Now! (2009) [online]. Available at: www.in-control.org.uk (accessed November 2010).

Murray P (2010) *A Summer Like No Other*. Halton: Halton Children's Services.

Further reading

Brewis R, Crosby N & Tyson A (2010) *A Whole Life Approach to Personalisation, Policy and Procedures No.4* [online]. Available at: www.in-control.org.uk (accessed January 2011).

Cowen A (2010) *Personalised Transition*. Sheffield: Centre for Welfare Reform.

Centre for Welfare Reform [online]. Available at http:www. centreforwelfare.reform.org (accessed November 2010).

The Learning and Skills Council ceased in March 2010 and funding for post-16 learning is now managed within the local authority. Currently funding for residential colleges, the money which was allocated as individual Learning Support Funds in Sheffield is currently controlled by the Young People's Learning Agency. The work in Sheffield continues to grow and develop. A full report of 'personalised transition' is available from the Centre for Welfare reform.

Chapter 15

Thinking community

Clare Wightman

Clare Wightman is director of Grapevine, a charity working in Coventry, where she has established a reputation for expertise in making the changes needed to enable people with learning disabilities to be more fully included in their communities. Grapevine is currently a partner in a national project with the Foundation for People with Learning Disabilities looking at ways of achieving inclusion for people with high support needs. She has been inspired by the work of the pioneers of citizen advocacy and particularly by Tom Kohler and others in Savannah, Georgia.

'The answer to what is usually who.'

(Tom Kohler, citizen advocacy organiser in Savannah, Georgia, USA)

Introduction

Putting People First (Department of Health, 2007) divides personalisation into four parts: choice and control, universal services, prevention and early intervention and social capital. In many local authorities, however, it is identified simply as the take up of personal budgets, together with the use of universal, not niche, services. The coincidence of its implementation with the worst economic recession for over 60 years almost certainly accounts for personalisation's narrowed meaning. However, this chapter argues that the neglect of social capital risks the failure of one of the most significant social policy developments.

By *social capital* we mean a person or a family's personal resources, their abilities and strengths, their social and professional networks or connections. As we will see, social capital is essential for a person to be genuinely able to shape and direct their social care provision. I will be using examples from the work of Grapevine, a charity for people with learning disabilities and their families based in Coventry.

Key points

▶ In a system where social care service users are supplied by the market, social inequalities are likely to persist or worsen.

▶ Building social capital is part of the solution to this challenge.

▶ Deep attention to who someone is precedes successful community building.

▶ You need social capital in order to realise the full potential of a personal budget.

▶ We can engage 'community' through conversation and listening.

▶ We then need to get from 'can do' to 'will do'.

▶ We need to help community members to learn and question the status quo.

Personalisation and social inequalities

There has been a too easily made assumption that swapping your civic right to publicly purchased provision for consumer rights and individual purchasing power will transform your life. As Daly (2008) makes it clear, it is people's use of economic and social capital that is the critical factor in enabling them to define meaningful outcomes, and direct their support to achieve those outcomes. Some service users and their families will be better able to make their voices heard in the social care market.

Well over half the families we at Grapevine have worked with in the last two years have experienced multiple disadvantages, the most common of which were low incomes and mental health issues. Many were isolated with no supportive networks of their own. The danger in a system where social care services are negotiated and purchased in a market (an underdeveloped one at that) is that such social inequalities are likely to persist or worsen.

The experiences of early pioneers who are motivated, energetic and resourceful will not be typical of the hundreds of thousands who follow as personalisation becomes mainstream. This is a cause for concern unless we are able to do something to redress it – one means is to help individuals and families build social capital. We will use some aspects of Tracey's life to illustrate this.

There is no question for those who have witnessed it that Tracey has fun and is welcomed by friendly people and is included in the action. However, whether she can go out is decided not by her but by the variable willingness, attitudes and convenience of staff and by staffing levels. Tracey, therefore, has no control over her membership of this community group. Taking part in a community activity and meeting new people who have warmed to her and her humour are features of an independent life which the service she pays for have undermined rather than supported. Her elderly parents are anxious not to rock the boat in case Tracey is returned to them and they are unable to cope again. Paid advocacy resulted in only short-term staff changes, which lapsed once the advocacy intervention ended.

The real problem for Tracey and others like her is indifference – it doesn't matter enough to the staff around her whether she gets to do something she loves with people who like her. Whether they are funded by a block contract or a group of direct payments doesn't matter; they don't care about her, they just do their shift. Tracey needs people who care about her to take her and see the joy she gets from it. If they did that then they might wonder where else Tracey could find joy and her life will start to grow. The only way a person can be protected from indifference is by another person deciding she or he really matters. If nobody thinks you matter as a person there is no policy that can help your life to improve.

The work of engaging others to know and to care is where community building starts. Grapevine tackles the isolation, loneliness, and separation experienced by those with a learning disability and their families. We do this because we know that no deep and lasting change can result from policies and services which fail to address these fundamental difficulties. The jaws of institutional life will always be open for those who lack real friends and allies, believers and admirers.

One of the things Grapevine has considered carefully is the relationship between the culture of the organisation – what we value and how we behave – and our work of relationship building. Grapevine's work starts from the organisation's values and beliefs, which are as follows.

▶ A life that grows because most of the people we serve have lives that have stood still for decades.

▶ Connections that matter because we all need to stand on the firm ground provided by relationships built up over a lifetime. Our goal is having people around who aren't paid to care, they just do.

▶ Everyone's contribution because most people with a learning disability are defined by what they need rather than by what they can offer. To make change possible we must believe in each person's ability to contribute.

▶ Learning on the journey because most people with a learning disability are protected from experiences for fear of the risks.

▶ Standing together because to create change we need a warm relationship of solidarity – not one which is over protective, or task-centred.

▶ Passion because it fosters new connections as our enthusiasms touch others. As workers, our belief in what we do helps us to do it better.

We try to ensure that these values are lived through how we relate to each other as a team as well as how we relate to the people we serve. It helps that these values were created by the current team and not 'imposed'. Values of course can not be imposed – they come from within.

The steps Grapevine has taken to connect people to community have been described elsewhere (Wightman, 2009). In this chapter I want to add thoughts on how organisations like ours can connect people and their families to community so that personalisation truly transforms lives.

Know how to be with someone

In building community, your sense of the right thing to do comes from knowing who the person is, and knowing who someone is comes not from questioning them but from time spent attentively with them.

It may seem obvious but the first step in any relationship is getting to know the other person properly and this applies to people working as community connectors. Ask permission to spend time with them and figure out the times of day and places the person is most likely to enjoy. Gradually be with them at different times or places and during different activities (or none). Being with someone in different places is a good way of learning more about them. It gives you the chance to identify their qualities naturally, rather than just talking about them.

Thomas and his connector Darren would sit and observe people going about their business in public places in the city centre and in country pubs positioned near junctions and roads. Any signs of paperwork and officialdom are left out as Thomas is frustrated by the attempts of 'services' to improve his life. He responds compliantly so asking lots of questions won't get to the heart of him. He senses he is in the spotlight and must perform when you begin to talk about life and its possibilities for growth.

A middle aged man and life-long day centre user, Thomas, lives alone now with his elderly mother. He exercises very little control over his own life as she does most tasks a man would normally do himself. In the words of his connector, being with Thomas makes you feel reflective and calm. In bars and pubs he enjoys randomly joining in with songs and seems most at ease slowly drinking a pint of lager, twisting the glass between his fingers as he watches the little stories of other people's lives open up before him. Those lives he sees in the community make him think about his own life: *'They have all the girls, the money and power'*. He will make statements after 10–20 minutes of silence and these short phrases need to be listened to. You have to hold them in your thoughts and respond to them, not ask him why. An example of this is when Thomas said, *'Architecture, good lines, built for Coventry, Coventry people good, built together'* to which Darren responded, *'Nice clock, nice roof'*.

The connector's task with Paul was to turn on its head a personal reputation that was given to him by some people in his home and work life. Support workers and care managers spoke of his negative and cocky attitude, his history of theft and a general sense that he was a loud mouth who was bad news. Attempts to connect him in a place where there was a need to be in physical contact with other people (a first aid course) didn't suit Paul. He does not always see personal boundaries, but perhaps that is no wonder as no one has offered him compassion in decades. So Darren sat on Friday mornings eating sausage sandwiches in Paul's favourite café in town – 'Snax in the City'. He revealed a lot of hurt he had experienced from all members of his family from a young age and a need for feeling safe personally and safety in the community surfaced. They talked about the last time he laughed and his favourite colours, and his face widened into a smile. In their time together Darren noticed him using his phone to take pictures of things he liked so he thought about Paul's passions for community, safety and photography and they went along to the local residents' association. From there they found a photographer working in the area and Paul is now being mentored by her to produce photos for the local newsletter.

Someone with a learning disability may not tell you directly what they want; natural connectors do not need obvious or verbal direction. They can, from their deep attention to who the person is and who they might become, spot the right people and the best opportunities for them.

Connect your planning to experiences of community

The answers you get when you plan depend on the questions you ask. If the main question is 'what will I do?' the answer will be activity. If the main question is 'who can help me do this?' then the answer will be new relationships. For example, the father of a young man with autism told us that when his son was small they would race up and down the road on a bike; Jordan loved the wind on his face. The planner played basketball with someone whose father-in-law owns a bike shop, and he thought maybe he could help them adapt an adult bike. He also considered the fact that there are fantastic grounds at the Excel Sports Centre including woodland, and we know how Jordan loves to be around grass and trees and it would provide a safe cycling space and a place to camp. Questions like, 'Maybe Cath [operations manager and sister of a man supported by Grapevine] could help?' and questions like these started to produce new answers involving new people and places in Jordan's life.

Jordan spent some time with his parents at the sports centre along with the planner meeting staff often enough to get acquainted and recognised – they also tried a spinning class. The planner spoke to the instructor and group members beforehand explaining why Jordan would love the experience of the wind stream at the back of the class. He walked up and down the line with his arms outstretched feeling the breeze before settling behind the person cycling the hardest. Jordan stared hard and the cyclist laughed. *'He wants me to go faster doesn't he? Good – he can tell me if I'm slacking'.*

These experiences were not just aimed at Jordan but at those around him too. His mother needed connections, new ideas and the moral support to carry them out. By the time Jordan got his personal budget, planning in this way had shifted his family's focus from building a sensory space in the back garden towards a set of places, activities and people that he could start to build his life around. Importantly it was not the personal budget that released Jordan's capacity to be with others, it was the relationship building which preceded it.

Without proper attention to the relationships in a person's life, personal budgets will not deliver better lives. We know from experience that those with a wide supportive circle of family and friends are able to define interesting new 'outcomes' and to plan for how the budget can be spent achieving them. Those who don't, and there are many, risk paying for a service much like the service they would have had before.

The power of conversation

Building connections in community happens through the right kind of conversation. Increasingly, Grapevine has turned from hoping that relationships will grow from a person's passions and interests to deliberately inviting others into a relationship with a person and their family. One of the things we can learn and regain from the origins of advocacy is the value of one person from a shared local community standing alongside another. Without someone who is willing to be alongside us in our life, we remain isolated and without power. Nowhere is citizen advocacy practised better than in Savannah, Georgia, USA. *'Can you and will you take the life of another person more seriously?'* That's the question Tom Kohler has been asking Savannah residents for more than 30 years and his work involves asking people to align themselves with the interests of individual people through personal relationship. Conversations that start to bring the 'can do' out of people and move it into the 'will do' are not easy to have and we have listened deeply to how Tom and Chatham from Savannah Citizen Advocacy do it.

First off we are clear that what we are not doing is 'recruiting volunteers' and that what citizens do for each other is not volunteering. We are talking about the distance between *friendship* and a *befriending service*. We are clear that we are looking for long-term commitments between people.

How we talk about people with a learning disability matters; we have to help others to get beyond stereotypes. We invite people to think about the parts of a person's character that others don't get to see right away and the qualities that others don't immediately see. Many of the people we support at Grapevine depend on others for their personal presentation. They also have a lot of preconceptions to overcome before others can really see who they are, not just what they have been called. It is important to work hard to become aware of these preconceptions and attitudes, so that we can listen effectively to what it is the person is telling us and particularly to what they tell us drives and motivates them, and what makes life interesting for them. Tell us a story about a time and a place you were together and point the common values and experiences as well as to the difficulties. Learning disabled people are strong and interesting people who our culture views as weak and marginal.

How we listen to community members matters too. In these conversations we are listening out for experiences of being judged, labelled or isolated; we are listening for experiences of overcoming those struggles. We ask questions like, what helped your life to grow and what connections matter to you? We talk about first impressions and it isn't just people with learning disabilities who are judged in society, people are judged on many grounds including on the basis of their race, sex and class.

Our aim is to encourage reflection on what it is like when you have no help to make your life grow and you have no connections. If the community member has overcome struggle and hard times we show them what they have in common with other people in our community who struggle against the odds. We are not so different from each other really.

It is important to establish the relationships and connections a community member has and can bring to the table together with how long they plan to stay. So too is establishing values through talk about upbringing and the big lessons of your early life.

It helps to illustrate or explore the rewards someone might find in such a relationship. Stories from Savannah show us that people have found joy when they have aligned themselves with someone in their town living a hard life. Benefits must flow both ways in relationships.

Anticipate people's schedules as a way to explore the difference between having control over one's time and being busy. A busy person may still have enough control over what they do and when they do it to be useful to another person at a time of need. You can encourage a longer, less intense perspective by pointing out that you don't have to build a close relationship instantly. If people saw each other a couple of times a month for 10 years how well would they know each other then? Listen for the reasons why people say no and help them unravel their limitations in these ways.

There are plenty of people who will and do go the extra mile for community already. Of these people you might have a conversation to get them thinking about, in Tom Kohler's words, the following.

- ▶ How much of the service I offer within the community is personal vs. professional?

- ▶ How much of the service I offer within the community draws me closer to people who live lives different to mine?

- ▶ How much of the service I offer within the community is freely given rather than quid pro quo?

- ▶ How much of the service I offer within the community involves my hands and my heart more than my wallet?

- ▶ How much of the service I offer within the community is transforming me?

(Chatham Savannah, Citizen Advocacy blog)

We know that we are asking a lot and that more people will say no than yes, but the goal of a freely given long-term relationship is important enough to keep us asking. That doesn't mean that we don't create other, smaller ways for community members to be involved, for example, a group of six people with and without learning disabilities just having dinner three times a year in the host's home. It doesn't mean that we have stopped helping people join and truly belong to community groups and community spaces. It simply means that we have supplemented those approaches with one which is more direct and intensive. A variety of ways of getting to the same goal are needed.

Social learning

We use opportunities to affirm, inform and remind community members about the power of what they do, planting seeds for future action and returning back to key themes like protection from indifference. It inspires people when you point out the bigger meaning of the action they took and the cultural pattern that they are challenging. When Grapevine works with young people we are careful to ask the young woman who goes with someone to get their nails done, what are you challenging when you do that? If two young people have a great time together we start a conversation about those who live on the thick ice and those who live on the thin ice.

Conclusion

Whether social inequalities can be overcome sufficiently to allow personalisation to work as successfully for one person as it does for the next, there are more factors to consider. It is important to decipher whether civil rights to care have been undermined in favour of market rights which operate unequally. Are personal budgets, for example, unleashing citizenship or subtly undermining it, or both?

Without relationship building, unequal experiences of personalisation will flourish. Without supports that can build social capital being commissioned and available, personal budgets will separate individuals and potentially create lobbying for segregated support (Gillespie & Dearden-Phillips, 2010). Already agencies supporting personal budget holders with the highest needs are creating small day centre style spaces 'because people can't just be out all the time'. Will community be an experience of relationships or will it be a place you visit when it's not raining?

In our experience learning disabled people seek what they most need: an enduring encounter with trust at its heart. Services can emulate that encounter but only community can truly provide it. The answer to 'what?' is usually 'who?'

----

*All names have been changed except where already published.

References

Daly G (2008) Is choice the right policy? *Health Matters* **72**.

Department of Health (2007) *Putting People First: A shared vision and commitment to the transformation of adult social care.* London: Department of Health.

Gillespie J & Dearden-Phillips C (2010) *Total Place, Community and Social Capital* [online]. Available at: www.adventuresincommunity.com/publications.html (accessed November 2010).

Tom Kohler's blog (2010) [online]. Available at: www.savannahcitizenadvocacy.org/ (accessed November 2010).

Wightman C (2009) Connecting people: grapevine. In C Poll, J Kennedy & H Sanderson (Eds) *In Community. Practical lessons in supporting isolated people to be part of community.* Stockport: HAS Press.

Further reading

Daly G & Woolham J (2010) *Do personal budgets lead to personalisation and what can their promotion tell us about the nature of citizenship and public accountability in relation to social care? Reflections from a study of the impact of self-directed support and personal budgets.* Coventry University: unpublished.

Grapevine (2010) [online]. Available at: www.grapevinecovandwarks.org.uk (accessed November 2010).

Inclusion Press and Network (2010) [online]. Available at: www.inclusion.com (accessed November 2010).

Mike Green (2010) [online]. Available at: www.mike-green.org/ (accessed November 2010).

Mills L & Messinger G (2005) *Sharing Community: Strategies, tips and lessons learned from experiences of community building at options.* Madison, Wisconsin: Atwood Publishing.

Pitonyak D (2007) *The Importance of Belonging.* Blacksburg, Virginia: Imagine.

Wightman C (2009) *Connecting People: The steps to making it happen* [online]. Available at: www.learningdisabilities.org.uk (accessed November 2010).

Chapter 16

A movement for change: the role of In Control and Partners in Policymaking

Julie Stansfield

Julie Stansfield was one of the founders of In Control and is now its chief executive. She has studied change management and has extensive experience in strategic and cultural change in local authorities. In this chapter, she describes the history of the movement for change, in which In Control is a part of and sets out her vision for a changed world.

The term 'Partners in Policymaking' as used in this chapter refers to a US licensed programme which was developed and adapted by Lynne Elwell in the UK. It includes a number of other courses within the overall programme, including 'Making it Happen', Kindred Spirits', 'Sharing Knowledge' and 'All Together Better'.

'Why doesn't anyone cut through all these silos in social services and health or diagnosis related support and get to the crunch of what all human beings need which is freedom and respect?'

(A woman's comment on the current systems and supports offered to her brother)

Introduction: a parallel world

Cries like the one quoted above are heard over and over again from people encountering what often seems to be a parallel 'service world' that exists for people who require support due to disability, ill health, age or other circumstances. These pleas come not only from the recipients of services, but increasingly from those who are paid to work in the alternative world – social workers, support workers, commissioners and service providers.

Many good, thoughtful people have heard these protests and tried to help and In Control is part of this attempt to respond. Movements of people struggling for full inclusion in society and for a dignified old age have existed now over many years. The organisation, In Control, began in the early 2000s as part of a grass-roots movement made up of people receiving services and of their allies working within those services. It went on to develop, test and refine the system that became known as 'self-directed support' and at the same time it built a strong alliance with the 'Partners in Policymaking' network of family and citizen leaders. This led to the In Control public membership initiative that we called People Power, an initiative which is now the heart of our work to unite people for change.

Key points

▶ We must respect, use and build on the skills of *experts by experience* as well as experts with professional or academic skills.

▶ We need to change the relationship between the citizen and the state, which means changing how people needing support are seen by those paid to commission and provide services.

▶ We need to change ingrained cultures, bottom up and top down. This requires visionary leadership.

▶ We need a new approach, a servant-leadership approach to replace the old service system approach that sees people as 'whole people' and as members of communities.

▶ We need to unite a grass-roots movement for change, focusing on people more than systems.

1. Respecting and utilising the skills and experts by experience and those with professional or academic skills

In Control began its work in 2003 when a small number of people came together to try and change things with a few local families with disabled members in Wigan. This group found inspiration in the independent living movement that had created direct payments and in the inclusion movement that had created the Partners in Policymaking family and citizen leadership courses.

Partners in Policymaking, perhaps the greatest influence on In Control, was developed initially in the USA in the 1980s by Colleen Wieck and brought to England in the mid 1990s by Chris Gathercole, Paul Taylor and Lynne Elwell. In 1996 the first Partners course was run in the North West of England, led by Lynne Elwell and supported by Owen Cooper, Martin Routledge and Julie Stansfield.

In that year I was working as a service manager in 'respite services' and was asked to present on the first English Partners in Policymaking course, alongside a mum who used the respite service. This experience was new and utterly scary for me. However, the style and content of presentations on the course were deliberately designed to create a shared understanding of the purpose and power of uniting experts by experience with people like me – an expert by profession. In managerial terms this may well be described as 'bringing a stakeholder group together' but my experience was that it was much, much more than this. Done properly, this approach generates and builds mutually respectful attitudes between the two types of experts and brings them together in a way that creates a genuine power shift.

We tried very hard to replicate this sort of approach in the early days of In Control beginning in 2003. The small committed group who came together included Partners graduates who were using services, family 'carers', development workers and trainers, government officials, managers, academics and the CEO of a local authority. In Control, at that stage a virtual group, developed the Seven Step Model of 'self-directed support' referred to throughout this book, based on the fundamental organising principles of self-assessment, transparent resource allocation, support planning and review. This model was successfully tested by English local authorities, first in services for people with learning disabilities, then across the whole social care spectrum. In all cases, independent evaluation showed hugely positive outcomes for people, with no increase in costs (see In Control's three major reports, published as Poll *et al*, 2006, Hatton *et al*, 2008 and In Control, 2010a). In 2007 these ideas influenced government policy in the form of the *Putting People First* concordat. In Control went on to develop as an independent social enterprise with charitable status and it began to work actively to promote self-direction for people at all stages of life and in all situations and circumstances. This included children and young people and users of health services. As we did this we learned that our focus needed to be more and more clearly on what it was that *communities* need to promote choice and control for all.

The role of 'uniting experts' is little talked or written about; and yet without the experience of 'Partners' and the many other leadership courses based on similar values and techniques, I am sure we would not have achieved so much nor had the same level of influence.

Much of this is rooted in how we see ourselves and how we understand the world, relate to those around us and how we make use of language to organise our thoughts and conduct our interactions.

The language of us and them
Mayer Shevin

We like things – they fixate on things
We try to make friends – they display attention seeking behaviours
We take a break – they display off-task behaviour
We stand up for ourselves – they are non-compliant
We have hobbies – they self-stim?
We choose our friends wisely – they display poor peer socialisation
We persevere – they perseverate
We love people – they have dependencies on people
We go for walks – they run away
We insist – they tantrum
We change our minds – they are disorientated and have short attention spans
We are talented – they have splinter skills
We are human – they are...?

(Courtesy of Mayer Shevin (1987) Available at: www.nursefriendly.com/ nursing/inspiration/the.language.of.us.them.mayer.shevin.htm (accessed January 2011).)

'[sic] *Unless we are careful. Difference is seen and treated as deficiency and the person is devalued which leads to being excluded and controlled by others.'* (O'Brien & Mount, 2005)

Today we are all asked to place much greater emphasis on what we now call co-production. The idea is that we work in partnership with people who are experts by experience, both for their intrinsic value and the power of their contribution, but also because these experts are far more committed to seeing things through in the long term. These are people who have strong motivations to ensure the mistakes of the past are not repeated. Many of them tell us difficult things in uncompromising terms: and this means that in many places we back off and continue to repeat the patterns of the past, doing no more than pay lip service to the contribution of many of the most talented and committed people. In these places superficial co-production resembles the shallow 'user involvement' and 'stakeholder engagement' approaches of the past that failed to build true partnerships or share real power.

The most recently developed course in the Partners programme, 'Altogether Better' is aimed at families and the people who support them through work in social care, health, education and leisure services. It first ran in 2009–2010 with the avowed intent of creating a 'national network of champions' to promote inclusion and self-direction. Reflections from participants included:

'I have never been on a course like this: it was an utter rollercoaster of emotion with inspirational speakers. I have done professional courses as a nurse for many years but nothing has had such impact on my practice. Of course, we are told to listen to patients, but listening and understanding how to use that to help their recovery has without a doubt resulted in better recovery and happier patients and a happier me at work.'

'I now view parents and disabled people as colleagues.'

'I never knew there were so many good fairies inside the service, which are human too, thank you for giving me the opportunity to see and understand what they have to work through to get my son some support.'

'Altogether Better' and other Partners' courses give participants the confidence to believe that people who use services and those who work in services both have something valuable to offer; they enable people to learn about the realities of how services operate; about how decisions are made and who is accountable to whom and for what – so they can put their learning into practice directly in their local communities and to influence their local services.

2. Changing the relationship between recipients of services and those who commission and provide them

There is now an emerging political consensus that the relationship between citizen and state needs to change. This was clear in the statements of the last Labour government and is (if anything) even clearer from the 2010 Coalition government. Everything we have described in the above section and many of the other changes we talk about in this book are steps on the road to this changed relationship, as manifested in a transformed set of protocols and arrangements between people who use services, and those who commission and provide them.

> 'Partners in Policy Making' are leaders and innovators in ensuring people who use services and their carers move towards an equal relationship with service providers and commissioners. I believe they have developed an approach, which can teach us much as we design the new National Expert Carers Programme. For years, we have struggled to genuinely empower people. 'Partners' have transformed rhetoric into reality. Their work is an inspiration to policy makers and professionals who are committed to changing the balance of power as we create modern health and social care systems. (Ivan Lewis, Social Care Minister, 2007)

> I want other forward thinking, entrepreneurial, community-minded people and neighbourhoods in our country to come forward and ask for the same freedoms, the same support too.
>
> If you've got an idea to make life better, if you want to improve your local area, don't just think about it – tell us what you want to do and we will try and give you the tools to make this happen.
>
> I passionately believe what we have begun here will spread right across our country – covering it in innovation, local inspiration and civic action.
>
> (David Cameron, Prime Minister, 2010)

There remain, however, many factors slowing or diverting us from this path. Some of the current systems we have inherited act to perversely prevent families from supporting each other and from enabling staff to really get to know and have a relationship with the people they are supporting.

One mum said, '*I have to say I can no longer care for my son in order for him to meet the FACS criteria to get some independent support to live his life. Can you see how hard this is to say, after I have cared for my son since his diagnosis of Down's syndrome since birth.*'

A worker said, '*I was disciplined for popping round to an individual's house after work for a brew, they said I was getting too personally involved with her and I have to keep a professional distance from clients, but I know that a five minute brew would prevent another admission to the mental health acute ward, so how can that be wrong!*'

There is no doubt that it will be challenging to bring about these new relationships, as we have operated for so long now an 'us and them' system between service workers on the one hand and people and their families on the other, and this is now deep set in the attitudes and behaviours of both groups. In Control has worked to develop a resource allocation system that starts by assessing people in terms of how their disability impacts on their life – rather than the old method of assessment focusing on functional deficits, an approach which aids neither the individual in taking power and responsibility nor the council in defining good outcomes for their services. The resource allocation system uses a supported self-assessment questionnaire, which was built around the key attributes that define citizenship – broad outcomes such as meaningful relationships, real work, a home of your own, and the ability to make your own decisions.

Much good work is happening in a number of local authorities across England, and the Law Commission is currently reviewing the law on adult social care which underpins this. We have confidence that the legislative changes that result will go at least some way to supporting the new approach which we have championed – but unless some of the existing perverse local authority systems also change, the relationship between citizen and state will remain far from equal and will continue to subtly disempower people who need support.

The Borough of Hartlepool in northeast England is one of the places where the shift in local authority culture has been strongest, and where self-reported 'outcomes' for local people are most positive. We believe that the success in Hartlepool is largely due to the inspirational leadership provided by Nicola Bailey, the Social Services Director and her team. This has been based upon the broad vision of changed relationships and shifts in power which they have set out, and the common and business sense they have used (rather than any sophisticated programme planning methodology) to make the necessary changes. Our evidence suggests that the relationship between the individual and the authority in Hartlepool has changed significantly with people now controlling their money, their supports and their lives with more effective and streamlined processes for individual people to find their way through the system (see Tyson, 2009 for more detail on the changes that have taken place in Hartlepool). Our view is that Hartlepool is unique only in the sense that every locality in the country is unique – if they can do it, so can each and every other.

3. Changing ingrained cultures, bottom up and top down

If we are serious about moving to a world where 'the most important thing is people' (In Control, 2010b), then there is serious work to be done to change society's attitudes towards those who may need additional support.

'The way we are, we are members of each other. All of us. Everything. The difference ain't in who is a member and who is not, but in who knows it and who don't.' (Burley Coulter, a character in Wendell Berry's The Wild Birds, 1986)

In all the work we've seen in recent years, attempting to move to a more 'personalised' way of doing things, a miniscule amount of time, money or effort has been spent on the most basic change of all – that is to say on cultural change. Our experience is that relatively few local authorities, PCTs or service providers have taken up this challenge and made wholehearted use of the body of learning about culture and innovation to help them bring effective change. In Control and Partners in Policymaking see this as one of the fundamental failings of the 'transformation programme' to date and are working to reverse it – to make cultural change and the tools needed to manage change through innovation the main focus of the shift. Those that have taken this up are now well on their way to achieving real transformation.

What does this mean in practice? As we found in Hartlepool, the quality of the leadership needed in order to make the change is crucial. Martin Luther King said I have a dream – not I have aims or objectives. What moves people is a vision of how things should look and feel. If we are serious about shifting the culture for the new 'big society' or towards 'People Power' then a *servant leadership* approach has to be developed to embrace the change.

The traditional 'service system' approach takes people through a functional assessment process which treats them as separate individuals with needs to be met. Sometimes they have 'family carers' to help but essentially they are alone. This old system provides a means to form a very basic 'diagnosis' that describes the person's needs and which leads to a 'service prescription'. In doing this it fails to consider the person's whole life or their real wealth (in the sense explained in Chapter 14) and it focuses exclusively on what they can't do ie. their 'deficits'. *A servant leadership approach* differs in two important ways: it sees the person as a *whole person*, with strengths and resources as well as needs; and it recognises the *community* around the individual as an important part of their life. This approach thus seeks to *serve* people in a genuine and compassionate way taking into account the full potential both of the person and of the community of support around them. The person is defined less as a 'dependent client' and more as a true citizen with their own rights and responsibilities.

Figure 1: This illustration shows the shift in culture needed for both the service leaders and the citizens.

(Taken from Ackoff R (2001) In: J Pearpoint (2001) Tools for Change. London: Inclusion Press.)

'There is nothing harder than starting something new apart from ... stopping something old' R Ackoff In: Pearpoint J (2001) *Tools for change.* London: Inclusion Press.

In Control has shown through our work with many councils and communities that the four corners of the jigsaw that need to be in place for change are leadership, legitimacy, support and entitlement. Andrew Tyson discusses this approach in some detail in Chapter 11. What does this mean in practice for councils wishing to embrace cultural change?

Figure 2: The transformation jigsaw

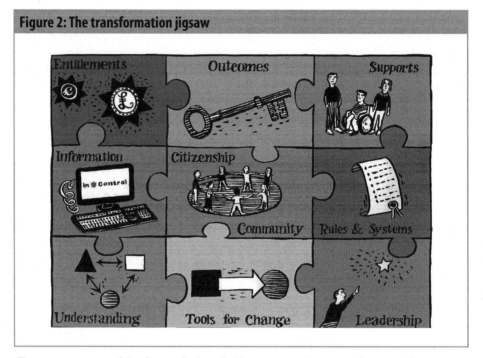

(Image courtesy of In Control. Available at: www.in-control.org.uk.)

We have referred to both *entitlements* and *supports*. We have clear evidence now that personalisation does not cost more money; what we find, in fact, is that the vast majority of people who are in control of their personal budgets are far more effective at getting the money to be used directly and efficiently to achieve a positive outcome than traditional commissioning arrangements and traditional services. Also, we have developed a simple, effective technology for resource allocation. Having the right *supports* in place is critical in terms of support to plan for someone to get what is in their plan and to help them manage their budget. All of this is important but not especially difficult.

The latter two jigsaw pieces, *leadership and understanding* now need much more focused attention in order to bring about the cultural change necessary. The *understanding* (or legitimacy) is now there in some sense, in the way academics and policy makers are talking about the changes that need to come about in society and community – and in government policy in *Putting People First* and the Coalition Agreement, but we are still very far from securing a similar level of understanding among the population at large, or indeed among local authority staff. And to return to our main point: *leadership*, the right kind of leadership, visionary and inspiring remains critical, and the picture here is mixed to say the least.

As challenging as this may seem, being as it is, about intangible attitudes rather than a system, it can be done. Look at society's attitude now to smoking in comparison to 10 years ago. Look at how people collaborate in recycling now as compared to five years ago. Look at the online social networking field compared to two years ago. Cultural change and changing attitudes are possible.

4. Uniting a grass-roots movement for change

To bring about the changes we want to see, the wider public needs to recognise that there is a problem with the old way of doing things. Sadly, there is little public focus on social care. When you mention social care, people think either about social workers taking children away, or about older people in residential homes. Of course the scope of social care is far wider than this, but public attitudes are hard to shift when their attention is elsewhere. This is the more so because many of our major charities and community groups have grown up in the shadow of the medical model, and have defined what they do around a particular medical diagnosis or condition. Thus we have many influential groups which focus purely on 'Down's syndrome' or 'MS' or 'Alzheimer's' or 'mental health' and so on. The difficulty is that these groups then often compete with one another to show that their cause is the best and the people they support have the greatest needs and therefore they need the highest level of funding, charitable or otherwise. When in fact, you actually talk directly to people you find that irrespective of diagnosis, they generally all want the same things – love, respect and value – and they gain opportunities for achieving these in many different ways, but not through their medical diagnosis. This is something that should not be difficult to sell to the public.

We do need to be wary here. In Control and Partners in Policymaking are sometimes accused in these matters of being 'evangelical', 'purist' or 'utopian'. In Control does not pretend that self-direction will cure all ills or that personalisation will lead to utopia. We are well aware that humans who need love, respect and value also exhibit greed, envy and cynicism. People are pessimists, as well as optimists, uncaring as well as caring. But these realities of human nature should surely encourage us to accentuate people's positive attributes, encourage them to develop their 'assets', and to see their medical diagnosis for what it is, a useful tool to understand what is happening to their body now and in the future rather than a complete summation of their personal identity. Partners in Policymaking embraces all people regardless of diagnosis, it unites people who have visual impairments with people who have complex life limiting health issues, with people with brain injuries and people with histories of abuse – and it works. These people are united in a quest to understand more about why things are the way they are for people who need additional support; about how to influence things and gain confidence in their own ability, skills, rights and responsibility to shape policy and practice. It also enables the parents of young children with disabilities to hear about the experiences of adults with disabilities and learn from them. Crucially, it does this in a way that does not blame individuals who work in services, because the process is based on an understanding of the context and the culture within which those people are asked to operate.

In all my time working in services, I have yet to meet a member of staff who comes into a job with the aim of making life difficult for people using the service – everyone comes to the work to help others. With this in mind, In Control's work starts by seeking to build common ground and a common understanding between helpers and those seeking help. We aim to identify problems, difficulties and what is not working – and then to use these alliances to address the issues together. This is what we mean by co-production. We also work in partnership with other organisations which share the vision and are on the same journey: with Mencap, MS Society, Together, NCIL and many others.

Our approach is not to compete with other groups but to unite with them in the common aim of enabling people in need of support to gain control. Working with Partners in Policymaking gives people the opportunity to change things directly in their personal, home and work life and it encourages and nourishes natural leaders to take on more of a role locally, regionally and nationally. We now see this network of leaders growing in strength across the country and beginning to influence the process of change. The grass-roots network of 'people power', which is now beginning to take shape comprises graduates from the many Partners programmes, individuals who work in local authorities and provider agencies, senior managers, civil servants and politicians, media, and many other ordinary members of the public who believe that 'people matter'.

5. Focusing on people more than systems

In Control and Partners in Policymaking focus more on people than on systems. The attitudes and approach of people who lead – from the ground up or from the top down – are the key influences on change. 'It's not what you know it's who you know' would be one view, but it's 'who you know and what they know' that we see really making the difference.

In Control and Partners are determined to continue to build and support the network of people who believe and embody 'people matter'. This does not mean that new technical systems and new operating systems are not necessary, but what we have learned is that how people operate these systems is the thing that makes the real difference.

'I have an individual budget but I have been told I can only spend it on buying my support from agency a or agency b.' (Direct recipient of social care)

This way of operating a new system keeps the old culture and keeps the power imbalance in place. It not only prevents people taking control, but it is also unnecessarily costly as there is no incentive for the individual to manage their budget. Freedom and flexibility along with the right to the cash are essentials.

'You can use your individual budget on x respite unit costing £500 per week but you're not allowed to take just £200 and spend it on an extended family holiday where your wife might also get a break.'

These are the sad and too common examples where statutory services have changed systems to 'give people a personal budget or a direct payment' – but where the culture remains as traditional as ever, focusing on service solutions rather than the outcomes individuals define for themselves. In Control continues to take this message from Number 10 'Any Street' to Number 10 Downing Street.

It has become clearer as our work has progressed over the last couple of years that a major social change is underway, one not confined to the workings of the social care system, but a deeper and wider change. We have observed the beginnings of a new set of relationships emerging between disabled people, their families, politicians and professionals. These new relationships now appear to be crystallising in the form of a social movement, with networks of support and a 'community of learning' at its heart. This movement is made up of people who need support, their families, professionals and government all working together for change. All of which share the goal of a fairer more open and nurturing society.

This feels like an historic moment, a point when things could change dramatically for the better, or could slip back. The mission of In Control is to serve the movement for change and the community. If the work is to realise its potential, then we must continue to reflect upon the core values of compassion, freedom and fairness that have motivated In Control through its short history; and as we do this, we need to find imaginative ways to join with people with learning disabilities and their families, and also with professional people, managers and community leaders. The aim of this process of reflective engagement is to address hearts and minds – hearts and minds that become open to a new way of seeing the world and a new way of engaging with it; a way of seeing the world that understands this process – reflection, discussion and engagement – as the critical steps on the road to choice and control for all.

References

Ackoff R (2001) In: J Pearpoint (2001) *Tools for change*. London: Inclusion Press.

Berry W (1986) *The Wild Birds, Six Stories of the Port William Membership*. San Francisco: North Point.

Cameron D (2010) Unspecified speech. For more information contact author.

Hatton C, Waters J, Duffy S, Senker J, Crosby N, Poll C, Tyson A, O'Brien J & Towell J (2008) *A Report on In Control's Second Phase, Evaluation and Learning 2005–7*. London: In Control.

In Control (2010a) *A Report on In Control's Third Phase, Evaluation and Learning 2008–9*. London: In Control.

In Control (2010b) 2020 *Vision*. London: In Control.

Lewis I (2007) Unspecified speech. For more information contact author.

Poll C, Duffy S, Hatton C, Sanderson H & Routledge M (2006) *A Report on In Control's First Phase, Evaluation and Learning 2003–5*. London: In Control.

Putting People First, toolkit [online]. Available at: www.puttingpeoplefirst. org.uk (accessed November 2010).

Shevin M (1987) Available at: www.nursefriendly.com./nursing/inspiration/ the.language.of.us.them.mayer.shevin.htm (accessed January 2011).

Tyson A (2009) *Self-Directed Support in Hartlepool, 2006–2009*. London: In Control.

O'Brien J & Mount B (2005) *Make a Difference*. Toronto: Inclusion Press.

Further reading

Elwell L (2009) *Partners' Co-ordination booklet revised* [online]. Available at: www.in-control.org.uk/partnersinpolicymaking (accessed November 2010).

O'Brien J & O'Brien L (1996) *Members of Each Other*. Toronto: Inclusion Press.

See www.in-control.org.uk/partners/ for full programmes of: Making it Happen, Kindred Spirits, Sharing Knowledge and All together Better.